# The Dynamics of the Language Classroom

# CAMBRIDGE LANGUAGE TEACHING LIBRARY

A series covering central issues in language teaching and learning, by authors who have expert knowledge in their field.

In this series:

# The Dynamics of the Language Classroom

*Ian Tudor*

*Université Libre de Bruxelles*

CAMBRIDGE
UNIVERSITY PRESS

CAMBRIDGE UNIVERSITY PRESS
Cambridge, New York, Melbourne, Madrid, Cape Town, Singapore, São Paulo

Cambridge University Press
The Edinburgh Building, Cambridge CB2 8RU, UK

Published in the United States of America by Cambridge University Press, New York

www.cambridge.org
Information on this title: www.cambridge.org/9780521772037

© Cambridge University Press 2001

First published 2001
Reprinted 2002

A catalogue record for this publication is available from the British Library

ISBN 978-0-521-77203-7 hardback
ISBN 978-0-521-77676-9 paperback

Transferred to digital printing 2008

# Contents

# Contents

# Abbreviations

| | |
|---|---|
| *AKL* | American Kernel Lessons |
| ESOL | English as a second or other language |
| EFL | English as a foreign language |
| ESL | English as a second language |
| CLL | Community Language Learning |
| CLT | communicative language teaching |
| LSP | languages for specific purposes |
| TL | target language |

# Acknowledgements

The author would like to express his gratitude to two anonymous reviewers and to Andrew Littlejohn for constructive advice and suggestions made at different stages in the preparation of the manuscript; thanks go also to Mickey Bonin of Cambridge University Press for his support throughout. Special thanks go to Gill Lucy for many interesting ideas on the content of the book and for her support during the writing process.

# Introduction

This is a book about language teaching which is meant for teachers and other language educators involved in the practical realisation of language teaching programmes or in organising teacher education courses. It rests on the belief that language teaching is a complex, dynamic activity, and that this complexity is frequently underestimated both in the popular imagination and in much of the official discourse of language teaching. The goal of the book is to explore the complexity of language teaching as it is lived out in classrooms and, in this way, to provide teachers and other language educators with guidelines for exploring the dynamics of their own teaching situations, and, thus, of developing what Elliott (1993a) refers to as 'situational understandings'.

Few practising teachers would consider as particularly remarkable the suggestion that language teaching is a complex activity: many, in fact, would see it as a statement of the obvious. I feel, however, that this point deserves to be made for at least two reasons. First, although practising language teachers are well aware of the complexity of their task, the same cannot always be said for the other actors who, in one way or another, play a role in the endeavour of language education; these are, for example, political and educational authorities, the management or administration of teaching institutions, clients, sponsors, parents, and many others. This may result from ignorance in the sense that these actors may simply be unaware of the precise details of what teaching entails. It may also, however, result from a more or less conscious will not to see or acknowledge the realities of teaching: the elegance of clear, rationally formulated curricula or the confident claims of current 'best practice' having a greater attraction than the complex and often untidy nature of teaching as it is lived out in real classrooms. And yet, it is often within frameworks set up by these actors that teachers have to live out their tasks in the classroom. If only for this reason, then, there is a good justification for recalling the complex nature of language teaching. Second, and more fundamentally, there is the question of whether the complexity of language teaching is something incidental – grit in the machine of pedagogical efficiency – or whether it is an inherent feature of the activity itself. This book suggests that the latter is the case, and that acknowledging and working openly with this complexity is fundamental to any honest attempt to understand language teaching as it really is.

Fortunately, there is a growing trend in thinking on language teaching which explicitly acknowledges and seeks to work constructively with the complexity of language teaching as it really is, as opposed to how we might like it to be or feel it should be according to one idealised schema or another. This trend is discussed in Chapter 1 in terms of what is referred to as the ecological perspective on language teaching. This perspective involves a fairly substantial shift in approach from that which has dominated (and in many ways still dominates) much thinking on language teaching. The ecological perspective offers an alternative to a positivistic and hierarchically based approach to the conceptualisation and planning of teaching programmes. It portrays language teaching as an emergent phenomenon, i.e. a reality which emerges dynamically from the actions and interactions of very many individuals working within specific contexts which operate according to rules that are proper to each as a reality in its own right. The ecological perspective on language teaching has parallels with the concept of sustainable development in economics, and with the call for more local forms of democracy and decision-making in the political field. It also shares a good deal of common ground with insights which have been developed in recent years in many fields of science and which have found expression in complexity theory, or the study of complex adaptive systems.

Viewed from this perspective, if we wish to understand language teaching as it is lived out in real classrooms, we need to explore the meaning which teaching and learning procedures have for individuals in their own terms and not against a template of abstract, situation-external precept and generalisation. We then need to explore the dynamics which arise out of the interaction between the individuals present in each specific situation. This can, of course, vary considerably from one context to another, but the totality of language teaching emerges from this vast kaleidoscope of detail and diversity. The elegant plans of educational planners and the generalisations of theorists can and do influence the reality of teaching as it is lived out in classrooms. However, they are not the full reality, nor can it be assumed that they represent a canonical view of what this reality should be. They are simply elements of the complex dynamics of teaching and learning, i.e. elements that reflect the perspectives on language teaching of certain groups of participants, but that interact dynamically with the perspectives of many other participants. In this view, language teaching is less a matter of the hierarchical, top-down realisation of ideal curricular structures and methodological principle than the emergent product a very large number of local, dynamically self-organising systems.

This book works within this perspective on language teaching and has the goal of providing teachers and other language educators with guidelines for exploring the dynamics of their own teaching situations and of their own interaction with these situations. The book is organised as follows.

Chapters 1 and 2 establish the theoretical background within which the book is placed. Chapter 1 briefly surveys trends in language teaching over the last few decades in terms of the shift in emphasis from a technological to an ecological perspective on language teaching. Chapter 2 introduces the dynamic perspective on language teaching which will underpin the subsequent chapters.

Chapters 3 to 5 examine some of the more frequent visions of language (Chapter 3), of learning (Chapter 4), and of the classroom (Chapter 5) which teachers are likely to encounter among their students, in teaching materials, in educational programmes, and in their own individual conception of teaching. These chapters do not argue for any one vision of language, of learning, or of the classroom. The goal is rather to evaluate a variety of perspectives not only in terms of their own inner logic, but also and crucially with respect to their interaction with various aspects of context. These chapters argue for an inclusive acknowledgement of diversity in pedagogical decision-making and seek to highlight the dynamic interaction between methodology and context.

Chapters 6 to 8 build on Chapters 3–5 to study the dynamics of classroom teaching from a number of perspectives. Chapter 6 focuses on the interaction between methodology and context, Chapter 7 on the exploitation of local traditions of learning and Chapter 8 on the concept of 'negotiation' in the creation of classroom realities. These chapters make use of the categories of methodological choice discussed in Chapters 3–5, but do this with reference to a number of case studies (two in each chapter). Not all of these studies could be considered to have happy endings; nor are they intended to be seen as exemplars of 'best practice' to be put in a display cabinet for admiration. They are simply slices of the complex, dynamic reality of language teaching as lived out by flesh and blood people working together in one particular setting or another. These chapters explore the dynamic nature of classroom interaction between students and teachers as lived out in specific contexts, with the goal of providing teachers with insights which they can then use to explore these realities in their own classrooms.

Finally, Chapter 9 briefly sums up the main points made in the previous chapters and provides a number of guidelines for methodo-logical decision-making and for teacher education.

As already stated, this book rests on the hypothesis that language teaching is an activity whose complexity is often underestimated, and that a key factor in understanding language teaching as it really is involves exploring the dynamics of teaching and learning as they are lived out in the specifics of individual settings. On this basis, it seeks to provide teachers with guidelines for exploring their own teaching context and the 'local' meaning which methodological choices can assume for their students in the specifics of this context. The book therefore questions the idea that pedagogical choices can be made on the basis of situation-external criteria or notions of 'best practice'. Specifically, it suggests that pedagogical decision-making needs to rest on a critical analysis of methodological principles in the light of their local meaning, and on the exploration of the dynamic interaction of students and teachers with the teaching–learning process in the full context of their lives within but also beyond the classroom.

This book is first and foremost a 'teacher reflection' text whose goal is to help teachers explore and respond to the dynamics of their own situations in an open and realistic manner. The book pursues this goal in two ways. First, the main text seeks to establish a framework of reference and to provide stimulus for thought. Second, the tasks (which are boxed in the text) invite readers to use this input as a basis for reflection on their personal interaction with aspects of language teaching and for the exploration of their own teaching situation. If teachers are following a professional development course at the time of reading, they may wish to relate these tasks to one or more situations in which they have worked previously. In the case of novice teachers, these tasks may be used projectively as a guide to their interaction with concrete teaching situations and to their personal development as teachers. Some tasks, to be approached systematically, call for a degree of data collection, and may thus provide a starting point for action research projects. These tasks can also, however, be used more lightly as input to the ongoing type of curiosity and observation which is so important in the teacher's professional life.

# 1 A changing perspective on language teaching

## 1.1 A new technology of language teaching

People have been learning languages other than their first language throughout history. How they did this, however, is something which remains shrouded in mystery as the long history of language learning is largely unrecorded. It is likely that a very large part of this learning occurred in a naturalistic manner by means of contact with speakers of another language with the goal of interpersonal communication for purposes of trade, social organisation or the conveyance of a belief system. There have also been attempts to help language learners by means of structured approaches to the presentation of the target language (TL) or the practice of elements of this language. That is what we would now call approaches or methodologies.

Neither the learning nor the teaching of languages, then, are novel activities. The period of language teaching history which stretches from the 1960s to the present, however, is probably unique. To begin with, the scale of the learning and teaching of languages is in all probability greater than has ever been the case previously; this is as a consequence of the expansion in international exchanges of all types which characterises the modern world. This period has also witnessed an unprecedented intensity of reflection and experimentation in all fields of language teaching. In this respect, it is useful to bear in mind that language teaching is a social phenomenon and is therefore influenced by the sociocultural context in which it occurs. It is therefore useful to look at the reasons for the development of language teaching in recent decades, and also at the general directions that thinking on language teaching have adopted over the same period.

The period around the 1960s witnessed a number of significant changes in the map of the world and in international relations. On the international level, colonial empires were disappearing, and a large number of states which had recently obtained their independence were investing heavily to provide their populations with improved standards of education and to develop their economies in order to be able to compete on the international market on more equal terms. This led to the need for knowledge of foreign languages as a means of gaining access to information in the fields of science and technology, and of enabling citizens to communicate with people from other countries in various aspects of economic and commercial life. In view of the role of English as an international language in the fields of science, technology and business, a significant part of the expansion in the demand for language learning involved English. At the same time, the countries of Europe, which were still emerging from the destruction and trauma of the Second World War, were rebuilding their economies and seeking to create greater mutual understanding and cooperation in both economic and social fields. One of the manifestations of this effort was the setting-up in 1963 of the Council of Europe's Modern Languages Project, an ambitious scheme which was designed to promote language learning throughout Europe. Increasing prosperity gave further impetus to this drive as a result of increased economic exchanges as well as by providing the bases for the expansion of travel for leisure and cultural purposes.

These changes in society influenced language teaching in two main ways. First, they increased the overall demand for language teaching dramatically. Second, they altered the nature of this demand. Before this period language teaching had been marked by a focus on the language code and by a strong scholastic and literary orientation. The changes alluded to above, on the other hand, set primarily functional goals for language teaching. In many cases, they related to the development of specific competences in more or less restricted domains of usage such as basic transactional skills for travel or tourism, the ability to read specialised material in a given domain of activity, oral communication skills in a particular field of economic life, and so on.

In order to be able to respond to this changing demand, the language teaching profession had to develop a new set of procedures for establishing goals, constructing learning programmes, and realising these programmes at classroom level. This led to work on needs analysis (cf. Richterich, 1973; Munby, 1978) and on functionally based approaches to course design (cf. Wilkins, 1976; Mackay and Mountford, 1978; Widdowson, 1978), as well as on the development of a new approach to classroom methodology (cf. Strevens, 1977; Brumfit and Johnson, 1979; Savignon, 1983; Brumfit, 1984a). These efforts led to the creation of what could fairly be described as a new 'technology' of language teaching, as seen in the options that were made available to language educators for investigating students' learning needs, constructing coherent learning programmes, and realising these programmes in terms of learning tasks and activities. By about 1980, the theoretical landscape of language teaching had undergone a significant change, and what came to be known as the communicative approach had established itself as the dominant paradigm in language teaching. This intense work of reflection and development has continued into the present and there is no reason to believe that it will stop in the near future.

The period since the 1960s has been marked by a considerable amount of creativity and energy in language teaching. This has manifested itself in terms of the theoretical developments mentioned above, and also in an impressive productivity in terms of teaching materials and learning aids of many types, including the use of various technical facilities such as video, computer-assisted learning, and multimedia. With respect to methodology, it is fair to speak of an explosion in the range of materials which are available to teachers. A parallel expansion has taken place in terms of the number of professional journals, language teaching associations, and courses in applied linguistics or language teaching methodology which are available. The world of language teaching is now a very much richer and more diversified place than it was in the 1960s. What could be described as the 'technology of language teaching' – namely the theoretical perspectives and practical options which are available to language educators for designing and implementing learning programmes – has expanded dramatically.

In one sense, the language teaching profession has good reason to feel satisfaction with this period of creativity: it points to the considerable efforts that have been made in response to the demands of society to develop new means of approaching the task of language teaching in an effective manner. In many ways, these developments reflect the positivistic belief in the power of human reason to find solutions to the various challenges of life and, thus, parallel developments in the fields of medicine, science, and technology. As a result, the language teaching profession has a much richer array of options at its disposal at the start of the twenty-first century than was the case a few decades ago. A teacher faced with the request to set up a learning programme for a given group of students thus has a varied and well-developed set of resources to choose from in terms of investigative and course design procedures, teaching materials, and learning aids; he or she also has an impressive array of methodological ideas as a source of inspiration. It would thus be reasonable to say that over the last few decades the profession has developed what could be seen as a new technology of language teaching.

This, however, is not the whole story. Having a rich technology at one's disposal is certainly a help. Technology, however, offers a potential but does not in itself guarantee that a given result will be obtained, not in a complex human activity like teaching, at least. The real effectiveness of educational technology lies not just in the inherent logic and potentiality of the technology itself but in the appropriacy of its use, and this involves consideration of a variety of 'soft' data relating to the perceptions and attitudes of the people who will be using it and to the type of context in which it will be used. This in turn calls for a different perspective on language teaching, one which is complementary to but, nonetheless, separate from the development of the 'technology' referred to above.

---

Evaluate your own interaction with the technology of language teaching in terms of the approaches, methodologies, materials, or learning aids with which you have worked.

- In which ways has this technology facilitated your task as teacher?
- Have you ever felt tensions or dissatisfaction with elements of this technology? Specifically, have you ever felt that technology did not appear to offer you what you might have expected it to?
- If so, try to identify the origins of these tensions or dissatisfactions.
- In which ways have you responded to situations of this nature?

---

## 1.2 Towards an ecological perspective on language teaching

If it could be assumed that learners were 'simply' learners, that teachers were 'simply' teachers, and that one classroom was essentially the same as another, there would probably be little need for any approach other than a technological perspective on language teaching. Objective differences – such as the age of learners, the specific goals being pursued, or class numbers – could be included in a pre-established matrix and accommodated in a reasonably straightforward manner as departures from a given norm, rather in the way that the same production machinery can be recalibrated to produce different cars. In this scenario, a well-developed technology of language teaching would be sufficient to guarantee a fairly predictable set of results.

This, of course, is not the case. Learners are not 'simply' learners any more than teachers are 'simply' teachers; teaching contexts, too, differ from one another in a significant number of ways. In other words, language teaching is far more complex than producing cars: we cannot therefore assume that the technology of language teaching will lead in a neat, deterministic manner to a predictable set of learning outcomes. For the technology of language teaching to produce effective results, it has to work with people as they are in the context in which they find themselves at a given point in time. The technology, then, has to be used appropriately, and deciding on what is or is not appropriate calls for consideration of the total context of teaching in both human and pragmatic terms. Certain writers (Holliday and Cooke, 1982; Van Lier, 1997) have referred to this as an 'ecological' perspective on language teaching, i.e. one which looks at language teaching within the totality of the lives of the various participants involved and not as one sub-part of their lives which can be examined in isolation. Van Lier expresses this in the following terms:

> An ecological perspective on language learning offers an alternative way of looking at the contexts in which language use and language learning are situated . . . It proposes to be a radical alternative to Cartesian rationalism, body–mind dualism, and the anthropocentric world promoted for several centuries. It replaces these views with a conception of the learning environment as a complex adaptive system, of the mind as the totality of relationships between a developing person and the surrounding world, and of learning as the result of meaningful activity in an accessible environment. (1997: 783)

In an ecological perspective on teaching, technology is simply one element among others, an essential element indeed, but still only one. Furthermore, it is unsafe to assume that the effects of educational technology can be predicted confidently from the inner logic of the technology alone, as this inner logic inevitably interacts with the perceptions and goals of those involved in using it. This means that in order to understand precisely what takes place in our classrooms, we have to look at these classrooms as entities in their own right and explore the meaning they have for those who are involved in them in their own terms. In other words, a classroom is not just an exemplar of a certain pedagogical idealisation: it is something living and dynamic which does not necessarily fit into an idealised picture of what a classroom should be. Consequently, understanding the reality of teaching involves exploring the meaning it has for students, for teachers, and for the others who, in one way or another, influence what is done in classrooms.

The ecological perspective has gained more attention and has come to assume a more dominant role in mainstream thinking on language teaching in recent years. It has, however, been present for some time, running parallel with the development of the new technology of language teaching mentioned above. Indeed, the two are by no means incompatible. The technology of language teaching as seen in approach, methodology, materials, and learning aids provides language educators with options from which they can choose in setting-up a course or planning a class. The ecological perspective, on the other hand, focuses attention on the human and pragmatic factors which influence the use and likely effectiveness of this technology. There can, however, be a tension between the two perspectives. A technological approach to education seems positive and confident, and it promises a specific product. An ecological perspective, on the other hand, often calls upon us to 'Wait a moment' and has many instances of 'It depends'. Perhaps for this reason, the technological perspective has the most attraction for those who are further removed from classroom realities, i.e. planning committees, educational authorities, and so on. Practising teachers, however, are in (and part of) one small ecosystem which is the classroom, and it is much more difficult for them to ignore the 'rules' or inner logic of this system and simply to 'apply the technology' according to the instruction manual. The teacher's reality is an ecological one which is shaped by the attitudes and expectations of students, of parents, of school administrators, of materials writers, and of many others including, of course, each teacher as an individual in his or her own right.

Understanding what takes place in classrooms therefore involves understanding what different participants – students and teachers in the first instance, but many others, too – bring with them to the classroom, and how this influences what they do within it. This, in turn, involves exploring participants' identities and listening to their voice. The next three sections therefore look at trends in research in recent years which have explored this aspect of teaching, namely the identity of participants and how this influences the voices they express.

---

This book works within an ecological perspective on language teaching and seeks to provide teachers with guidelines for negotiating a shared and sustainable approach to teaching within their classrooms. Think about the two perspectives on language teaching which have been outlined here.

- Which do you work with more?
- Which was dominant in your training?
- Have you encountered tensions between the two?
- If so, analyse the origin of these tensions and how you have dealt with them.

---

## 1.3 Learner identities

A significant part of the new technology of language teaching which was developed in the 1960s and 1970s reflected the demand for a functionally oriented approach to teaching. The development of the new technology of language teaching was thus strongly influenced by pragmatic considerations which focused on 'hard', objectively observable phenomena. Within this framework, students were seen primarily as social actors whose identity was defined in terms of the social role in which they would have to use the language, e.g. a tourist needing to organise travel and accommodation, a student needing to read a certain type of specialist material, a businessperson needing to describe his or her company's products or negotiate a contract, and so on. The main emphasis was thus on students' objective needs, what they would have to do in the language, and the translation of these needs into a coherent pedagogical form. As far as it goes, this is a perfectly valid perspective on the final goals of language teaching.

The functionally based approach to teaching had not been in use for long before it became apparent that the objective relevance of learning content is no guarantee in itself that effective learning will occur. The latter depends on the willing and active involvement of students in the learning process: students therefore need to perceive the relevance of learning content and be willing to interact meaningfully with the learning activities in place. This, however, depends on factors of an affective and attitudinal nature, which have come to be studied under the heading of subjective needs. This area of concern relates to the identity of learners within the learning process itself, not just as future language users, but as language learners who are involved in developing a certain competence in interaction with a given set of teaching procedures and learning activities.

This is clearly a complex area and has been investigated from a number of angles. One of the first was the learning strategy research of the 1970s (for an overview of the earlier work in the area, cf. Rubin, 1987; for subsequent developments, cf. Reid, 1995). Early work on learning strategies arose out of the observation that some learners seem to be more at ease with and achieve higher levels of success in language study than others. It therefore seemed reasonable to investigate whether it would be possible to identify those behaviours which were typical of more and of less successful learners. One motivation of this research was to assess whether the behaviours of successful learners could be pinpointed as the basis for a sort of ideal learning strategy agenda which could be used to provide guidance for less successful learners. It did in fact emerge that more successful learners manifest a certain number of characteristic behaviours. At the same time, it also became apparent that these behaviours are expressions of a certain attitude to the learning process which is deeply rooted in the personality and experience of each learner. Students' interaction with the learning process therefore arises out of a complex of attitudes which is specific to each one as an individual. For this reason, it was realised that the behaviours characteristic of more successful learners could not be transformed into a discrete set of steps to be learned and imitated by others like an aerobics routine. The learning strategy research of the 1970s was pivotal in that it opened up a research agenda which has led us to explore the complexity of students' interaction with their language study, an agenda which has made us appreciate the individuality of each learner, and of their interaction with language study.

One of the main lines of investigation in this area has related to individual differences among learners (for overviews, cf. Skehan 1989, 1991). Individual differences are those factors of a psychological, cognitive or attitudinal nature which influence the way in which learners perceive and interact with their language study. Individual differences studied with respect to second language learning include motivation (Dörnyei, 1990, 1994, 1998; Oxford and Shearin, 1994; Tremblay and Gardner, 1995), anxiety (Scovel, 1978; Horwitz and Young, 1991), tolerance for ambiguity (Chapelle and Roberts, 1986), and field dependence–independence (Abraham, 1985; Chapelle, 1995). Another area of research is learning style, even if there is some disagreement as to the status of this concept. One perspective (Oxford and Ehrman, 1993) is that learning style is an individual difference alongside others. Another (Willing, 1988) sees it as a more powerful concept which encapsulates the combined effect of a number of individual differences as they relate to language learning. Since the 1980s a considerable body of research has been built up in this area. Attention has also been devoted to 'theories' or beliefs about language learning that students bring with them to the classroom, and how these may influence their interaction with teaching and learning procedures (Wenden, 1987).

This line of research has made us aware that factors of a subjective nature exert a significant influence on how learners perceive and experience the learning process and, therefore, how they are likely to react to various learning activities or modes of teaching. For example, for one student an oral production task may represent a welcome opportunity to express his or her personality and/or to experiment with his or her ability to use the language for its 'real' purpose, namely to exchange ideas with another human being. For another student, the same activity may be a stressful and unwelcome experience in which he or she feels judged on his or her use of a language that has not as yet been 'learned properly'. This means that what the teacher has in mind when preparing a class may not be what students perceive or experience during the class itself. The reality of teaching therefore arises out of the meaning that methodological choices assume in the minds of students and the dynamics that this generates within the learning group.

Research in individual differences has played a valuable role in increasing our understanding of the factors that make language teaching and learning what they are in the minds of our students. Nonetheless, much of this research has focused on one specific aspect of learners' perceptions of language study at a time. This is understandable in research terms, but it leaves us with the unresolved problem of knowing how to put the various elements together in the moment-to-moment dynamics of classroom teaching.

Williams and Burden (1997: 89–95) make a number of pertinent remarks in this respect about the variables which are studied under the heading of individual differences. To begin with, they point out that these variables are hypothetical constructs. In other words, researchers agree to speak about factors such as intelligence, anxiety, or risk-taking in order to gain insight into the psychocognitive reality of students' interaction with language learning. However, these terms are not the reality itself, nor can we be sure whether they are the best way of encapsulating this reality. Williams and Burden also suggest that while individual differences tend to be viewed as fixed or at least relatively stable phenomena, most are better viewed as 'variable, context specific, and amenable to change' (1997: 90). They point out, for example, that anxiety is highly situation specific, that it is affected by a variety of factors, and that a behaviour that would be seen as anxious in one culture might be construed differently in another. Indeed, they suggest that 'the whole area of individual differences is fraught with unan-swered questions' and argue for an approach which focuses on 'the unique contribution each individual brings to the learning situation' (p. 95). For Williams and Burden, such an approach would involve a change in the way in which the psychocognitive aspect of language learning is considered:

> So, instead of asking the question: 'How are learners different from each other and can we measure these differences?', it would be more helpful to seek answers to such questions as: 'How do learners perceive themselves as language learners?', 'What effect do these "personal constructs" have upon the process of learning a new language?', 'How do individuals go about making sense of their learning?', and 'How can we as

teachers assist learners in making sense of their learning in ways that are personal to them?'     (Williams and Burden, 1997: 96)

These are all valid questions, and they frame the investigation of students' subjective interaction with the learning process in terms which are pertinent to the concerns of the practising teacher. They are not, however, easy questions, and we are some way from settling on adequate answers to them. Nevertheless, the fact that they are being posed is in itself an indication of how far our awareness of the role of learners' subjective interaction with the learning process has developed over the last few decades. We can no longer assume that our students are 'simply' students, nor that they are bundles of discrete variables. They are complex human beings who bring with them to the classroom their own individual personality as it is at a given point in time, and this influences how they interact with what we do as teachers.

Attempting to disentangle and analyse the many strands which make an individual who he or she is is a valid strategy for researchers. Practising teachers, however, deal with individuals integratively. The inner coherence of a learner's classroom identity has to be explored and understood in its own terms, and as it is at a given point in time and in a given setting. Stevick's (1989) *Success with Foreign Languages*, which is built around an exploration of the perceptions and strategies of seven successful language learners, provides an insightful illustration of how complex an undertaking this can be. Stevick describes the seven learners under the following headings: intuitive, formal, informal, imaginative, active, deliberate, and self-aware. It is unlikely, however, that Stevick would feel too attached to these terms as such: they are an attempt to encapsulate a certain learner identity, but this is a reality which can never be fully pinned down and which is unique to each learner as an individual. Stevick also gives some very useful advice about helping different learners to build on their basic disposition to learning in a productive manner. His last piece of advice (1989: 150), however, – 'Beware of building a system of teaching around one type of learner' – seems to be crucial in that it points to the importance of working with the diversity of learners as they are and their attempt to find personal meaningfulness in their language study.

Over three decades of research into learners' subjective interaction with language study has led us to acknowledge the uniqueness of each language learner, and therefore of the need to accommodate this uniqueness and, in this way, the learner's identity, in our pedagogical actions and choices.

Consider your own experience as a language learner.

- To what extent do you feel that your individuality as a person and as a learner was acknowledged in the learning programme or programmes you followed?
- Analyse your answer (which may vary from one programme to another) to evaluate what did or did not make your learning experience(s) congenial to you as an individual.
- In which way could you make use of these insights to help you cater for the individuality of your own students?
- Do you feel that there might be obstacles to this? If so, what are they, and where do they come from?

## 1.4 Teacher identities

Research into the subjective needs of language learners has made us aware that our students are not 'simply' language learners but complex human beings whose interaction with language study is influenced by a variety of attitudinal and experiential factors. Our students are not therefore blank sheets of paper onto which a pre-ordained body of knowledge can be transferred in a neat, predictable manner. They are human beings who interact with teaching procedures in an individual manner as part of the broader goal of creating a personal understanding of language and of language learning in the here-and-now of their lives. The goal of language teaching is not to iron out differences among learners but to work with them in a constructive and educationally informed manner. More recently, we have also come to realise something similar with respect to teachers.

In itself, this may not seem a particularly startling discovery. No one would seriously question that each teacher is an individual in his or her own right, nor would it be reasonable to assume that a teacher leaves his or her individual identity on a clothes peg on entering the classroom. At the same time, there is an implicit assumption in much curriculum design that the perspectives on language teaching contained in approach and materials feed through in a relatively direct manner to the classroom via the actions of the teacher. In planning terms, this is clearly a very convenient assumption. It does, however, suppose that teachers are 'simply' teachers who act in accordance with the plans of others in a dutiful and predictable manner. This is at best somewhat simplistic, and it also underestimates the very specific contribution which the individual teacher as a person makes to the teaching process and to the creation of classroom realities.

Richards (1996), for example, points to the importance of understanding teaching 'from the inside', i.e. of the 'need to listen to teachers' voices in understanding classroom practice' in order to be in a position to 'understand teaching in its own terms and in ways in which it is understood by teachers' (pp. 281–282). He contrasts this perspective with 'earlier research traditions which presented an outsider's perspective on teaching and sought to identify quantifiable classroom behaviours and their effect on learning outcomes' (p. 282). Richards thus stresses the need to accord attention to the subjective realities of teaching from the point of view of the individual teacher. This involves exploring teacher attitudes and perceptions and the way in which these influence teachers' classroom behaviours. Richards focuses in particular on teachers' 'maxims', or the principles which teachers use, consciously or unconsciously, to guide their pedagogical decisions. Other writers have looked at teachers' 'conceptions' of teaching (Freeman and Richards, 1993), teachers' 'understandings' (Almarza, 1996; Burns, 1996; Freeman, 1996), the teacher's 'sense of legitimacy' (Moran, 1996), and the role of the teacher's language learning autobiography (i.e. teachers' own experiences as language learners) on their teaching philosophy and practice (Bailey *et al.*, 1996). A related line of research has focused on teacher learning and decision-making (e.g. Johnson, 1992; Pennington, 1995, 1996; Numrich, 1996; Woods, 1996). This line of reflection paints a picture of teaching which is no less complex than that which has emerged from the studies of learners' subjective needs reviewed above. We are thus coming to acknowledge that both students and teachers are human beings whose involvement in the process of language study is shaped by a complex set of beliefs, attitudes, and perceptions, and that this can no more be ignored with respect to teachers than it can with respect to students.

This realisation clearly has implications for curriculum planning. Freeman and Richards (1996: 22) suggest that 'the external prescriptive views of method that generally prevail in the field of language teaching bear little resemblance to teachers' and students' lived experience of methods in the classroom.' In a similar vein, Woods (1991) suggests that the reality of classroom teaching is not what is found in official curricula or recommended materials, but results from individual teachers' interpretations of these. The official syllabus certainly does influence what takes place in the classroom, but not in a linear or easily predictable manner. The reality of classroom teaching and learning emerges rather from the teacher's interpretation of the syllabus or materials in use, and how this interpretation interacts with the perceptions of the learners involved, as well as with forces present in the broader context in which teaching is conducted. Woods (1991) contrasts two models of education: the input model and the process model. The former assumes that a programme is implemented:

> in a linear manner from top to bottom: overall educational objectives are set by a ministry or planning body, a syllabus is designed to carry out these objectives, materials are developed to instantiate the syllabus, the teaching is carried out to teach the content presented in the materials, and, finally, the learners are evaluated on the degree to which they have learned the content. (Woods, 1991: 1)

This describes the classic approach to curriculum design and implementation, and assumes the presence of a single set of rational principles which are subscribed to by all participants. The process model, on the other hand, sees classroom learning as operating in a multidirectional manner, so that 'learners interact with teachers and materials to determine what and how they learn' (1991: 1). In this view, two of the key factors which go to create classroom realities are the way in which teachers interpret materials and how they interact with learners. Both of these factors engage teachers as individuals with their own particular attitudes and beliefs about the nature of learning and teaching.

Kennedy and Kennedy (1996: 351) make a similar point with respect to the implementation of change. They point to the 'importance of teacher attitude and the interconnections [of attitude] with beliefs and teaching behaviour'. Any form of educational innovation is put into practice by teachers and is understood (or 'interpreted' to use Woods' term) by them in the light of their own attitudes. Kennedy and Kennedy also point out, however, that teacher attitude should not be seen as a static phenomenon, but rather as something which interacts with 'the social norms and the perceived behavioural control which is specific to a particular context' (p. 359). This parallels the remarks of Williams and Burden (1997) cited above with respect to individual differences among learners. Teachers may have a certain attitudinal disposition towards teaching and a number of behavioural preferences, but these are not static: They represent an underlying orientation that is realised dynamically in response to the specifics of each situation.

These observations indicate that teachers cannot be taken for granted or viewed simply as skilled technicians who dutifully realise a given set of teaching procedures in accordance with the directives of a more or less distant authority. Teachers are active participants in the creation of classroom realities, and they act in the light of their own beliefs, attitudes, and perceptions of the relevant teaching situation. This realisation has set our profession the challenge of working with teacher individuality and teacher identity just as much as with the individuality and identity of students. Indeed, we are coming to realise that we need to be as aware of the 'unique contribution which each individual brings to the learning situation' (Williams and Burden, 1997: 95) with respect to teachers just as much as learners.

---

- What do you feel that you as an individual bring to your task as teacher? In which ways does this influence your actions and choices in the classroom?
- Have you ever felt any tensions between your personal attitudes or philosophy of teaching and the expectations of other participants? If so, identify what these tensions are and analyse their origins.

---

## 1.5 Identity and context

Students' and teachers' identities are in part the result of factors of a purely individual nature, but they are also influenced by aspects of the context in which they live and work. The language classroom is not an other-worldly entity divorced from human culture and society. Language teaching is conducted among individuals interacting with one another in a specific socially defined framework, i.e. in a classroom, school, language centre, or whatever. This framework in turn is part of a larger entity which is the society and culture in question. In this way, context influences what takes place in classrooms in a variety of ways. Context, however, is a complex phenomenon, which may be seen as having two main sets of components: pragmatic and mental.

In the first instance, there are the objectively observable pragmatic features of a given teaching situation. These include a wide range of factors. Class size is clearly one: teaching a group of 100 students is a very different affair from teaching a group of 10, even if the objective learning goals that the two groups are pursuing are the same. Then there is the question of the teaching–learning resources which are available, and which can vary from a blackboard (with a more or less reliable supply of chalk) to classrooms equipped with audio and video equipment backed up by a self-access centre with CALL and multimedia facilities. Other factors include the type and level of training that teachers have received, their salaries, their status in society, and their decision-making role in their institution. The presence of an examination may also be an important contextual factor in terms of the vision of language it contains, its role in students' careers, the type of study habits it generates, and so on. These and other factors can play a powerful role in influencing what takes place in the classroom, both directly in terms of what can or cannot be done, and indirectly in terms of participants' attitudes to the teaching situation.

The second main constituent of context are the attitudes, beliefs, and behavioural expectations which participants bring with them to the classroom. The language classroom is certainly a pedagogical entity, but one which is embedded in the society and culture of which it is part. The classroom therefore needs to be understood with reference to the broader context of the beliefs and expectations of the relevant culture. Brumfit highlights the close connection between participants' attitudes and belief system and their evaluation of classroom behaviours in the following terms:

> Schooling, which includes teaching, is a co-operative activity performed by human beings. Participants in this enterprise are constrained by the micro-social context in which they operate, so any teaching will have limitations on available options imposed by the nature of the classroom . . . These constraints favour particular kinds of social interactions, but the negotiation of appropriate interaction that goes on within them is also subject to the macro-sociological context, which will reflect larger ideologies of the time . . . Factors of these kinds, mediated through the views of students, their parents, administrators, politicians and others will necessarily constrain any teaching. It is only within this context that matters of the nature of language and the nature of language learning become important. (1991: 141)

The way in which participants perceive classroom realities and interact with one another are therefore influenced by their socialisation, and their belief and value systems. The language classroom is thus one part of a much broader sociocultural reality. Hayes (1996: 174) observes that 'meaning is a socio-cultural construct' and stresses the importance of 'an understanding of the meaning for participants of their experience of a situation and their participation'. A similar point is made by Cortazzi, who uses the term 'perspective' to describe 'the matrix of assumptions by which someone makes sense of their world'. Cortazzi stresses that 'perspectives' are not:

> simply reflections of reality, but [are rather] constructed in the course of social interaction in terms essentially given by the

> culture. In this view, culture serves as a framework for the perception of others and guides the interpretation of classroom interaction and, more broadly, the construction of meaning in the classroom. (1990: 55)

Context, then, includes more than just the externally observable pragmatic features of a situation. It also relates to the mental context which is created by participants' attitudes, beliefs, and expectations. Furthermore, and crucially, it involves the interaction of the two. Holliday (1994), for example, in a discussion of certain study habits current among Egyptian university students, points out that these habits derive in part from aspects of traditional Egyptian culture, but also reflect cooperative modes of behaviour which have arisen out of relatively recent developments in Egyptian society, in particular rapid urbanisation, an overburdened infrastructure, and the consequent need for people to develop networks of mutual support and assistance.

The acknowledgement of the role of contextual factors has given rise to a number of studies which have explored the way in which these factors influence the behaviours and, indeed, the 'personality' of participants in the classroom. With respect to language learners, this has taken the form of investigation of the learning style preferences of certain culturally homogeneous groups of learners (e.g. Reid, 1987; Melton, 1990; Oxford *et al.*, 1992; Hyland, 1993), of culturally-specific learning traditions (Erbaugh, 1990), and of the modes of classroom interaction characteristic of certain cultural groups (Coleman, 1996a; Sullivan, 1996). Other studies have examined the way in which learners' socialisation and their culturally based expectations interact with particular methodological approaches such as learner autonomy (Riley, 1988; Ho and Crookall, 1995) and communicative language teaching (Ellis, 1996). It would be unhelpful to oversimplify the results of these studies, but they indicate that the sociocultural traditions of learning to which students have been exposed exert a real influence on how they perceive the teaching–learning process, how they define their goals, and how they interact with methodology, including the relative roles of teachers and students. This may be more marked when learners are studying in their home culture, where their own socioculturally based beliefs and expectations receive reinforcement from the attitudes and behaviours of other participants (including their teachers), as well as from various institutionalised aspects of the education system.

A smaller number of studies have adopted a similar approach to teacher behaviours, in the attempt to explore the cultural content of teachers' perceptions of their pedagogical tasks (e.g. Burnaby and Sun, 1989; Langfeldt, 1992; Richards, 1992). Other studies have focused on the way in which teachers and students interact with one another to create classroom realities in response to various aspects of context (Young, 1987; McCargar, 1993; Muchiri, 1996; Shamim, 1996a), including political or ideological factors (Adendorff, 1996; Chick, 1996; Duff, 1996).

Interestingly, Cortazzi and Jin (1996) point to the way in which the different expectations of students with respect to teachers from their own and from a different cultural group interact with differences in the behaviours of the two groups of teachers to create different classroom dynamics. This study reminds us that, while both students and teachers appear to bring to the classroom perceptions and expectations that arise out of their sociocultural backgrounds, these factors operate dynamically, i.e. they interact with and around the expectations and behaviours of other participants and with aspects of context. Cortazzi and Jin also point out that cultures evolve over time and thereby warn against a stereotypical or static view of culture.

It emerges from these studies that the context, both pragmatic and mental, in which students and teachers operate exerts a very real influence on what they do and how they evaluate the options that are available to them. These factors contribute to the participants' identity in the classroom and need to be taken into account both in understanding a situation as it is at a given point in time and in evaluating the likely effects of change.

---

Select one situation that you are familiar with either as a teacher or as a learner and try to identify the main contextual factors which make this situation what it is.

- Initially, do this separately for the two categories of contextual factors outlined above, viz. pragmatic and mental.
- Then try to evaluate the interaction of the two. For example, how do participants react to poor resourcing or large class numbers? Which strategies do they adopt, and what are their attitudes to the pragmatic aspects of the situation? In which way does the presence of an examination influence approaches to teaching and students' motivation and study strategies?

---

## 1.6 Emerging responses, emerging challenges

The trends reviewed in this chapter reflect a significant change in thinking on language teaching. They arise out of an increasing acknowledgement of the role played by human perceptions and expectations in both learning and teaching. This clearly alters the role which is attributed to the technology of teaching, and to methodology in particular. The reality that methodology assumes in the classroom is not simply a reflection of its own inner logic (or that which was in the mind of its originators) but of the meaning it assumes for participants. This meaning results from participants' own perceptions of the teaching situation and the goals they will be pursuing within it, not simply as students or teachers in the abstract but in the totality of their lives. It cannot therefore be assumed that methodology operates in a linear, deterministic manner: a given methodological option leading in a more or less direct and predictable manner to a specifiable set of learning outcomes. Methodological choices need to be made in the light of the human and contextual factors which are specific to each teaching situation. Decision-making therefore has to be local and situation-specific; this clearly has a number of significant implications for educational planning.

This section begins with a survey of the pedagogical responses which have emerged in recent years as part of the move towards a more ecological perspective on language teaching. It then briefly surveys some of the challenges which these responses have raised, not simply in a strictly pedagogical sense, but with respect to the overall organisation of learning programmes.

## 1.6.1 Responses . . .

Our recognition of the importance of learners' subjective interaction with language study has made it clear that no one methodological approach can be considered to be equally suitable for all learners. This implies that a given activity or mode of learning is likely to assume quite different meanings for the various learners who use it, and therefore it cannot be assumed that it will lead to the same or perhaps even to comparable learning outcomes. One response to this has been to cater for variety in methodological approach and activity type so that most students have the opportunity to find at least some aspects of their learning programme which correspond to their own learning preferences; this represents a meaningful step towards the accommodation of learner diversity. A teacher working from a coursebook or a range of sources which offer a variety of activity types is clearly in a better position to respond to different learning preferences than if the source material caters for just one mode of learning. A varied and strategy-rich (Tudor, 1996: 197–201) learning environment is therefore a real asset in the goal of accommodating learner diversity. This having been said, the availability of a variety of learning options offers a potential which has to be realised locally as part of the day-to-day interaction between teacher and students and among students themselves; this calls for a reflective involvement of learners in their language study.

For this reason, considerable attention has been devoted to the means of engaging learners actively in their language study. A key aspect of this process is the fostering of their ability to articulate their insights and preferences, and to develop their understanding of language study so that they can engage in an informed dialogue about the learning options available to them, a process which is generally referred to as learner training (cf. Ellis and Sinclair, 1989). Learner training, however, is not an end in itself, but one stage in the broader involvement of learners in their language study. The latter has found expression in concepts such as syllabus negotiation and the learner-centred curriculum (Nunan, 1988). The acknowledgement of the role of subjective factors in learning and of the individuality of each language learner has thus given rise to a concern with the quality of learners' involvement in their language study and a desire to develop learning frameworks which cater for an active and reflective involvement of learners in the shaping of their study programme.

A parallel change has taken place with respect to the role of the teacher. In part, this is a logical consequence of the move towards a more learner-centred approach to teaching. The difficulty of accommodating learner diversity in a pre-programmed, technocratic manner means that the move to a more learner-centred approach to teaching involves a greater degree of negotiation and decision-making at classroom level between teacher and students. This places a greater decision-making responsibility with the classroom teacher as opposed to the more or less distant curriculum designer or materials writer (Tudor, 1993, 1996). It is for this reason that Kumaradivelu (1994: 27) speaks of a 'post-method condition' which has arisen out of the move away from the traditional concept of method and which 'may potentially refigure the relationship between theorizers and teachers by empowering teachers with knowledge, skill and autonomy'.

Furthermore, as indicated in Section 1.4, research into teacher decision-making has revealed that teachers interpret methodology and understand their own teaching situations on the basis of a variety of affective, attitudinal, and experiential factors. It cannot therefore be assumed that teachers will simply 'do as they are told', if only because they are likely to interpret 'what they are told' in different ways. Teachers are active participants in the creation of classroom realities and will do this in an individual manner. Teacher awareness and skills are thus crucial factors in the quality of teaching. These factors, however, cannot simply be written into a set of materials, and need to be explicitly fostered and supported. The acknowledgement of the crucial decision-making role played by the classroom teacher has given rise to interest in the concept of reflective teaching (cf. Wallace, 1991; Graves, 1996; Nunan and Lamb, 1996) and to the exploration of teaching 'from the inside' (Richards, 1996). The idea of reflective teaching is thus in part a consequence of the move towards reflective learning. It also points to our profession's growing acknowledgement of the complexity of teaching. Teacher awareness and teacher development have thus become key 'methodological' issues.

A number of studies, as well as the experience of practising language educators, have drawn attention to the role of context in language teaching. As already indicated, context includes both the pragmatic aspects of the teaching situation and the attitudes and expectations of participants. As teaching situations can differ significantly on both counts, it cannot be assumed that what works well in one situation will necessarily work equally well in another. This realisation has given rise to interest in 'appropriate methodology' (Holliday, 1994), which takes the pragmatic and mental realities of each teaching situation as the starting point for decision-making. In part, this concept may be seen as paralleling on a sociocultural level the concern with subjective needs on the individual level. In other words, it acknowledges the role played in language teaching and learning by participants' sociocultural background, and the attitudes and expectations to which this gives rise. It also reflects the fact that the practical conditions within which teaching is conducted exert a significant influence not only on what can or cannot be done, but also on participants' attitudes to the teaching situation and to the actions of other participants.

Concern with appropriate methodology has drawn attention to what could be called the contextual relativity of methodological choices. This means that methodological choices cannot be made simply on the basis of abstract principles, but need to accommodate the mental and pragmatic realities of each teaching situation in its own right. Achieving this calls for exploration of local realities and the adaptation or reformulation of existing methodology around these realities. This requires flexibility and open-mindedness both from individual teachers and in terms of curriculum design and revision. On the latter count, Kennedy (1987) argues for a collaborative approach to innovation which integrates the insights of both insiders and outsiders; he also suggests that it is the former – and, in particular, the teachers – who will be responsible for realising change in the classroom, who should decide on the degree and pace of change. These suggestions, although very reasonable in themselves, have significant implications for educational planning.

## 1.6.2 . . . *and challenges*

Acknowledging the identity of participants both as individuals and as members of a given community clearly offers a much more promising path in educational terms than attempting to squash these many poles of diversity into a single mode of teaching and learning. It does, however, raise significant questions of both a pedagogical and an organisational nature. One question relates to the locus of control in language teaching. A learner-centred approach makes local decision-making crucial and calls for teacher empowerment. This, however, has implications both in terms of support for teachers and with respect to the organisation of teaching programmes. It can, for example, be difficult to obtain the time and resources needed for teacher development, and there are powerful forces of a political and organisational nature which emphasise control, accountability and standardisation. There may therefore be resistances within educational hierarchies either to the costs entailed by teacher empowerment or even to the very idea itself. The pedagogical impetus towards localness of decision-making can thus encounter significant obstacles of a social, organisational, or ideological nature.

In more general terms, the research reviewed in this chapter involves an acknowledgement of the complexity of language teaching in both human and contextual terms. Should this be seen in positive or negative terms? Is it an indication that our profession is suffering from postmodernist confusion, or that language teaching has fallen victim to the much discussed 'crisis of values' which is (apparently) threatening our societies? This is one interpretation. Alternatively, it is equally plausible to suggest that by acknowledging the complexity of language teaching in a more open and constructive manner, we are simply showing that our profession is coming of age and demonstrating the willingness to see things as they really are. The trends reviewed in this chapter reflect a growing awareness of the complex and dynamic nature of language teaching which has parallels with developments in many other fields of research. These are often discussed in terms of complexity theory or the study of complex adaptive systems. Much of what is written on these topics is specific to fields of research far removed from the direct concerns of language teaching, but accessible and engaging accounts are given in Waldrop (1992), Lewin (1993), and Kauffman (1995); Larsen-Freeman (1997) is also well worth reading for a discussion of these trends of thought with respect to aspects of language teaching. Our profession is thus by no means alone in calling into question the general framework of reference in which we have worked in the past.

In fact, one can seriously question whether it is reasonable to see language teaching as anything other than a complex activity. To begin with, all participants (students, teachers, heads of department, materials writers, and so on) are individuals in their own right. Each has his or her own personality, attitudes, beliefs and life experience, and these factors all influence how the participants interpret and interact with the activity of language teaching. Each participant is also a member of one or more sociocultural or socioprofessional groups, and this, too, influences the identity which they manifest in the classroom, staff meeting, planning committee, or whatever. On this level, then, language teaching can never be less complex than the individuals who are involved in it. In addition, language teaching involves human beings in interaction with one another. This may involve direct face-to-face inter-action in the classroom, or the interaction may be indirect, as when a coursebook which reflects a given writer's perspective on language teaching is recommended for use in dozens or possibly hundreds of classrooms. In this case, the materials writer, although not physically present in the classroom, exerts strong influence on modes of interaction in the classroom.

This is the reality with which teachers and other practising language educators have to live and work. At the same time, while acknowledging that the complexity of language teaching may bring us closer to the reality of the activity, it also raises a variety of questions, not the least of which is where we should look for the guiding principles we need in order to help us approach our many tasks as teachers, teacher trainers, and so on. The technological response is to look outside of the specifics of each situation for general principles which can then be used to guide decision-making within these situations. However, as we have seen in the last three sections, this approach soon runs up against the problem of diversity: general principles are precisely that: general. All too frequently they do not fit the specifics of any one situation, and it is with specific situations that individual teachers work and in which decisions have to be made.

Another response is to look into each situation in its own right, to try to understand the dynamics which make the situation what it is, and to work with and from these dynamics. This may seem to confront us with a kaleidoscope of detail which may often seem confusing, contradictory and, at times, rather trivial. And yet, this is where language teaching is lived out, and where the value of principle is put to the hard test of reality. The essence of an ecological perspective on language teaching is precisely to understand situations in their own terms and in the light of the dynamics which operate within each situation. This clearly implies a change in orientation from the search for generalisations which has guided much thinking in language teaching. It does, however, open the door to better understanding of the uniqueness of each teaching situation and, thereby, to an approach to teaching which is locally relevant and meaningful by virtue of it being rooted in local realities. It suggests that we look at classrooms not as more or less perfect exemplars of an ideal classroom, but rather as complex adaptive systems in their own right. I have suggested elsewhere (Tudor 2000) that 'Local is beautiful' is a useful motto for language teaching. However, in order to be able to work locally, we need to explore the dynamics which make each teaching situation and, indeed, each classroom, what it is. This book has the goal of helping teachers to do this. It does not propose a grand theory of language teaching, but more modestly seeks to provide teachers with a few guidelines for developing a local understanding of their own teaching situations as they are in their own right, and in terms of their own inner logic and dynamics.

# 2   The dynamics of teaching and learning

## 2.1 Locating language teaching

One fairly fundamental question that arises in discussions of language teaching is what precisely one is talking about. On the one hand, there is a large and ever-growing body of theoretical writing and advice to teachers on how they could (or should) approach their tasks in the classroom. This is often translated into language curricula and finds expression in coursebooks and syllabuses. On the other hand, there is the daily reality of language teaching as lived out in thousands of classrooms throughout the world. This, too, is clearly an aspect of language teaching, and by no means the least important one. What, however, is the relationship between the two? And when we talk about language teaching, which of these two aspects of it are we in fact referring to? Freeman suggests that the relationship between the two may not be what we may wish to assume it is:

> In order to examine processes and to assess outcomes as products, researchers often create detached, stylized images of the messiness of teaching; they can then stand outside of these images to examine what is going on within them. The study of teaching becomes the examination of images of what is done in classrooms, of teachers' and students' behaviours and activity . . . However, these orderly relationships may lie more in the images themselves than in the world they are meant to capture. (1996: 91–92)

A technological perspective on education focuses on potentialities and assumes a fairly linear relationship between input and uptake. An ecological perspective, on the other hand, focuses on realities as they are lived out in particular contexts. It is less concerned with generalisations than with local realities. The shift in emphasis from a technological to an ecological perspective on language teaching (Sections 1.1 and 1.2) involves a change in the focus of attention, and therefore a change in what we are primarily concerned with when we talk about 'language teaching'.

Nunan (1989: 9) suggests that the term 'curriculum' can be understood in two ways. The first is the curriculum 'as a statement of intent, the "what should be" of a language programme as set out in syllabus outlines, sets of objectives, and various planning documents'. The other is the curriculum 'as reality', or 'what actually goes on from moment to moment in the language classroom'. A relationship is of course likely to exist between the two. The official curriculum can influence day-to-day classroom realities in a number of ways, if only because a certain pedagogical approach or set of materials may be recommended for use in classrooms. Classroom teaching, however, involves more than the elegant application of theoretical precept. It is something much more complex and, to use Freeman's (1996) expression, 'messy'. One problem, of course, is that while the official discourse of language teaching as found in methodology texts and curriculum descriptions is accessible to scrutiny and discussion, the day-to-day reality of teaching is far less accessible and infinitely dispersed. It is thus difficult to discuss it in a systematic manner, which does not, however, mean that it does not merit discussion at least to the same degree as the official discourse. The question therefore arises as to what the reality of language teaching is, and where we should look for it. Is it the 'official' version we find in academic publications and curriculum descriptions? Or is it something else, something more complex and about which we know relatively little?

Hayes (1996) makes an interesting contribution to this debate by distinguishing between 'vision' and 'voice' in language teaching. Hayes sees 'vision' as the prescriptive perspectives on language teaching generated by academics, and which he feels are imposed on teachers via theoretical precepts and ideal curriculum structures. 'Voice', on the other hand, relates to teachers' personal perceptions of their role within the specific context in which they are operating. For Hayes, teacher 'voice' arises out of a variety of factors including teachers' status in society, their motivations for choosing a career in teaching, teacher socialisation, teacher development, and:

> the whole complexity of teachers' lives within the classroom – their methods, their interaction with students, and so on – and the relationship of this with their lives outside the classroom.
>
> (Hayes, 1996: 185)

Hayes believes that 'vision' has predominated in discussions of language teaching, and that insufficient attention has been paid to 'voice', thereby ignoring a crucial element in the creation of classroom dynamics and thus of the reality of language teaching. For Hayes, then, we have two different perspectives on language teaching. One is the official discourse as expressed in theory and policy statements of different kinds. The other is that of the practitioners most directly responsible for realising language teaching at classroom level. The first perspective rests on generalisations and on abstract principle; the second is local, situation-specific and diverse.

These remarks imply that an honest understanding of language teaching as it is lived out in real classrooms needs to take account of the many and varied factors which assume prominence for the students and teachers immediately present in these classrooms. The official discourse of language teaching clearly plays an important role in the creation of human and pedagogical realities in the classroom. It is not, however, the whole story. The day-to-day reality of language teaching is something far more diverse and is lived out amid a mass of details which are often untidy and difficult to put together into a coherent whole. This reflects the multifaceted interaction of students and teachers with one another, with methodology and materials, and with the broader context in which teaching is conducted. The reality of language teaching emerges from this meeting of different actors and different perceptions of the nature and goals of learning and teaching. The result is anything but tidy, but that would seem to be the way it is, which is a good enough reason for trying to explore this reality openly and in its own terms – untidiness and all.

It is tempting – especially perhaps for educational authorities, course designers and others responsible for planning teaching programmes – to think of language teaching as a classical symphony in which the various participants faithfully and devotedly render the notes as laid down by the composer: a margin for interpretation exists, but Beethoven's Fifth is always Beethoven's Fifth. In practice, language teaching is more like a jam session in which the musicians respond intuitively to one another's ideas to create a reality which is novel and at least partly unpredictable at the start of the session. Tuning in on what different participants bring to the classroom, how they perceive and experience classroom realities, and the interactive dynamics which arise out of their attempt to find personal meaningfulness within it would thus seem to be the starting point for an honest understanding of language teaching as it really is.

In a book entitled *Metaphors We Live By*, Lakoff and Johnson (1980) highlight the role played by metaphor in our thinking and mental organisation of reality. With this in mind, think about the two metaphors used in the last paragraph to refer to language teaching.

- Which corresponds more to your own view of teaching?
- If you are dissatisfied with these metaphors, what would be the metaphor which you would use to describe language teaching as you have experienced it? (For a discussion of metaphors relating to teachers, cf. Oxford *et al.*, 1998.) Compare your choice with those of a few colleagues and discuss the differences that emerge.

## 2.2 Diversity and rationality

One of the main ideas on which this book rests is that diversity is a fundamental component of language teaching. One rarely has far to look to discover this diversity. If a teacher pauses a moment to look at the class they have been teaching for the last week, it soon emerges that 'the class' is in fact a collection of 15, 20 or however many individuals. Each of these individuals differs from the others in one way or another, and these differences mean that what the teacher does or asks the students to do in the classroom is likely to assume a somewhat different reality for each of the students concerned. These differences may be more or less marked, but they are certainly there. The diversity which characterises language teaching is also likely to have struck teachers who have worked in different contexts, especially perhaps if these have included cultural settings other than that in which the teacher was brought up and educated. The teacher may have found that learning activities or materials which worked smoothly and effectively in another context seem not to fit in the new one, or that they elicit unexpected reactions from the students. In addition, the teacher may come to feel that the new setting operates according to a set of rules which they seem unable to grasp, or may come to feel that in one way or another they are 'getting things wrong', but without being able to understand why or even in which ways. Then there is the diversity which we encounter among our fellow teachers. How often have we felt that there are as many differing perspectives on language teaching as there are colleagues in a meeting? There are of course common points, too. All of our students and colleagues share their basic humanity and have a very large number of human aspirations in common. The path to this shared humanity, however, frequently passes through the acceptance and exploration of diversity.

To a large degree, it is this diversity which makes language teaching a complex activity. If all participants saw language teaching and learning in the same way and defined their goals in the same terms, a technological approach to teaching would probably be quite adequate. Objective differences such as the age of learners, their learning goals, or class size could be dealt with in a relatively straightforward manner within a single decision-making matrix. Language teaching would thus be marked by differences at the surface level, but there would be little reason to speak of it as complex. In reality, of course, the various participants involved in a language teaching situation do not necessarily see either the nature or the goals of the activity in the same way. It is here that language teaching becomes complex, less because of the externally observable differences that exist among learners, teachers, or teaching situations, than as a result of the differences in the way in which participants perceive the nature and goals of language teaching, and the behaviours and interactional patterns to which these different perceptions give rise.

Faced with this situation, questions inevitably arise when one tries to think of language teaching as a 'rational' activity. In essence, which set of rational principles is one to work with? One response is to think of rationality as a single entity, i.e. to assume that there is one rational way of viewing situations and of interacting with them. To begin with, this raises the question of what this one rational perspective should be. Then one has to think of how one should react to those who do not see things the same way, and one never has to look far to find them: students, fellow teachers, the management of a given institution, the author of a coursebook, or even a whole educational system. If there is one rational way of seeing a situation, then other ways of seeing the same situation must logically be flawed to one degree or another. Or, to paraphrase Orwell, some are more rational than others, and we generally tend to place ourselves in the category of those who are that bit more rational.

A more tenable standpoint is that each language teaching situation will exhibit a number of different rationalities (Tudor, 1998). In this sense of the term, a rationality represents an internally coherent set of beliefs about the nature and goals of language teaching. These beliefs may or may not be explicitly formulated, but they constitute the framework of reference within which participants evaluate and interact with language teaching. It will be suggested here that the starting point for decision-making in language teaching is an open and constructive understanding of the diversity of perceptions which meet and interact in the language classroom. In other words, decision-making needs to rest on an understanding of the rationalities of the various participants present in the situation in question, rather than the appeal to the authority of a supposedly universal set of rational principles.

There are two main reasons for adopting this perspective on language teaching. The first is simply a matter of honesty: participants do frequently see aspects of teaching and learning in different ways, and this alone is sufficient reason for working with this diversity in an open and constructive manner. The second is that it enables us to understand the motivations and behaviours of participants better, and thereby to see situations in terms of the meaning which they have for these participants. Taking any one perspective on a situation as canonical entails the neglect, trivialisation or, worse still, the stigmatisation of others. Accepting that the reality of a situation has multiple interpretations, or that there are several rationalities at play in this situation, opens the door to improved mutual understanding and a sharing of insights.

In this section, a brief survey is made of some of the main 'rationalities' that teachers are likely to encounter in the practice of teaching. This has two purposes. The first is to identify certain key groupings of actors whose perceptions and goal structures intervene in language teaching. The second is to point to the fact that these actors will be operating according to a set of more or less explicitly formulated principles, and that their actions will therefore have their own inner coherence. A willingness to explore the inner logic which underpins the actions of the various actors involved in language teaching is thus the basis for constructive dialogue and the working out of a shared understanding of the activity.

## 1 Student rationalities

As was pointed out in Section 1.3, students are not 'simply' language learners. They are all individuals, each of whom has his or her own psychocognitive make up, personal history and life goals, and his or her own experience of education in general and possibly of language education in particular. These factors combine to influence students' attitudes to the process of language learning itself and also the way in which they define the goals of learning. In this way, each student can be said to have his or her own rationality of language learning, something which emerges from the studies of learner beliefs conducted by Wenden (1987) and Willing (1988). These rationalities may not be explicitly formulated in the way we find in writing on methodology or in official policy statements, but nonetheless influence the meaning which class-room learning activities assume for students, and therefore how they react to what we as teachers do and ask them to do.

Each of our students will thus have his or her individual perspective on language teaching and learning. In addition to this, there may also be rationalities which are shared by a larger number of students. Teachers may thus feel the presence of a shared set of beliefs and attitudes among their students. In this way, a group personality emerges in addition to the personalities of each student as an individual. These shared beliefs and attitudes may have roots in the cultural background of the students concerned, or may emerge from the interpersonal dynamics of a given class group. Effective teaching depends crucially on teachers being able to tune in to the meaning which language learning has for their students both as individuals and as members of a learning group.

## 2 Methodological rationalities

As Richards and Rodgers (1986) point out, approaches and methods are internally coherent constructs which rest on and exemplify a set of assumptions about language, language learning, and how the latter is best fostered by means of teaching and learning activities. In certain cases these assumptions are formulated with great precision and are linked to a closely defined set of teaching–learning activities, whereas in other cases the link between underlying principle and its classroom realisation is less closely defined. In either case, however, the teaching–learning activities which are recommended in a certain approach or method derive from an underlying set of assumptions about the nature of language and of language learning, and thus embody a certain rationality of language teaching. Methodological choices are therefore never neutral.

For this reason, when a teacher adopts a given approach to teaching or uses a certain set of materials, a specific educational rationality enters the classroom. This influences patterns of interaction and thus the dynamics of teaching and learning. In itself, this is a statement of the obvious: methodological choices are designed to promote a certain set of interactional patterns and learning-related activities and thus inevitably influence what takes place in the classroom. Two points do, however, need to be borne in mind. The first is that no approach is 'right' in an absolute sense – it is simply one way of conceptualising language learning and of promoting the process of learning a language (however this is defined), and may coincide more or less closely with the way in which students or teachers view language learning. The second is that the nature of the change in classroom dynamics to which a given approach gives rise does not depend solely on the inner logic of the approach in question, but rather on the meaning which it assumes for participants, and this is situation-specific. It is for this reason that a given methodology can assume a very different reality in the classroom from that which it may have had in the mind of the course designer or materials writer.

The main point with respect to the concept of methodological rationalities is therefore that a given methodology represents one perspective on the nature and goals of language teaching. Consequently, when a given methodological approach is adopted, the assumptions on which the approach is based interact dynamically with the perceptions and expectations of the teacher and students, and the nature of this interaction may be difficult to predict in advance. It is therefore unwise to make methodological choices on the basis of the inner logic of methodology alone, without consideration of the attitudes and expectations of the teachers and students with whom it will be used.

## 3 Sociocultural rationalities

Two main categories of rationality have been considered so far: those of students and those of methodology. For fairly obvious reasons, these two rationalities have received the greatest amount of attention in the literature. It is, however, difficult to understand the dynamics which arise from the interaction between students and methodology without considering the other rationalities which can and do play a role in the practical realisation of language teaching. To do this, however, it is necessary to look beyond the classroom in the narrow sense.

To begin with, as was pointed out in Section 1.5, the classroom is a socially defined reality and is therefore influenced by the belief systems and behavioural norms of the society of which it is part. Van Lier makes this point in the following terms:

> The language classroom itself is only one segment of the social world of the learner, and it is only one – though central – component of the organized institutions that are involved in education and training. The classroom researcher must therefore study the classroom as embodying a specific set of functions and values from the point of view of the learner, and also from the point of view of social institutions at large. Ideals, expectations, and conceptions of the properties that a classroom must possess so that it can be regarded as an ordinary, good classroom, play an important role in determining what will happen in the classroom.
> (1988: 81)

These 'ideals, expectations, and conceptions of the properties a class-room must possess' are not optional frills, something quaint added on to a 'basic' classroom, but represent powerful forces which make the classroom what it is. Van Lier (1988: 78) is therefore correct in suggesting that they influence factors such as how the purposes of teaching and learning are defined, the roles of and relationships between participants, and the rules according to which appropriate classroom behaviour is evaluated. They thus constitute a diffuse but nonetheless powerful rationality which is rooted in the attitudes, behavioural norms, and expectations of participants such as students, teachers, administra-tors, parents, sponsors, policy-makers, and potentially many others.

Sociocultural rationalities can be very difficult to pin down, partly because they are diffuse and partly because they are more often than not implicit: they are what participants take as being 'the way things are done', and it may in fact be difficult for an insider to articulate their principles. Sociocultural rationalities may, in fact, be more apparent to someone from outside the sociocultural group in question. The outsider will realise that certain things operate differently from what they would expect from their own cultural background, which gives these factors a prominence that they may not have for insiders. This having been said, sociocultural rationalities are not monolithic, and participants interact with them in different ways. Nor are they immutable: cultures and social systems evolve and a dialectic may emerge between different sub-groups within the same general culture, which may lead either to the development of new ideas or to a call for a renewal of 'traditional' values.

At this point it is difficult to avoid the thorny question of where education ends and politics begins. Van Lier (1996) points out on a number of occasions that the political or ideological climate can influence classroom realities in a significant manner, not simply with respect to questions of funding but also in terms of the way in which goals are defined and classroom behaviours are evaluated. For example, he reproduces (1996: 84, from Carter, 1992) the comments of a leading Conservative politician in the 1980s, Norman Tebbit, on language teaching:

> We've allowed so many standards to slip . . . teachers weren't bothering to teach kids how to spell and to punctuate properly . . . if you allow standards to slip to the stage where good English is no better than bad English, where people turn up filthy . . . at school . . . all those things cause people to have no standards at all, and once you lose standards then there's no imperative to stay out of crime. (Norman Tebbit, Radio 4, 1985)

These comments clearly express a certain perspective on language, on the role of the teacher not just in a 'strictly' pedagogical sense but also as a member of society, and on society itself. If officially sanctioned and used to guide curriculum design, such attitudes can have a direct influence on what is done in classrooms, e.g. an influence on the materials that are used, the way in which tasks are structured and outcomes evaluated, not to mention the way in which teacher performance is assessed. Sociocultural rationalities can therefore play a powerful role in shaping the context in which teachers and students operate.

## 4 Institutional and corporate rationalities

Language teaching is more often than not conducted in an institutional setting, and for this reason the ethos and goal structure of the institution – the rationality of the institution in question – can play a significant role in the creation of classroom dynamics. Institutions are of course likely to reflect aspects of the sociocultural rationalities which prevail in the society of which they are part, but most have their own corporate culture and ways of defining their goals, whether this finds expression in the form of a mission statement or in the form of a more or less implicit set of assumptions and norms of behaviour. With respect to language teaching institutions this can influence the way in which an institution defines the nature and goals of language teaching, its decision-making structures, and various aspects of teacher–student relations. It is therefore useful to look at the rationality of language teaching that is operant in a given institution and to evaluate the way in which this influences classroom teaching and learning.

One pole on which language teaching institutions differ is whether they are state run or privately run. In the state sector – at primary and secondary levels at least – education is compulsory, teachers have a number of clearly defined and legally binding social responsibilities, and learning programmes are often drawn up by the relevant educational authorities. Furthermore, the institutional structure of state education introduces into the decision-making process a variety of participants such as headteachers, school inspectors, administrators, government officials, and politicians. These participants have their own role and perceptions of teaching, and exert an influence on what occurs in classrooms, including the criteria according to which classroom realities are evaluated. A change in government or in educational policy may thus lead to changes in the goals which are set for language learning, in the methodologies which are favoured, and also in the general ethos of teaching and learning with which educational institutions are required to work. Especially in the state sector, institutional rationalities often have a close relationship with the prevailing sociocultural rationalities.

Language teaching in the private sector differs in a number of respects from state education: attendance is by free choice, students are generally able to select among a range of courses offered by one or more schools and, at institutional level at least, the traditional pedagogical relationship between teachers and students is coupled with that of supplier and client. Furthermore, private language schools often have more freedom to define their goals and approach to language teaching than state-run institutions, even if they may take an external examination as a reference point. Furthermore, it is not uncommon for language schools to work with a fairly specific approach to language teaching, to have a preference for a certain type of materials and learning activities, and to promote a specific professional and interpersonal ethos. Teachers who work in a given school may thus be expected to adopt the school's approach to teaching and learning and to contribute to the classroom relations and interpersonal ethos promoted by the school.

In certain contexts, aid or development agencies and their rationalities can assume a significant role in the organisation of language education programmes. This can relate to the way in which the objectives of language education programmes are defined and also to the methodologies which are favoured. Even if the aims of such agencies are laudable, the choices they make are never value-neutral, and the pedagogical expression of these choices generally reflect the value system and norms of the agency in question and those of its source country or countries.

Other corporate groupings which exercise a significant influence on the landscape within which teachers work are the publishing houses responsible for commissioning and marketing coursebooks and teaching materials. Considerations relating to the popularity and effectiveness of materials are inevitably combined with concerns of commercial risk and viability. Thus, while publishing houses are attentive to their users, the materials which are available on the market at a given point in time reflect the publishers' perceptions of the market and their own corporate goals and concerns. The range of materials from which teachers may choose therefore reflects both the educational and the corporate rationalities of publishing houses.

## 5 Teacher rationalities

Teachers, like students, are individuals and their actions in the classroom reflect their individuality and their own personal philosophy of teaching. Each teacher thus defines the nature and goals of language teaching in a certain way and may therefore be seen as having his or her own rationality of teaching. This exerts a significant influence on what teachers do in the classroom and also on how they interact with the actions and the attitudes of other participants. From the point of view of materials writers, educational authorities, and institutional authorities this can be seen as a reminder that teachers do not necessarily perform their tasks 'on cue' (cf. Woods, 1991), but interpret and go about these tasks in the light of their own vision of teaching. From the point of view of the individual teacher, it is a reminder that what we as teachers do in the classroom reflects our own vision of teaching and that, while this vision has its own inner logic, it is only one among potentially many others. Teachers therefore need to examine their own beliefs and assumptions, and how these contribute to the dynamics of their teaching.

---

This section has worked with the concept of 'rationalities' as a means of exploring the inner logic of the perspectives which various (groups of) participants have on language teaching. With reference to a teaching situation with which you are familiar:

- Identify the various groups of participants who played a role in the relevant situation and the rationality which underpinned their actions.
- Analyse the inner logic of these rationalities to assess whether they can explain any tensions or disagreements which may have arisen among participants.
- Compare your findings with those of one or more colleagues who have performed the same task. What does this suggest to you about the nature of language teaching?

---

## 2.3 A changing research agenda

Much educational planning operates as if a fairly linear relationship exists between the methodological principles contained in a curriculum or set of materials and the reality which these will assume in the classroom. This rests on the assumption of normality which, in our field, implies that participants have the same (or at least fairly similar) perceptions of the nature and goals of language teaching. In certain contexts there may genuinely be a large degree of consensus among students, teachers, materials writers, educational authorities, and other members of society about what language teaching involves and the goals it should pursue. In these contexts, the assumption of normality, although never fully tenable, may at least provide a reasonable working hypothesis.

As was suggested in Section 2.2, however, normality cannot be taken for granted, and diversity is more likely to be the norm than the exception, as has been shown with respect to ELT projects in countries with different educational traditions to the Anglo-Saxon world (cf. Holliday, 1994). Even within a given culture, however, it cannot be assumed that all participants share the same perceptions and goal structures, particularly during periods of change when social groupings and ideologies are in a state of flux. Rather than the elegant realisation of one rationality, then, language teaching is likely to involve the meeting and interaction of different rationalities. Murray (1996) is therefore right in speaking of the 'tapestry of diversity' which makes our classrooms what they are. It is therefore necessary to explore what the classroom means to the different participants involved, and how these various understandings influence participants' choices and decisions. It also makes it necessary to explore the network of relationships which arises out of the meeting of these different perceptions and goal structures.

Doing this, however, clearly calls for an investigative methodology which makes it possible to gain insight into different participants' perceptions of a situation in their own terms and not simply with respect to those of another group of participants. This is true of the formal type of research that is reported in specialist journals, and also with respect to the applied, situation-specific type of research which is involved in preparing a teaching programme for a given class, institution, or region. Experienced teachers know that whatever the theoretical potential of a given methodology or set of materials, these are unlikely to lead to meaningful learning unless they fit into the mental realities of the students in question. Creating this link is a key aspect of teaching, and calls both for an understanding of the mental realities of the students involved and also for the ability to react to these realities on a moment-to-moment basis. The move to a more ecological approach to language teaching therefore calls for a research orientation which is able to look beyond observable behaviours to their origins and, in this way, to seize the inner logic which underlies participants' actions.

An important distinction in this respect is that between 'etic' and 'emic' approaches to research (cf. Van Lier, 1988: 16–17; Bailey and Nunan, 1996: 3–4). The first approach, which has tended to dominate in language teaching research, adopts the standpoint of the outsider concerned with general principles and objectively verifiable phenomena: it represents what is generally seen as the 'scientific method' and is strongly influenced by positivist thinking. Emic research, on the other hand, accords more attention to the perspective of insiders, i.e. how participants perceive a situation and their place within it. It is also concerned with discovering local coherence, or how a system operates in terms of its own inner logic and rules. This type of research is sometimes referred to as naturalistic inquiry in that it works with systems as they are, and seeks to discover how they operate from the perspective of those who are involved in these systems, as opposed to studying them in the light of criteria derived from outside the system. Not surprisingly, this type of research is frequent in ethnography as a means of discovering the belief and value systems of societies unfamiliar to the observer. Bailey and Nunan, referring to Lincoln and Guba (1985), list five axioms for naturalistic research.

1. Realities are multiple, constructed and holistic.
2. The knower and the known are interactive and inseparable.
3. Only time-bound and context-bound hypotheses are possible (in contrast to the positivist desire for time-free and context-free generalisations).
4. It is impossible to distinguish causes from effects since 'all entities are in a state of mutual simultaneous shaping'.
5. Inquiry is value-bound (in contrast to the experimentalist notion that legitimate inquiry must be value free, which is, in itself, a value statement). (1996: 1–2)

One justification for adopting an emic or naturalistic approach to research in language teaching is that while there is no lack of advice about what could or should happen in classrooms, we are coming to realise that we know relatively little about what does happen in reality. Van Lier makes this point in the following terms:

[Classroom research] is a commitment to go into the classroom and find out what goes on in it. It is probably the most difficult place to do research in, as witnessed by its long history of neglect and its status as a 'black box' between input and output measures . . . Researchers have tended to avoid it as a particularly 'messy' source of data, and walked around it in the hope that, eventually, its walls would come tumbling down.'

(1988: 14)

Whenever choices have to be made – from a teacher's decision to select one activity as opposed to another, to curriculum design at institutional or national level – the first consideration must evidently be the objective relevance of the choices made to the learners' present or future needs in the language. At the same time, these choices have to be viewed in conjunction with the perceived reality which they will have for the participants involved at a given point in time and in the specific context in which they are operating. This involves working, in part at least, with 'soft' data which can provide insight into the understandings and motivations of participants. Such data may arise from diary studies or personal accounts of learning and teaching experiences, or from open-ended discussion with participants about their individual perceptions of a situation. It may also involve study of the educational traditions of a given culture or institution, the interpersonal norms and decision-making structures in place, or the ways in which change is generally realised (by whom, at what pace, and via which channels), as well as of factors such as the perceived status of the target language (TL) or the socioeconomic status and self-image of either students or teachers.

The importance of insider insights does not, of course, mean there is no place for the gathering of information on externally observable phenomena. It simply reminds us that the observation of a given phenomenon does not necessarily tell the whole story. This needs to be sought beyond the surface script of interaction in the classroom in the meaning which events have for participants. Indeed, the move towards an emic or naturalistic emphasis in research has brought the concerns of researchers closer to the day-to-day experience of practising language teachers. Teachers know that their task is rarely straightforward, and that the key to effective teaching is the ability to feel and respond to the dynamics of each class as it is in its own terms. It is perhaps for this reason that practising teachers sometimes express a certain scepticism about the confident generalisations put forward in the theoretical literature. They know that each class is unique, and that the teacher must learn to respond to this uniqueness, whether it corresponds to an ideal picture of what a classroom should be or not.

It is only recently that we have begun to acknowledge just how complex an activity teaching is, and that the implicit, instinctive reactions of the experienced teacher may tell us more about the reality of language teaching than the elegant generalisations found in methodology texts. As Freeman pertinently suggests:

> The complexity of teaching cannot be cleaned up simply by pretending it is not there; order cannot be forced on to it by writing and talking in a detached manner about its messiness.

> (1996: 107)

An acknowledgement of the complexity of language teaching does not promise neat, unambiguous solutions or paths of action. It does, however, point our energies in the right direction, which is presumably a first step towards finding appropriate and sustainable responses.

Think of one or two questions that you have often asked yourself about language teaching with respect to a specific group of students, a given methodological approach, or any other topic.

- To begin with, try to identify as precisely as possible what you consider to be at the heart of each question.
- How would you go about exploring this question? Where would you look for answers? Which investigative procedures would you use?
- Would your approach be more etic or more emic in orientation? Justify your choice as if you were speaking to a proponent of the other orientation, whichever it may be.

## 2.4 A dynamic perspective on the classroom

So far in this chapter it has been suggested that language teaching is a complex activity, and that this complexity derives primarily from the diversity of perceptions and goals of the various participants who, in one way or another, play a role in the teaching–learning process. Indeed, if all participants could be assumed to see the nature and goals of language teaching in the same way, teaching would be a much more straightforward undertaking than it generally is. In some contexts, of course, there is a high level of consensus among participants about why a given language is being learned and how this should best be under-taken. This degree of consensus, cannot, however, be taken as the norm. It is for this reason that it was suggested in Section 2.2 that language teaching can be understood more meaningfully in terms of the inter-action of different rationalities rather than the enactment of a single canonical rationality.

The classroom is a place where a variety of participants with potentially differing perspectives on the nature and goals of language teaching meet and interact, which gives rise to a dynamic tension between their differing perceptions of the nature and goals of language teaching. Teaching and learning are thus dynamic phenomena (cf. Prabhu, 1992) in that they involve the attempt of various actors to live out their own perceptions of the activity and to pursue their own goals within a context which is shaped by the perceptions and goals of a variety of other actors. The dynamic nature of teaching is thus a logical consequence of the diversity of perspectives which meet and interact in the language classroom.

43

Teachers are most immediately confronted with this diversity among their students. It is perhaps for this reason that even experienced teachers can feel slightly apprehensive when they meet a new group of students for the first time. The programme may be established and the materials chosen, but teachers know that their task is to bring these alive with the particular students that they have in front of them, and how this can be achieved depends on the specific individuals who are present and the group dynamics that emerge. A teacher may, for example, achieve a fairly stable and shared understanding of teaching and learning with a class during one course, but find that a year or perhaps even a semester later, a new modus vivendi and a new understanding need to be worked out with the very same class. There may be many reasons for this. The students may be that little bit older or may have entered a different stage of their studies, and they may thus see either the TL or the learning process itself in different terms. Alternatively, the students may react in a different way to the course goals which they have to pursue or to the coursebook that they are now required to use. The teacher may therefore find it necessary to re-initiate an exchange of perceptions and to attempt to develop a new sense of shared meaningfulness in the learning process.

The dynamic nature of language teaching may emerge most clearly when a change is introduced into an educational system. The participants present in the system may have worked out a fairly stable way of approaching learning and teaching. This modus vivendi may, however, satisfy some participants more than others, or external events may precipitate a re-evaluation of the terms in which goals are defined or the way in which teaching is approached. This in turn can lead to a change being introduced into the system, which often takes the form of a revision of programme content or methodology at the initiative of one group of participants. The system in place will therefore be disrupted, and the various participants will react to this change and to the new roles which are assigned to them in a variety of ways.

Holliday (1991), for example, uses the term 'tissue rejection' to describe the fate of a learning programme which, as a result of being insufficiently embedded in local realities, fails to take root and has to be abandoned or at least radically revised. There is more likelihood of this occurring when the programme is developed by agents from outside the local context, or whose perceptions either of the situation or of language teaching in general do not coincide with those of the participants directly involved in the realisation of the programme. This type of outcome is generally viewed in terms of the failure of the programme in question, and can be a rather painful experience for the programme developers. In reality, however, it is simply one outcome of the dynamic interaction of different participants with one another in a situation where local participants may have no other means of manifesting their unease with the perceptions contained in the programme than by a withdrawal of support. Furthermore, if a given programme suffers tissue rejection and 'fails', it generally needs to be replaced by another, and this gives rise to another set of dynamics that may allow local participants to move the new programme in a direction which is more in tune with their own perceptions of the situation. Indeed, if explicit channels for an open exchange of perceptions among participants do not exist, then a withdrawal of support may be the only way in which teachers can express their dissatisfaction.

The term 'token adoption' is used to refer to another type of outcome. In this case, aspects of a programme are adopted, but in a manner different from that which was intended by the programme designers. Teachers involved in the realisation of a programme may, for instance, use a certain type of materials or of learning activity, but in a manner which differs from the logic in which they were conceived. A superficial survey of classroom activities may thus indicate that an innovation has been adopted, whereas a more detailed study of class-room interaction would reveal a discrepancy between official intention and pedagogical reality. Token adoption is likely to occur more often in contexts where the planning authorities have disciplinary power over teachers, so that teachers may feel a degree of pressure to adopt what is recommended in at least formal terms, even if they then work out their own modus vivendi around these elements. This may reflect a difference between the perceptions which teachers (and possibly students, too) have of the situation, and the perceptions and goal structures of the relevant educational authorities (cf. Prabhu, 1987).

These examples relate to programme reform at institutional or regional level. It is important to bear in mind, however, that the implementation of educational reform takes place in each classroom of the institution or educational system in question: the whole therefore emerges from a mass of specific actions and choices. The content of a language learning programme may be decided in ministerial planning committees, but its success is decided by the dynamic interaction of teachers and students in the dozens or hundreds of classrooms in which it is implemented. The real strength of a language teaching programme therefore emerges from the network of shared meaningfulness which binds it together in the minds of students and teachers.

So far in this chapter it has been suggested that language teaching is far more complex than it is often acknowledged to be either in popular imagination or, which is more serious, in many aspects of the official discourse of language teaching as found in policy documents, course descriptions, and methodology texts. The reason for this complexity is that language teaching can mean different things for the various participants who, in one way or another, are involved in it. Understanding language teaching as it is lived out in real classrooms therefore involves exploring the meaning it has for participants and the dynamics which arise out of the meeting of their more or less differing perceptions of the nature and goals of the activity. These dynamics may at times coincide with the ideal script found in methodological principle or in a given planning document, but it neither can nor, indeed, should it be assumed that this is the norm.

Idealised visions of language teaching postulate normality and operate on the assumption that teaching and learning can be planned fairly neatly in advance. The reality of language teaching is, of course, very different, and it is sometimes a distinctly untidy affair. Nevertheless, it is in the untidy world of the classroom that the success or failure of educational programmes are decided, and the classroom teacher plays a central role in this process. Furthermore, the teacher's task involves a great deal more than 'simply' teaching in a naive sense of the term. Effective teaching depends crucially on teachers' ability to negotiate a shared and mutually meaningful understanding of language learning with their students, but within a context which is shaped – and often powerfully so – by the perceptions and goal structures of a variety of other participants, many of whom may be physically distant from the classroom as such. The reality of classroom teaching and learning emerges dynamically from this complex set of interactions among participants.

---

It has been suggested in this section that language teaching is a dynamic activity which involves the reconciliation of a variety of potentially differing perceptions and goals.

- How far does this perspective on teaching correspond to your own experience of it?
- In which ways have you experienced the dynamic nature of language teaching in your classroom practice? (In this respect, it may be helpful to focus on one or more specific incidents which struck you as unexpected or surprising in one way or another.)

---

## 2.5 Exploring classroom dynamics

In Section 2.4 it was suggested that the classroom is a place where a variety of potentially differing perspectives on the nature and goals of language teaching meet and interact. For this reason, what takes place in the classroom cannot be fully understood from the perspective of any one participant or group of participants in isolation. It is therefore necessary to explore what situations mean to the various participants involved in them and how these meanings interact dynamically with one another. This does not in itself provide solutions, but offers the possibility of understanding situations as they really are, and thus of being in a position to make appropriate and sustainable decisions. As already suggested, the dynamics of teaching and learning in a given setting, and the reality which emerges from them may not fit in with official plans or with conceptions of methodological best practice. And, yet, it is in this reality that teaching and learning are lived out and where the ultimate effectiveness of teaching programmes are decided. This is sufficient reason for attempting to understand this reality in its own terms.

In order to understand language teaching as it is really lived out in classrooms we therefore need to explore two main sets of factors. The first relates to the different rationalities of language teaching which underpin the actions of the various participants who, in one way or another, exert an influence on the classroom, i.e. educational or institutional authorities, materials writers or course designers, sponsors or parents, teachers and, last but certainly not least, students. The second relates to the way in which classroom participants interact with one another and with the choices of other participants who, more or less directly, influence the context in which they are operating.

Methodology is the means by which the language is presented to students, teaching–learning activities are organised, and classroom relations are defined; it therefore plays an important role in this process. This does not mean that methodological choices feed through to classroom realities in a linear manner. Nor, indeed, can it be assumed that all participants see the classroom in the same terms that are habitually employed in the professional literature. Nevertheless, methodological choices constitute a pivot around which students and teachers interact with one another and negotiate their classroom behaviours and identities; they therefore play a key role in classroom dynamics.

With this in mind, Chapters 3–5 are structured around three fundamental areas of methodological choice, namely the nature of language, of learning, and of the classroom. The exploration of each of these areas of choice will be organised around a number of categories drawn from the literature on language teaching. These categories are not, however, proposed as received knowledge, or set methodological principles to be accepted as such. They are put forward rather as poles of attraction around which methodological choices tend to revolve and, crucially, as starting points for exploring the dynamics which such choices can generate. These chapters adopt a relativistic perspective on methodology. The developments discussed in Chapter 1 make it clear that no one methodological approach can be assumed to be equally appropriate with all learners and in all contexts. The perspective that is adopted in the following chapters therefore involves exploring methodological options in terms of their contextual and thus their local meaning. The goal is to help teachers to explore the meaning their methodological choices can assume for students and, in this way, the contribution they make to classroom dynamics.

# 3 Visions of language

## 3.1 The language is the language: Or is it?

If we were to ask a non-specialist layperson what language teaching is about, we might, not wholly unreasonably, be told that language teaching is about teaching language. When we are in the classroom, then, we are teaching language. What seems a fairly simple question soon becomes less straightforward when we think about it a little more closely. There are a variety of perspectives on the nature of language both in the theoretical literature and in the coursebooks and materials we use. These perspectives may in certain cases be stated explicitly, while in others they may remain implicit. In either case, however, they are present and influence how the language is presented to students and which aspects of it are selected for study. Then there are the ideas which our students have of language, i.e. of what we are asking them to learn. These, too, may or may not be explicitly formulated, but they are certainly present, even if they come to the surface only when the vision of language we are working with fails to match students' expectations. And then, of course, we cannot forget the vision of language which we as teachers subscribe to and which, explicitly or implicitly, influences our choices and priorities.

Our non-specialist's answer that language teaching is about teaching language is thus a pertinent one, but it does not provide us with the sort of guidance we need in order to approach the task of teaching this phenomenon in a coherent manner. Nor does it help us to understand the way in which our choices can be perceived by our students, and the dynamics which can arise out of the meeting of potentially different conceptions of what language is. The chapter surveys a number of different perspectives on the nature of language. The goal is not to suggest any one as definitive, but to consider each perspective in its own terms and then to raise a few questions about the reality which this vision can assume for different participants and in different learning contexts. This survey centres around four main visions of the nature of language:

1. language as a linguistic system;
2. language from a functional perspective;
3. language as self-expression; and
4. language as culture and ideology.

Other perspectives exist, and this chapter does not claim to provide a comprehensive overview of all theories of language, but simply to examine some of the more frequent ways of seeing language which teachers are likely to encounter in the daily practice of teaching.

## 3.2 Language as a linguistic system

The growth of the communicative approach in the 1970s emphasised that language is a tool for achieving communicative goals, and not simply a linguistic system in its own right. At the same time, language is a system, and mastering this system (or parts of it at least) is a prerequisite for any meaningful form of communication. A coherent approach to language teaching therefore calls for choices to be made about the language system itself. This, however, as Cunningsworth points out, is less straightforward than one might at first sight imagine:

> It is generally necessary to analyse language and divide it into small units for effective teaching and learning to take place. Yet it is notoriously difficult to separate individual aspects of language from the whole, and isolate them, without losing authenticity and naturalness in the process. This is mainly because language is a complex phenomenon which operates at several levels simultaneously . . . The 'whole' of language in use is greater than the sum of its parts. (1995: 31)

Teachers and other language educators are therefore faced with the question of where to start and around which aspects of the 'complex phenomenon' of language to structure their teaching. In other words, how can the language be analysed and presented to students in an effective and meaningful manner? One answer is to look at the language as a linguistic system and to present this system to students. Once this choice is made, however, the question arises as to the elements around which the language system should be presented to students; this brings us back to the question of how we understand the concept of language.

### 3.2.1 Components of the language system

In an introduction to coursebook selection, Cunningsworth (1995) analyses the language content of coursebooks, focusing on six categories: grammar, vocabulary, phonology, discourse, style and appropriacy, and varieties of the TL. Cunningsworth's categories are used here because they result from an analysis of published coursebooks, and may thus reflect a certain practical consensus among at least two influential groups of participants in language teaching, i.e. coursebook writers and publishers. In this respect, it is worth noting that as a result of the role coursebooks play in very many teaching situations, they can become a significant constitutive element of classroom dynamics.

## 1 Grammar

Johnson and Johnson (1998: 143–144) say that the first of these categories, grammar, is 'a protean term, meaning different things to different people, but often used with varying references by the same speaker'. This point needs to be borne in mind in discussions of grammar and its role in language teaching. The word is, for example, sometimes used to refer to aspects of the language system, while at others it relates to aspects of the teaching process or to a certain type of learning activity. (Indeed, as Brindley, 1989, points out, the demand for more 'grammar' may in fact relate more to a certain mode of learning than to a certain content of learning.) In the present context, the term is used to refer to the structural regularities or patterns in language by which speakers organise messages. It typically involves the study of areas such as morphology and word formation, the tense system, modality, and the expression of quantity. Together with vocabulary, it is probably the aspect of language which is most often associated in popular imagination with knowing or, at least, with learning a language.

Cunningsworth makes two significant points about grammar. The first is that it is 'a major component of any general language course, whether it is acknowledged as such, or disguised as something else' (1995: 32). The second is that it is the effective teaching of grammar which makes a language course what it is and distinguishes it from a phrasebook. This results from the generative nature of grammar, namely that a knowledge of grammar provides learners with the ability to structure their language usage beyond any discrete collection of utterances to which they may be exposed. Cunningsworth also suggests (1995: 55) that structural syllabuses, i.e. those which are organised around language content, emphasise grammatical structure in particular. Lexis and phonology are taken into account, but within an overall framework this is defined in primarily grammatical terms. Cunningsworth is thus suggesting that there is a fairly large degree of practical agreement among coursebook writers and publishers that grammar constitutes the basis for learning a language or, at least, that it constitutes a convenient principle around which to structure a learning programme, possibly with the addition of other elements.

## 2 Vocabulary

Together with grammar, the second of Cunningsworth's categories, vocabulary is probably an aspect of language whose importance would rarely be questioned. Cunningsworth is, however, correct in pointing out that vocabulary has been relatively neglected until recent years. This may result in part from the open nature of the vocabulary of a language. Whatever the theoretical debates about the nature of grammar may be, there is a fair degree of practical agreement in teaching materials about which aspects of the grammar of a language constitute 'the basics'. The same cannot be said of vocabulary. Vocabulary allows us to express meaning, and what is or is not relevant in terms of vocabulary therefore depends to a large degree on the messages which students wish to understand or express. Vocabulary choice is thus more straightforward in specific purpose courses, where target areas of meaning are directly linked to the learners' interests or needs. Corpus-based studies of vocabulary offer the possibility of establishing an objective basis for vocabulary selection. In many cases, however, vocabulary selection in general courses operates around situations or topics which are chosen on the basis of their likely motivational value or future usefulness.

Thus, while vocabulary is clearly seen as being a major aspect of knowing a language, and will always be present in a course, it is less often used as a defining principle than grammar. Lewis expresses his dissatisfaction with the relative importance given to grammar as opposed to vocabulary in the following terms:

> The basis of language is lexis. It has been, and remains, the central misunderstanding of language teaching to assume that grammar is the basis of language and that mastery of the grammatical system is a prerequisite for effective communication.
> (1993: 133)

In the sense that he acknowledges the still dominant role of grammar in current approaches to teaching (general language teaching at least), Lewis would seem to be agreeing with Cunningsworth's observation of the role given to grammar as a defining principle in language teaching materials. He is, however, disagreeing with the relative importance which it should have. Lewis is therefore arguing for a more balanced treatment of grammar and vocabulary, with more importance being given to the meaning-bearing role of vocabulary. Lewis' comments are indicative of a disagreement as to the relative importance accorded to grammar and lexis in current language teaching practice. This still leaves us with the other elements of the language identified by Cunningsworth, namely phonology, discourse, style and appropriacy, and varieties of the TL.

## 3 Phonology

Cunningsworth suggests that phonology – within which he includes the articulation of individual sounds, word stress, sentence stress, and aspects of intonation – has tended to be 'sidelined' (1995: 41) in many general courses. He also points to a number of difficulties in dealing with phonology in pedagogical terms. Clear explanation of pronunciation and intonation can call for the use of phonetic transcription or a more or less complex metalanguage which can add to the total learning load of students. Nevertheless, the ability to understand the spoken language and to produce a comprehensible version of the language that is being learned are certainly very important aspects of 'knowing a language' and cannot be ignored. Furthermore, command of the phonology of a language can play an important affective role in language use.

## 4 Discourse

A command of discourse, which Cunningsworth defines as 'the features of language use that go beyond the domain of grammar rules and include areas such as the sequencing of sentences, cohesion, paragraphing, structuring text, participation in conversations, etc.' (1995: 45), is clearly essential to effective communication and thus needs to assume importance within a communicative approach to teaching. One tricky point in this respect, however, is the relationship between grammar and discourse. Both relate to the structuring of ideas and messages, and could thus arguably be seen as part of the same system. In practice, however, 'grammar' tends to be seen as an organising principle at sentence level, whereas discourse relates to larger segments of language. This distinction is probably more a matter of practical convenience of presentation, as sentences rarely exist in isolation, other than in language courses. Moreover, teaching discourse brings in considerations of context, which can be difficult to incorporate into teaching materials, especially at low proficiency levels. As Cunningsworth rightly points out (see above), language is a complex phenomenon, and this complexity emerges very clearly at the level of discourse.

## 5 Style and appropriacy

Similar considerations apply with respect to style and appropriacy and varieties of the TL. Language serves not only to convey factual information, but also to signal choices of an attitudinal and interactive nature. Style and appropriacy are therefore aspects of language which are more than just linguistic: they involve understanding situations and interacting with these situations in a purposeful manner. At the same time, they do have a linguistic component, and Cunningsworth is correct in pointing out that stylistic differences can be signalled by elements of grammar and vocabulary, discourse structure, and aspects of phonology. Using a language in a stylistically and contextually appropriate manner therefore calls for a command of various aspects of the language; it also, however, calls for an understanding of context. Style and appropriacy are thus linked to aspects of the language system itself, but they also involve factors which are related to contextual and sociocultural aspects of language use.

## 6 Variety or varieties of the TL

This brings us to the question of the variety or varieties of the TL which are presented to students. What, for example, does it mean to learn 'English'? Is this British English, American English, or the emerging phenomenon of 'international English'? There is also the question of the 'standard language', which is frequently defined around the dominant media channels in the target country. Is this an unmarked and purely linguistic phenomenon, or is it one which involves choices of a political and ideological nature? (cf. Section 3.5)

---

Which of these elements of language do you concentrate on most in your own teaching?

- Does this reflect a personal choice on your behalf, or does it result from choices which have been made by course designers, materials writers, or others?
- Does the relative focus of your teaching change in response to the level of your students or their learning goals?
- In practice, all of the elements surveyed above play a role in communication. How do you handle the tension between splitting up language into discrete chunks for teaching purposes while aiming at integrated language use?

---

## 3.2.2 *From convenience to meaningfulness*

In terms of the organisation of teaching materials, in general courses at least, there would seem to be a fairly broad practical consensus that grammar and vocabulary constitute 'the basics', and that one works 'upwards' from these basic elements to the more complex and context-sensitive elements of discourse, style, and appropriacy. Language in use is not, of course, like this. To begin with, a reasonable command of the phonology of the language, which may imply choices regarding regional or social varieties of the language, is essential for any form of spoken interaction. Furthermore, even in fairly simple transactions, familiarity with aspects of spoken discourse, style, and appropriacy is often crucial. Here, however, we need to distinguish between two factors. One is the 'complex phenomenon' of language itself, and the other is how it can be presented to learners so that they can, over time, acquire the ability to use it integratively. The latter calls for practical choices and possibly for compromises between visions of what language is and how it may usefully be presented to students for learning purposes.

An approach to teaching which is based on pre-selected elements of the language system is one option. It is the most traditional approach, which neither means that it should be accepted unquestioningly nor that it should be rejected out of hand. This approach has a number of practical advantages in terms of the organisation of teaching pro-grammes and the preparation of materials, if only because our profession has developed considerable experience in doing things this way. Orga-nising a course around aspects of the language system introduces a strong element of content study into language learning. It says, in essence, that the language is 'out there' and constitutes a body of knowledge that can be organised and structured for learning purposes. It does not, in itself, deny that language use is something both personal and interpersonal, but it places emphasis on those components of language which can be isolated out and presented to learners in an accessible pedagogical form. An approach to teaching based on the language as a system therefore offers a variety of practical advantages, which is a valid consideration from the point of view of those who are responsible for organising language programmes. It can also have advantages in terms of the learning process itself. Especially in situations where students are not in regular, functionally oriented contact with the language, a system-based approach allows at least a sample of the language to be structured and presented to them in the form of a coursebook or study programme, which can be a considerable support to learning.

These considerations relate to the practical advantages of a system-based approach to teaching. In addition to this, however, our students bring with them to the classroom a variety of attitudes and expectations about the nature of language. The effectiveness in learning terms of the vision of language we present to students therefore depends to a considerable degree on how they interpret and interact with this vision. Our decisions about the way in which we present language to our students therefore need to take account of what the language means to them.

Brindley sums up the beliefs about language learning of a group of learners of English in Australia in the following terms:

- Learning consists of acquiring a body of knowledge.
- The teacher has this knowledge and the learner has not.
- The knowledge is available for revision and practice in a textbook or some other written form.
- It is the role of the teacher to impart this knowledge to the learner through such activities as explanation, writing and example. The learner will be given a programme in advance.
- Learning a language consists of learning the structural rules of the language and the vocabulary through such activities as memorisation, reading and writing.                    (1984: 97)

Some of these comments relate to the learning process as much as to the nature of language itself and have common ground with the beliefs of the 'Learn about the language' group of learners identified by Wenden (1987). Nevertheless, they do indicate a concern with the language as a system, grammar and vocabulary, in particular, as the central component of language study. With such learners, then, there is a good chance that a strongly system-based presentation of language would be well received. In other words, the beliefs and attitudes which our students bring to the classroom influence how they perceive and interact with what we as teachers propose to them, and are therefore a significant constituent of the dynamics of classroom teaching and learning.

---

It is very likely that teachers' beliefs and attitudes influence the choices they make and how they evaluate the choices of other participants (cf. Borg, 1999).

- What are your attitudes to the vision of language as a linguistic system?
- What, in your opinion, are its advantages and disadvantages?
- Have you ever encountered disagreements in this respect with students or with other participants?
- What were they and how did you deal with them?

---

## 3.3 Language as doing things: The functional perspective

The change in the nature of the demand for language teaching which emerged in the 1960s and 1970s coincided with and was supported by a changing theoretical perspective on the nature of language itself as seen in the work of writers such as Halliday (1973, 1975) and Hymes (1972). Hymes' theory of communicative competence, in particular, played an important role in introducing a new perspective on language into reflection on language teaching. Hymes situates language in its social context as the medium by which members of a speech community express concepts, perceptions, and values which have significance to them as members of this community. Language, then, can only be understood within the framework of the meaning structures of the relevant speech community, and the study of language therefore needs to operate within a sociological and sociocultural framework. This implies that the teaching of language needs to accommodate this dimension of meaning and enable learners to operate effectively within the relevant speech community.

This perspective on language underpinned work on notional/functional syllabuses (Wilkins, 1976; Finocchiaro and Brumfit, 1983) and the communicative approach to language teaching (Widdowson, 1978). As a result of this line of reflection, language came to be seen as social action and the social or functional uses which learners were to make of the language became the starting point for the development of learning programmes. Communicative language teaching (CLT) arose out of this perspective on language and, on this basis, set out to develop an approach to teaching whose goal was to enable students to use the language in one or more socially defined contexts. In this view, language learners are social actors whose learning goals are defined by the contexts in which they will be required to use the language and the messages they will wish to convey in these contexts.

### 3.3.1 Bases of a functional approach to language teaching

The basic assumption in CLT is that students are learning a language in order to be in a position to do something in or with this language. On this basis, the goals of a learning programme are defined on the basis of the uses which students will have to make of the language. Students' target uses of the language are thus the starting point, and course content is selected in order to enable students to operate effectively in the relevant situations of use. These assumptions emerge most clearly in terms of specific purpose teaching (called 'languages for specific purposes', or LSP), and it is for this reason that the functional perspective on language is in the first instance discussed with respect to LSP.

Robinson (1991: 2–4) identifies two features which she considers to be criterial to LSP. The first is that LSP is goal directed, which means that students are learning the language because they need it for one or another pragmatic purpose, related in general to their academic or professional life, and not necessarily out of interest in the language itself or in the culture of the source country. The second distinctive feature of LSP is that it is based on needs analysis, which has the goal of specifying as accurately as possible what students have to do in the language. This is only logical: if a course has the goal of preparing students for a number of specific pragmatic tasks, it is obviously important to identify what these tasks are. Needs analysis thus plays an essential role in LSP.

Robinson (1991: 12–15) lists seven needs analysis procedures. Three involve information derived from the learners themselves:

- *Questionnaires* and *interviews*: These elicit information directly from learners.
- *Tests*: These provide information on learners' general abilities in the TL as well as on their relative abilities with respect to their intended uses of the language.
- *'Participatory needs analysis'*: This involves an open-ended discussion with learners of how they perceive their needs in the TL as well as of what they expect from their course of study.

Three procedures relate to the analysis of the learners' target situations of use:

- *Observation*: Information can clearly be elicited by means of observation of the behaviour of proficient native speakers in these situations.
- *Case studies*: These can be conducted by shadowing and observing a learner in the relevant situations of use, which can yield insights into the learners' relative abilities in their target situations of use.
- *Authentic data collection*: This involves the gathering and analysis of data from the target situations, by means of audio or video recordings of interactive exchanges or the collection of written materials that learners need to consult or generate.

It is also possible to make use of qualified informants, i.e. individuals who are able to provide insights into the learners' future needs, either in terms of the demands of the target situations themselves, or on the basis of their experience with the difficulties encountered by former students in the same situations. Informants may be employers, subject lecturers or tutors, fellow teachers who have experience with similar categories of learner, or former students.

The results of needs analysis feed into the definition of course objectives, which are generally expressed in terms of skills and functions. In the case of a businessperson needing to improve his or her ability to negotiate and take part in meetings in English, the main target skill would probably be speaking, and most likely with a listening component. On this basis, the target skill(s) would be analysed into a number of functions such as greeting and introducing people, keeping a conversation going, introducing and checking acceptance of objectives, creating a climate of confidence, and so on (examples from O'Connor *et al.*, 1992). Each of these functions would then be explored by means of carefully selected language work. Elements of grammar, vocabulary, and phonology would certainly be present. Attention would also probably be given to aspects of spoken discourse, style, and appropriacy. It might also be judged necessary to consider questions of varieties of English in function on whether the learner's interlocutors would be British, North American, or non-native speakers from a variety of language backgrounds. In all likelihood, then, most of the components of the language system mentioned in Section 3.2 would be included, but their selection would be contingent upon decisions related to an analysis of the functional needs of the learner in question. What distinguishes a functionally based approach to teaching from one based on the language as a system is not, therefore, the presence or absence of elements of language, but the principle upon which these elements are selected and sequenced.

The functional perspective on language and its expression in language teaching has a high degree of both intuitive plausibility and face validity. For many language learners, the language is first and foremost a means of achieving certain functional goals, e.g. reading specialist material, settling in to a foreign country, or performing professional tasks such as answering the telephone or providing information to customers. An approach to language teaching which is centred on these needs is thus precisely what is needed in many cases. A functional perspective on language and language teaching also makes it possible to justify investment in language teaching programmes in terms which are accessible to sponsoring bodies concerned with the achievement of practical goals. Furthermore, a clear statement of goals – where the course is going and what students can expect to get out of it in practically relevant terms – can serve a valuable motivational function for both students and teachers.

This having been said, the realisation of a functional approach to teaching is not always a simple affair. To begin with, needs analysis, the basis of a functional approach to teaching, is far less straightforward in practice than a superficial survey of models such as that put forward by

Munby (1978) or the techniques suggested by Robinson (1991) might lead one to believe.

To begin with, needs analysis, especially the techniques of observation, case study, and authentic data collection, can be extremely time-consuming, and relatively few teachers, or even institutions, are able to engage in this type of needs analysis on a regular basis. For this reason, teachers often have to rely either on acquired experience or on coursebooks which claim to offer a pre-pedagogised analysis of the skills, functions, and language elements which are needed in various fields of activity. Some textbooks reflect long experience and valid insights, but this cannot be taken for granted, as indicated by studies such as Burkhalter (1986) and Williams (1988). In addition to this, there is a growing acknowledgement that a significant part of needs analysis has to be conducted during the course itself between teacher and students on the basis of the specialist knowledge students bring with them to the course, their pragmatic awareness of language use, and possibly direct experience of their target uses of the language, as well as their own individual learning objectives.

Needs analysis, therefore, has to be seen as a two-stage process. The first stage rests either on a more or less detailed initial needs analysis conducted for a specific group of students or on a broader needs analysis conducted for a certain category of students; the latter is often expressed in terms of a course with a title such as 'French for Secretaries', 'Academic German', or 'Negotiating in English'. The second stage involves an ongoing form of needs analysis which is both developmental and experiential (Tudor, 1996), and which is conducted jointly by teacher and students on the basis of a sharing of insights and knowledge between the two parties.

Thus, while there can be little doubt as to the usefulness of basing a course on an analysis of the objectively observable needs of the students concerned, the practical realisation of needs analysis is far from straightforward. It often depends on the amount of time and resources the teacher or institution can invest in it, as well as the practical possibilities of gaining access to the students' target situations of use, and this may involve negotiation with sponsoring bodies with respect either to funding or in terms of access to information. In other words, the practical realisation of a functional perspective on language can be considerably more complex than some theoretical writing might lead one to believe.

---

If you have been involved in teaching an LSP course, examine the ways in which the goals of the course were decided upon.

- Which of the needs analysis procedures surveyed above were used? On which basis were materials selected?
- How far did this correspond to an 'ideal' view of needs analysis and LSP?
- Which possibilities existed during the course itself for ongoing input from students? Could such opportunities be enhanced and, if so, in which ways?

---

## 3.3.2 Distant needs, present realities

From a functional perspective, language is first and foremost a means of achieving a certain number of pragmatic goals: a functionally based course therefore focuses on the skills and functions which are most relevant to the uses which learners have to make of the language. In many learning contexts, however, students are learning a language for more or less distant and more or less uncertain uses. For a very large number of learners, the TL has little or no immediate relevance to them other than as another subject alongside others on their school or university programme. They are studying the language because the relevant authorities have decided that a knowledge of this language is likely to be of use to them at some stage in the future. The language is thus another subject alongside others on the students' programme. This raises a number of questions regarding the implementation in learning programmes of a functional perspective on language.

In situations where learners' needs cannot be identified clearly in advance, goal-setting in language teaching operates according to similar general principles to those used in other subject areas. Educational authorities try to work out a set of target competences which are likely to be relevant in themselves or which have an enabling function with respect to other competences. Students at secondary level may, for example, be required to study geography, history, and science in order to develop a knowledge base which will enable them to participate in social or political debates in an informed manner. In this sense, broadly based general education is a component of informed citizenship and of participative democracy. Students may also be required to study different elements of mathematics, even if relatively few make active use of the specific mathematical processes they have learned outside of their schooling proper. The study of mathematics, however, enables students to make subsequent, more specialised choices of study or work orientation, and also provides them with essential numeracy skills. Much the same applies to language skills: knowledge of a foreign language gives students access to another culture, which is enriching in itself, and it also provides them with a potentially useful practical skill.

Considerations of this nature cannot fail to have an influence on the practical realisation of a functional perspective on language. In essence, if no clear functional target can be identified, then on which basis can objectives realistically be set? (This is rather different from an LSP situation where students often have immediate pragmatic needs in the language.) In practice, a frequent response has been to aim at a fairly general communicative ability, often with emphasis on the spoken language as used in everyday interactive situations which might, one day, be relevant to the students concerned. Once such goals have been set, they become a given around which teaching is conducted and learning outcomes are evaluated. In this sense, the task of the language teacher at secondary school or even at university does not differ radically from that of teachers of other subjects. They are involved in imparting knowledge and developing skills which may well be useful to students at some stage in the future, but which may not necessarily have a direct link with their current life and concerns except as objects of study. In other words, future needs and present realities may not coincide. For learning to be effective, however, a link has to be established in students' minds between the two. Achieving this involves consideration not just of what language is in theoretical terms, but of what it means to students at a given point in time.

The pedagogical response developed in mainstream CLT involves the practice of communicatively oriented activities which are intended to bring the language and students' likely uses of it alive in the classroom. Thus, if a course aims at developing spoken interactive skills, the students are likely to be asked to practise around role-plays and simulations related to a certain number of pre-specified contexts of use. If the students can relate at least fairly well to their possible future uses of the language and are willing to engage in the relevant learning activities with genuine personal involvement, then this approach can work well. In this case, the projected uses of the language will have assumed at least a reasonable degree of reality in students' minds. In other words, the functional perspective on language found in their programme goals will have assumed a psychological reality in the here-and-now of students' lives.

If, however, the TL and the type of goals which are set for students are far removed from their daily lives, it can be difficult for students to engage in communicatively oriented activities with any real degree of involvement. This is more likely to be the case if the students have no contact with the TL or with speakers of this language outside the classroom, and even more so if the prospect of them doing so is distant or uncertain. It is therefore important to assess whether there may be a dissonance between the vision of language expressed in course objectives and learning activities and the meaning which the language has for students in the particular context in which they are studying it. The functional perspective may tell students that the TL is the means of expression of a given speech community and a tool for achieving certain pragmatic goals. The reality of their situation, however, may well be that the TL speech community is something foreign and distant – an object of study rather than a set of interlocutors – and that the language is primarily something they have to study in order to pass an examination. If the gap between the vision of language present in course goals and materials, on the one hand, and students' practical experience of the language, on the other, is too great, then it can have a negative influence on the authenticity of learning activities and, thereby, on their real learning potential.

I have looked at this phenomenon in a case study of undergraduate students of business at the Université Libre de Bruxelles in their first and fourth (final) year of English (Tudor, 2000). In their first year of English, the students viewed the language primarily as one component of their programme which they had to 'learn' and pass just like their other subjects. With this goal in mind, they wanted clearly structured learning content and easily revisable material that would allow them to make use of the study strategies they had developed within the evaluation system of their study programme as a whole; this was, at this stage, heavily geared around knowledge transmission and content learning. They expressed unease with heavy use of spoken activities in class saying that they did not know what they had learned or were supposed to learn. In the students' first year of English, then, the language was not primarily the means of expression of a given speech community, but another course on their study programme which they had to pass in their end-of-year examinations.

By the fourth year, however, the students' attitudes to both the language and the learning process had changed. Their business courses had become more practical in orientation, and the students had begun to perceive more directly the linguistic demands of their future careers. They had become much more receptive to a functionally based view of language and were more willing to engage in functionally oriented learning activities. By their final year of English, then, the students themselves saw English as the language in which many would be interviewed for their first post, and in which many of them would work.

In other words, the status of the language in their minds had changed from an object of study to a functional skill in their professional repertoire.

This case study suggests that developmental considerations relating to learners' current concerns, their self-image, and perceptions of the role of the TL in their lives need to be taken into account alongside objective considerations of the nature of language in goal-setting and activity development. This implies that different pedagogical approaches – and, thus, differing visions of what language is – may be appropriate at different stages of students' learning careers. In the situation described in the case study, the first-year course was revised around a heavy input of grammar and vocabulary with a dominantly content-learning focus. This allowed students to use their tried-and-tested study strategies and also fitted in with their somewhat tenuous perception of the pragmatic role English would play in their future lives. In successive courses, however, a more functionally oriented approach to learning was introduced in line with students' growing professional awareness. The case study therefore suggests that even if the ultimate goal of a course of study may be defined in terms of certain functional competences, it does not necessarily follow that these competences have to be given priority throughout the programme. For learning to be effective, it has to fit in meaningfully with the concerns and perceptions of the students as they are at a given point in time and in the context in which they are working. The decision to adopt a functional vision of language therefore needs to be evaluated not only in terms of objective relevance but also with respect to the dynamic interaction of this vision with the perceptions and concerns of the students in the here-and-now of their life both in and beyond the classroom.

---

Have you ever encountered a dissonance or tensions between the terms in which the goals of a course are defined and the current perceptions of students?

- If so, what do you feel to be the source of these tensions?
- In which ways did (or could) you try to resolve these tensions? Think about this in as much detail as possible, with reference, for instance, to a particular activity or the exploitation of a certain type of materials.

---

## 3.4 Language as self-expression

The functional perspective on language discussed in the Section 3.3 emphasises the role of language as a means of achieving pragmatic goals, e.g. reading specialised material in the TL, performing professional or academic tasks, settling in to another country, and so on. Language is not, however, used only for this purpose. It is also the medium by which we build up personal relationships, express our emotions and aspirations, and explore our interests. In other words, language is not simply a tool for achieving specific transactional goals, it is also a means of self-expression. Lewis puts this in the following terms:

> In addition to social identity, language is the primary means for our own personal self-definition. The language we use helps other people, and most importantly ourselves, to understand who and what we perceive ourselves to be.          (1993: 50)

A functional perspective on language portrays the learner primarily as a social actor and language as a form of social action, which is certainly a valid perspective. Language learners are also, however, individuals in the personal and affective sense of the term, which means that language is also a means of personal and affective expression.

This casts a different light on language and also, thereby, on the nature and goals of language teaching. A view of language as a linguistic system says that the goal of language teaching is to help students learn this system. A functional view of language says that the goals of language teaching are defined by what the learner has to do in the language. When language is viewed as self-expression, learning goals are defined by what the learner wishes to express, and this means that each learner has his or her own unique and personal learning agenda.

### 3.4.1 The humanistic perspective

The vision of language as self-expression is not a prerogative of humanistic language teaching, nor is it the only perspective on language which is found in humanistic teaching. Nonetheless, the humanistic movement has played a significant role in introducing a concern with the expressive and personal side of language use into reflection on language teaching. Stevick identifies five main strands or 'overlapping components' in humanistic thinking which, with differing emphases, have underpinned most humanistic approaches to language teaching.

- Feelings, including both personal emotions and esthetic appreciation. This aspect of humanism tends to reject whatever makes people feel bad, or whatever destroys or forbids esthetic enjoyment.

- Social relations. This side of humanism encourages friendship and cooperation, and opposes whatever tends to reduce them.
- Responsibility. This aspect accepts the need for public scrutiny, criticism, and correction, and disapproves of whoever or whatever denies their importance.
- Intellect, including knowledge, reason, and understanding. This aspect fights against whatever interferes with the free exercise of the mind, and is suspicious of anything that cannot be tested intellectually.
- Self-actualisation, the quest for full realisation of one's own deepest true qualities. This aspect believes that since conformity leads to enslavement, the pursuit of uniqueness brings about liberation. (1990: 23–24)

These principles establish the bases upon which humanistic approaches to language teaching rest. They set objectives which are internal to learners as individuals, and which relate to the concerns and aspirations of learners as thinking and affective beings. Language in this framework of ideas is a means of personal expression and a tool for personal fulfilment.

Discussions of humanistic language teaching are often somewhat impassioned, and so it is useful to point out that there is not necessarily a contradiction between underlying humanist concerns and the more pragmatically oriented perspective on language surveyed in the last section. Professional or academic achievement can be a means of personal fulfilment, and the successful organisation of an individual's daily life is an important enabling condition for self-realisation. It may be helpful to consider this with respect to the case of a group of refugees arriving in a new country.

A humanistic language teacher might quite justifiably feel that the first step towards empowering these students would be to provide them with the basic language skills they need in order to deal with administrative matters, find accommodation, be in a position to get a job, enter education, and so on. A large part of the students' language programme might therefore be functionally based, resting on a needs analysis of the practical tasks the learners have to fulfil in order to settle in to their new country of residence. This is in no way inconsistent with a humanistic view of the goals of language teaching. In addition to these elements, however, a humanistic teacher would wish to create the possibility for the learners to express their personal feelings, not as something incidental to their learning programme, but as an integral part of it. In this way, the programme would be a means of enabling the students to 'be themselves' in the full sense of the term. This might involve helping the learners to express and communicate to others their feelings of sorrow at the loss of their home and friends, their feelings of confusion and alienation in their new setting, their happiness at finding an old friend or family member, or their aspirations for the future. From a humanistic perspective on language and language teaching, this type of content is integral to the learners as human beings and therefore needs to find expression within the context of their language programme. A humanistic teacher would also try to create a warm and supportive atmosphere in the classroom so that students would feel confident to express their deeper personal feelings without fear of judgement or rejection.

The example of a group of refugees, with their often tragic histories, is possibly an extreme case (even if, regrettably, an all too familiar one). Even when circumstances are less extreme, however, it should not be forgotten that the desire to be oneself as a person and not simply as a social actor is a deeply rooted human need. Campbell (1996, referring to Moore, 1977), for example, describes the feelings of frustration of an academic working in Denmark at not being able to interact with colleagues as he would normally wish to, and suggests that 'Demonstrating one's personality appears to be a need that concerns some adult students, especially if they are new to a country . . .' (Campbell, 1996: 220). The reservation expressed by 'some' is a useful one that we return to later. Nonetheless, it is certainly a real and justifiable aspiration for a not inconsiderable number of language learners. It therefore merits consideration alongside other types of learning goal. Neglecting this communicative motivation would involve ignoring a part of the identity of the learner, and humanistic language teaching has served a valuable function in reminding our profession of this fact.

### 3.4.2 Operationalising self-expression

Acknowledging the importance of self-expression as a learning goal is one thing; incorporating it into programme design is another. In a system-based view of language, the learning goal is 'out there' in the form of the grammar, vocabulary, etc. of the language, and in a functional view of language in the form of the objectively observable uses that learners will have to make of the language. In a view of language as self-expression, the target learning content is specific to each learner as an individual. This poses a not inconsiderable problem in terms of programme design. One humanistic approach which attempts to do this in an original and creative manner is Community Language Learning (CLL), a method developed by Charles Curran (1972, 1976).

In CLL, there is no pre-set syllabus either in language or content terms: both arise out of the ideas or subjects which learners themselves wish to express in the classroom. In a CLL class learners typically sit in a circle and talk naturally about a subject that is of personal relevance to them. The learners express themselves either in the TL or, if their abilities in this language are inadequate to allow them to do this to their satisfaction, in their first language. The teacher stands behind the learner who is speaking and either provides the second language form of what the learner has said in his or her first language, or gently reformulates his second language utterance in an appropriate manner. Each learner then repeats his or her contribution to the conversation, and other learners make their own contribution in the same way. The conversation is recorded and replayed at the end of the class: it then forms the basis for various language tasks which are intended to consolidate the language used. The learning content of a CLL lesson is thus derived *post hoc* from what the learners themselves wish to express.

The approach to goal-setting adopted in CLL is consistent with a view of language as self-expression in that it takes learners' spontaneous expressive desires as the basis for their learning programme. Expression is the starting point, and language work follows on from this in two stages: the immediate input from the teacher (or 'counsellor', to use Curran's term), and then the follow-up work conducted on the re-cording of the conversation. Curran's ideas have had an influence on language teaching beyond the circles of those who are involved with CLL as a method in its own right. Deller (1990), for example, mentions CLL as one of the sources of inspiration for her book *Lessons from the Learner*, and a number of the activities contained in Campbell and Kryszewska's (1992) *Learner-based Teaching* have clear links with the approach which underpins CLL and also other strands of humanistic teaching.

The insights into the expressive role of language and the implications which this has for language teaching have therefore spread beyond the confines of humanistic language teaching as such to become part of mainstream CLT. There is nothing surprising about this: personal expression is one of the main functions of language, and it would therefore be rather strange if it had not found a place in mainstream language teaching. Indeed, the way in which this aspect of language is dealt with in a course can play a significant role in classroom dynamics. This can, however, vary from one group of learners to another.

On the one hand, some individuals – and some cultures, too – may not believe that the public arena of the classroom is the appropriate place for the expression of ideas or feelings of a personal nature. There is also the question of reconciling different priorities in language programmes, and personal expression may not assume a major role in the learning goals of all students. In such cases, an insistence on self-expression may be perceived by students (and possibly other participants, too) as inappropriate or intrusive. There are also the practical difficulties for the teacher of accommodating learning goals which cannot be predicted in advance and which are specific to each learner: in a class of 40, for example, this is no easy task. Furthermore, while self-expression may be a meaningful goal for individual learners, many educational authorities prefer to define the goals of a learning pro-gramme in terms that are more familiar or that fit in better with their broader socioeconomic agendas.

On the other hand, self-expression is a fundamental component of language use and the 'opening up' of a course to at least some degree of self-expression can help learners find a sense of personal meaningfulness in their language study. Or, to express this negatively, the absence of any scope for self-expression can make students perceive a course as being something 'out there' and indifferent to them and to their individual concerns, and thus make it difficult for them to relate to it in a personally meaningful manner.

---

What role do you accord to the expressive function of language in your teaching, and how does this realise itself in your choice of learning activities and materials?

- Does this change from one group of learners to another? If so, in which ways and for which reasons?
- In your own experience as a language learner, do you feel that the expressive function of language received sufficient attention? If so, in which way was this done? If not, why was this the case, and how did you react to this 'omission'?

---

## 3.5 Language as culture and ideology

The concept of a speech community reminds us that a language is not simply a linguistic system, but the means of expression and communica-tion used by a community of human beings. For this reason, a language will embody and express aspects of the culture and world view of its speakers. Full communicative competence in a language therefore

69

entails an understanding of and ability to interact with the culture and world view of the speakers of this language. This does not necessarily mean that the goal of language teaching is to turn learners into full members of the TL speech community. This is a choice which each learner has to make individually, and raises questions relating to the personal identity of the learner. Furthermore, whether the question arises at all depends a great deal on learning context. Second language learners who intend to spend the rest of their lives in the TL community may wish, or may feel pressures upon them, to assimilate fully into this community. In a foreign language context, the question may simply never arise. In either case, however, there are aspects of language use which have a sociocultural dimension and which play an important role in being able to function effectively in the language. In the daily practice of teaching, this affects goal-setting and evaluation criteria, as well as the selection of study material and topic.

### 3.5.1 Language and culture

Stevick makes the following remarks about 'Bert', a student learning Chinese:

> Bert was not only learning a new language; he was also learning a new culture. Learning Chinese culture meant becoming familiar with the range of meanings that other people might want to convey, some of which were different from the meanings Bert was used to at home. It also meant learning how those meanings fit together in the lives of Chinese people.  (1989: 25)

Anyone learning another language will have encountered this feeling of learning to see the world from a more or less different perspective. Indeed, learning to see the world through the eyes of a different culture may be one of the most broadly educational advantages of learning another language: it is a very practical means of exploring 'otherness' in the terms of 'the other'. Stevick is therefore correct in pointing out that learning a language involves learning a new culture, too.

The cultural aspect of language manifests itself on many levels. In part, it relates to the representation of external realities. This includes the way in which a language handles time relations; this is generally referred to as the tense system. It also involves the organisation of entities and phenomena in lexis, e.g. the same entities may be organised differently in two languages, or one language may have terms for phenomena which another does not seem to recognise. In addition, of course, the cultural aspect of language manifests itself with respect to the way in which social relations are encoded and expressed: in this respect, the language reflects aspects of interpersonal interaction which are often deeply rooted in the sociocultural traditions of the TL community. Some of these elements may be explicitly encoded in the language, such as the tu-vous distinction in French, or certain conventional modes of address related to the perceived social status of interlocutors. There are also more subtle factors relating to interactional conventions which may not necessarily be linked to specific linguistic forms (cf. Richards and Sukwiwat, 1985). In such cases, the question may, for example, not be what one says, but whether one says something or not.

Factors of this nature are far from quaint extras, as they can make the difference between successful or unsuccessful interaction with TL speakers. This is likely to assume particular importance when teaching focuses on language use in context, where questions of what is or is not appropriate behaviour (in both verbal and non-verbal terms) assume an important and possibly crucial role. It is for this reason that the sociocultural dimension of interaction receives very serious attention in the field of business communication, as failure to tune in to this aspect of language use can lead to misunderstandings or worse. The cultural and, more specifically, the sociocultural aspect of language intervenes significantly in language use, and thus has a real influence on students' ability to use the language in an effective and contextually appropriate manner. They cannot therefore be ignored in programme design and teaching.

This having been said, the relation between language and culture is far from straightforward, and is probably even less so in the case of an international language such as English. One basic question that needs to be addressed is which variety of English is to be taken as the target: a variety from the United Kingdom, from the United States, from Australia, or another of the widely spoken regional varieties of English? This influences the selection of linguistic forms which are specific to the variety chosen. It also touches on the sociocultural conventions and, in a broader sense, the cultural attitudes, which are proper to the speech community in question. Then there is the question of whether one should, in fact, link English to any one specific speech community of native speakers or rather view it as an international *lingua franca*, which is what it in fact is for a very large number of learners and users of English. This approach can avoid the problem of seeming to oblige learners to assimilate the sociocultural conventions of a speech community with which they may not wish to be associated culturally. At the same time, however, it runs the risk of presenting a rather impoverished means of expression which is largely limited to interaction of a more or less narrowly transactional nature.

These questions relate to the 'ownership' of English and also to the perceived identity of learners with respect to this language (cf. Norton, 1997). They are generally dealt with in curricula and published materials on two levels. One is by the choice of a given variety of English, often on the basis of traditional regional preferences for British, American, or Australian English. The other is by means of the selection of topics and of exemplificatory material which is more or less closely linked to the culture of the relevant variety of English. None of these choices, however, is unmarked, and they can have a significant influence on classroom dynamics. A sanitised and decultured presentation of the language, for example, can make it appear so lifeless that learners may experience difficulty in relating to it as a living medium of communication, even perhaps within the framework of practice activities. On the other hand, a culturally biased presentation of the language can give rise to negative affective reactions. Reactions of this nature are more likely to occur in situations where tensions exist or have existed between the TL community and that of the learners. In other words, the way in which the cultural content of teaching materials is perceived by learners is likely to be context-specific. A given vision of the TL or the TL community will thus interact dynamically with the attitudes and aspirations of the learners concerned, and possibly those of the broader community to which they belong.

### 3.5.2 Language and ideology

The comments made above point to the importance of sociocultural factors in language use. They also, however, indicate that there are serious questions to be addressed in selecting what is to be the relevant sociocultural content of learning, especially in the case of an international language such as English. These considerations relate in part to the sociocultural dimension horizontally, across national borders, but similar choices have to be made vertically, with respect to social and other differences within a given speech community or sociocultural group. No culture is monolithic, and there are always sub-groups within a given culture that have their own values and expressive preferences which differ to varying degrees from those of other groups. When we are presenting a given variety of a language to our students, we need to ask ourselves what this entails in sociocultural terms and what we are, in fact, presenting. Cunningsworth makes the following remarks in this respect about the messages which are communicated by coursebooks, but they apply equally to other aspects of pedagogy, including aspects of methodology:

If they have any subject content, coursebooks will directly or indirectly communicate sets of social and cultural values which are inherent in their make-up. This is the so-called 'hidden curriculum' which forms part of any educational programme, but is unstated and undisclosed. It may well be an expression of attitudes and values that are not consciously held but which nevertheless influence the content and image of the teaching material, and indeed the whole curriculum.

A curriculum (and teaching materials form part of this) cannot be neutral because it has to reflect a view of social order and express a value system, implicitly or explicitly. It has been claimed by some educationalists that this hidden curriculum is more effective than the stated official curriculum because it pervades most aspects of education. (1995: 90)

Cunningsworth goes on to suggest a few categories around which teachers can evaluate the representation of characters in teaching materials; these are gender, ethnic origin, occupation, age, social class, and disability. He also suggests that attention be given to the nature of the characters depicted, 'what makes them tick, what motivates them, . . . their fears, hopes, loves and hates' (1995: 91), and the vision of society and of social values that is presented.

No society is a single seamless entity made up of 'standard' members. We therefore have to question whether the image of the TL society we present to students is a real, living one or something shallow and stereotypical. We also need to question whether we are presenting a balanced view of this society or rather a selective and value-loaded vision of the way in which one group may wish to see it.

In a forcefully written and pertinent article, Grady (1997) considers these questions with respect to a coursebook series intended for immigrant learners of English as a second language (ESL) in the United States. Grady suggests that the characters and situations around which the series is constructed are shallow and likely to be far removed from the day-to-day experience of most immigrant learners of English. She therefore questions whether the series is likely to provide learners with the models of language and the interactional skills they need in order to make a success of their lives in their new environment. In essence, Grady says that the series in question is inappropriate because it fails to address the real communicative needs of its intended audience: in other words, it is not based on a rigorous use of the principles of needs analysis discussed in Section 3.3. Significantly, however, Grady is suggesting that this derives from an unwillingness in social or ideological terms to address the real needs of a significant group of learners. The conclusion to her article contains the following comments.

> What are the implications of trivializing the content of ESL textbooks and constructing 'communicative competence' for immigrants such as the ability to describe a wedding or use a TV schedule? Such language practices will not help immigrants who are living on the periphery of U.S. society gain access to political and economic power. Maintaining the status quo of great inequity and limited possibilities for language minorities was not the likely goal of the authors of this language series, but it most certainly supports that end in any classroom where the teacher and students use the series as it was apparently designed to be used.
>
> If the intent of the authors was not to position language teachers and their students as mindless consumers who have no lives or interests of their own worth discussing, the reduction of language learning and teaching to tightly controlled, 'neutral' competence contributes to the construction of teachers as mere technicians and offers students linguistic knowledge of simplistic, yes/no decisions, but no knowledge of the discourses that will enable students to actively participate in transforming their lives.                                              (1997: 10)

Similar remarks may be made here as at the end of Section 3.5.1, namely that choices regarding the ideological presentation of the TL or TL community can have an influence on teaching–learning dynamics, but are likely to do so in a context-specific manner. In one context, a rosy, 'Happy Families' view of 'traditional' British culture may be exactly what learners expect, and they might well not want to know about unemployment or inner-city deprivation. In another context, the same vision of society can induce a feeling of alienation from this culture and also, quite possibly, from its language. The teacher may thus experience tensions between the desire to portray the TL society as it really is, and the expectations of students and possibly of other participants such as publishers, educational authorities, or development agencies as to precisely what this culture is. This, too, is one of the factors around which teachers have to work out a shared understanding of language with their students and with other participants in the teaching–learning process.

Have you ever felt it necessary to question the cultural or ideological content of the vision of the TL community conveyed by the
teaching materials you have used?

- If so, what was the vision in question, and what disturbed you
  about it?
- Can you identify different cultural or ideological visions of the
  TL in the various coursebooks or teaching materials you have
  used?
- In which ways (if at all) might the remarks made in this section
  influence your choice of materials?

## 3.6 Overview

Four visions of language have been surveyed in this chapter. Each is
valid and makes a meaningful statement about what Cunningsworth
(1995) rightly refers to as the 'complex phenomenon' of language.
Language is both a linguistic system and a means of achieving functional goals. Language is also a means of self-expression – in their first
language for all students and in the TL for at least a certain number.
Furthermore, as the medium of expression of a certain speech community, each language is the bearer of a set of cultural values and of one or
more ideologies. Each of the visions of language surveyed above is thus
valid, and a full mastery of a language involves all of these elements. In
the practicalities of language teaching, however, choices need to be
made regarding the way in which language is presented to students and
practice activities are organised.

Discussions of language generally revolve around exactly what
language is, which is clearly a legitimate perspective. From a pedagogical point of view, however, this needs to be complemented by
consideration of a variety of other factors. Some of these are pragmatic
in nature and relate to factors such as the practicalities of materials
preparation and course development, or the feasibility of conducting a
reliable pre-course needs analysis. In addition, and crucially, attention
has to be given to what language means to students in the here-and-now
of their lives both within and beyond the classroom. This influences the
way in which students will interpret and interact with the vision of
language which is presented to them in the materials they are asked to
study and the learning activities they are asked to engage in. If the
vision of language that is presented to students is too distant from their

current realities, it is unlikely to take root in their minds; thus, learning activities linked to this vision stand less chance of leading to meaningful learning. For example, if students have little or no current contact with or need to use the language as a means of communication, one can question how meaningful learning activities based on a vision of language as communication or as self-expression is likely to be for them. Indeed, even if students do objectively need to use the language for communicative purposes in a fairly proximate future but do not perceive the language in these terms, then it is probably wiser to anchor learning activities in the students' current perception of language, and then to attempt to move on from there.

The attempt to establish a sense of shared meaningfulness, and thus constructive teaching–learning dynamics, involves a variety of considerations, some of which are discussed in subsequent chapters. Nevertheless, in the endeavour of language teaching, a first point which has to be explored is the nature of language itself. Various perspectives exist, and those surveyed in this chapter make a valid statement about the nature of language. None, however, offers a universal right answer or an automatic guarantee of pedagogical meaningfulness. This is something which needs to be sought locally, and arises dynamically out of the interaction between the perceptions and goals of the participants present in each teaching situation.

# 4 Visions of learning

## 4.1 The diversity of the learning experience

If we were to ask the imaginary lay person we met at the start of Chapter 3 what he or she understands by language learning, the response is less easy to predict than with respect to language, which is not surprising. To a degree at least, language is something that is 'out there': we see it on billboards and in newspapers, we hear it on the radio, in trams, in shops, and at our place of work, and we use it ourselves every day in spoken and possibly also in written form. Language learning, on the other hand, is something that we do not 'see'. It is a mental process which cannot be 'observed' in any direct or tangible manner. It is possible for us to observe the teaching procedures and learning activities which are practised in a given classroom, or to observe the study habits in which language learners engage; we may also be able to observe a given learner's progress in acquiring aspects of a language over time. We can therefore monitor changes in students' mastery of a language and hypothesise about the way in which various teaching or learning procedures may have influenced these changes, but we do not have direct and unambiguous access to the process of learning itself.

This is clearly not without consequence for language educators. Teaching is a goal-oriented activity, and the goal is to create conditions which help students to develop the ability to use a language effectively, however this may be defined in operational terms. What we do as teachers – the materials we present to students, the activities we ask them to engage in, the advice we give them, etc. – has this one purpose, namely to support effective learning. No serious approach to language teaching can therefore ignore the nature of the learning process. For this reason, various theories of learning have been developed and translated into teaching methods and materials. However, two points need to be made in this respect. The first is that, as we saw in Chapter 1, no one set of methodological procedures can be assumed to be equally appropriate for all learners. The second is that methodological choices relating to learning (as those relating to the presentation of the language) become part of classroom dynamics in a way which is related not simply to their own inner logic but also to the meaning which they assume for participants. Methodology as theoretical principle may not therefore correspond with the pedagogical reality it assumes in the classroom. The latter arises out of the way in which students and teachers interpret and interact with the methodology in question. It is therefore important to bear in mind that while the choices we make do not necessarily lead to an easily predictable outcome, they certainly contribute to the dynamics of teaching and learning. For this reason, methodological choices need to be made and evaluated not only on the basis of theoretical principle, but also in the light of the meaning which these choices assume for participants, and thus the way in which they contribute to classroom dynamics.

As was the case in Chapter 3, this chapter considers four visions of learning that have assumed a significant role in the discussions of language teaching in recent decades. The goal is not to recommend any one in a general sense but simply to survey some of the main methodological poles of attraction that teachers are likely to encounter. In part, this involves an examination of the theoretical underpinnings of these perspectives. This, however, goes hand in hand with an exploration of the contextual meaning that these choices can assume for students and other participants, and thus the way in which they can influence the dynamics of teaching and learning in the classroom.

## 4.2 Experiential learning

Whatever other factors make them different from one another, there is one thing which our students – adolescents and adults at least – have in common, namely their ability to speak at least one other language, their first language. In other words, they have already achieved in at least one language the complex task which we as language educators are trying to help them achieve in another. In addition to this, some of our students may have learned more than one language without the assistance of a teacher or of a formal course. Even if it is reasonable to view children's acquisition of their first language as a special case, it is clear that people can and do learn languages without the type of support associated with a formal learning context.

This naturalistic form of learning or 'picking up' of a language can take many forms, depending on the context in which the language is being learned and the purposes of learning. It would, however, be fair to suggest that it entails at least two main factors. The first is exposure to the TL in one form or another, and generally exposure to fairly substantial amounts of input in the language. The second is the use of the language for communicative purposes of one type or another. The acknowledgement that people can and do learn a language without the support of a formal learning environment raises the question as to whether aspects of a naturalistic form of learning built around contact with and use of the TL for communicative purposes could enrich or even form a model for language learning in formal contexts. In this section, this perspective on learning is referred to as experiential learning in that it revolves around direct experience of the TL for communicative purposes as a basis for learning.

## 4.2.1 Learning by doing

The idea behind the experiential vision of learning is that the use of the TL for communicative purposes is not only the goal of learning, but also a means of learning in its own right. This may clearly involve students using language which they may not have fully mastered, and contrasts with other more 'traditional' approaches which emphasise part practice (i.e. isolating parts of the whole for explicit study and learning) leading up in a more or less controlled manner to integrated language use for communicative purposes. An experiential approach to learning may therefore involve a degree of what Johnson (1982) refers to as an 'in at the deep end strategy'. Simply throwing learners into wholly uncontrolled and undirected language use is, of course, as dubious a strategy with respect to language learning as doing the same with someone who is learning to swim.

For this reason, considerable effort has been devoted by methodologists, materials writers, and teachers in recent decades to the way in which two sets of factors can be combined. One is the basic insight that language use can serve a significant role in promoting learning, and the other is the acknowledgement that use of the language needs to be structured in a coherent and pedagogically manageable way. The experiential vision of learning has evolved in a variety of ways since the 1960s and is now encountered in a number of differing forms. Nevertheless, most experiential approaches to learning rest on five main principles which were developed in the earlier days of the communicative movement, even if certain receive more attention in one variant than in another. These principles are the following: message focus, holistic practice, the use of authentic materials, the use of communication strategies, and the use of collaborative modes of learning (for a slightly different analysis, cf. Johnson and Johnson, 1998: 69–74).

## 1 Message focus

The first of these principles – message focus – posits that language learning activities should focus primarily on the processing and communication of messages. (This principle clearly differs from an approach in which learning is structured primarily around the language code itself, often in the form of a pre-set structural syllabus.) It rests on the belief that message conveyance and communicative practice are effective means of stimulating the learning process and of helping learners to develop their communicative skills. This principle manifests itself in a number of learning activities.

- One of these is the use of role-play and simulation, i.e. activities in which students are required to assume a certain communicative role and to use the language in conformity with the interactive or functional criteria established by the role in question. This can involve fairly simple role-plays of a transactional nature in which students have to ask for information about directions or train times, or can involve simulations of quite complex situations of use involving the processing of various forms of input data.
- Information gap or information transfer activities also involve message focus in that the information needed to carry out a certain task is unevenly divided among students, so that one learner has to convey the information that he or she has to another in order for the latter to be able to carry out a certain task. The idea here is that the shared performance of the target task sets a goal framework within which learners activate or acquire the linguistic resources relevant to the accomplishment of the task at hand.
- Message focus can also involve the use of students' personal interests, their affective concerns, or creativity as a source of communicative involvement. The logic behind such activities is that if students are exchanging ideas on a subject which is of personal relevance to them, they are more likely to experience a personal motivation to use the language and communicate their ideas.
- Some such activities are referred to as opinion gap activities, in that they involve the exchange of opinions as opposed to information, as a basis for communicative practice. These activities rest on the engagement of students' human curiosity and desire to share ideas with others.

The activity types mentioned above were developed fairly early in the communicative movement and, while they still remain part and parcel of mainstream CLT, they have since the 1980s come to be supplemented by other approaches to the generation of message focus. These developments include the process syllabus (Candlin *et al.*, 1981; Breen, 1984, 1987; Candlin, 1987), the procedural syllabus (Prabhu, 1984, 1987) and task-based language learning (Long and Crookes, 1992, 1993). In these approaches learning activities are centred on the resolution of problems or the completion of tasks involving the use of the TL. It is the problem or task which assumes centre stage, and the language syllabus arises out of the requirements of the problem or task in question, e.g. understanding input material, sharing insights or evaluating options with fellow learners, or producing a document, to cite just a few instances of language use to which these approaches can give rise. Although different in a number of respects from the earlier developments mentioned above, these approaches have in common a concern with making message conveyance (and not code study) the starting point for learning activities.

Message focus is probably the most important single feature of an experiential view of learning. It involves the creation of conditions in which students have to use the language to achieve goals or to share insights, as opposed to presenting the language as an object of study in its own right. To a degree, the other aspects of the experiential view of learning flow logically from this.

## 2 Holistic practice

The second principle of the experiential view of learning is its emphasis on holistic practice. Natural language use involves the simultaneous manipulation of a variety of communicative parameters and levels of linguistic information, and experiential views of learning favour holistic learning activities which reflect this multi-dimensional nature of normal communication. The centre point of learning is thus the ideas which are to be conveyed or the task to be performed, and not the language elements by which this has to be achieved. The latter are, of course, important, but they are meant to emerge from the attempt to convey a certain message.

## 3 The use of authentic materials

The third principle of experientially based views of learning is a preference for authentic materials. This has a number of origins. Widdowson (1978), for example, criticised the decontextualised showcase language characteristic of then current code-focused language teaching materials as being unrepresentative of real language, and therefore unlikely to provide learners with a meaningful model of language use. Other currents of thought, such as those expressed by

Krashen (1985) and Krashen and Terrell (1983), emphasise the importance of authentic input in language learning, pointing to the role which input plays both in child language acquisition and in naturalistic learning among adults. As a result of considerations of this nature, experiential approaches to learning favour the use of authentic or naturally occurring materials, i.e. materials not written for language teaching purposes.

## 4 The use of communication strategies

The fourth principle is the development of communication strategies (cf. Faerch and Kasper, 1983). By focusing students' attention on message content and engaging them in holistic practice, experiential approaches to learning can confront students with unplanned or unpredictable language needs, both receptively, in terms of the input material to which they are exposed, and productively, in terms of the messages they wish to convey. As a result, students find themselves having to 'negotiate' messages within their existing knowledge of the language. This calls for the use of strategies by which learners can make the most of their existing resources or get round deficiencies in their current command of the TL. Recourse to communication strategies is consistent with the experiential view of learning and also has the advantage of helping learners to develop strategic skills which can be helpful to them outside of the classroom when they encounter TL material which they do not fully understand, or when they are confronted with communicative tasks which may go beyond their current TL resources.

## 5 The use of collaborative modes of learning

Finally, an experiential approach to learning often makes use of collaborative modes of learning. The emphasis given to message conveyance frequently leads to the use of learning activities which involve collaboration among learners. This can manifest itself in the conveyance of messages from one student to one or more other students in the framework of role-play or simulation tasks, or in information or opinion gap activities. It may also involve collaboration among learners towards a shared goal, as found in drama production or the project work often associated with task-based learning. Such activities embody what has been called the interaction hypothesis (Allwright, 1984), which maintains that interaction with others gives rise to learning processes or, at least, creates conditions in which productive learning conditions are likely to arise.

How wide is the range of approaches to teaching and learning that you have encountered which could be described as manifesting an experiential vision of learning? (In answering this, you may find it helpful to use, as a check list, the five principles outlined above, i.e. message focus, holistic practice, the use of authentic materials, the use of communication strategies, and the use of collaborative modes of learning.)

- What are the differences, and to which factors (e.g. the age, learning goals, or the attitudes of students) do these differences relate?
- What does this suggest to you about the nature of experiential learning?

## 4.2.2 Experience in context

There is something intuitively attractive about the experiential view of learning. Most students are learning the language in order to put it to some sort of pragmatic use or, at least, with a view to doing this as and when circumstances may require them to. With this in mind, it does not seem unreasonable that the learning process itself could be enhanced by it being geared around the type of communicative activities that students will or may have to perform in the language, or around problem-solving activities or tasks which require learners to use the language in ways which are likely to be relevant to them in the future. Many of the methodological innovations which have appeared in recent decades have involved the development of more experiential forms of learning. In the sense that this general orientation has a clear and plausible rationale, it is not surprising that, in the theoretical literature at least, it has held the high ground in recent decades. Its practical realisation, i.e. how it is lived out in the classroom, has however raised a number of questions.

First, holistic practice and the concomitant use by learners of communication strategies to negotiate around difficulties or gaps in their expressive resources have a rationale and may be able to prepare students for real language use better than part practice and a dominant concern with accuracy of expression. Indeed, in strategic terms, if students have only a limited period of time to learn a language before having to make use of this language in communicative situations, there is a clear justification for holistic practice and the active development of students' communication strategies. However, when students have the time to build up a more rounded and accurate command of the language, there is no reason why this should not be taken as an objective. While faultlessness of speech is by no means the only criterion for success in language learning, a deliberate tolerance of correctible error and inaccuracy is also not an objective. Indeed, an experiential approach can fail to resolve quite a number of language problems and therefore leave students with levels of inaccuracy in their command of the language which can hinder their progression to higher levels of competence.

Second, developments such as the process syllabus and task-based learning call for an 'open' approach to course design. While coherent in methodological terms, such an approach can conflict with top-down educational structures where comparability across groups and institutions is required. It also has significant implications in terms of the practicalities of course design and materials development, not to mention factors such as levels of teacher training and the time required of teachers to engage in ongoing readjustments of course content around emerging learner needs. In other words, the theoretically plausible principles of the process syllabus or of task-based learning can enter into conflict with the practicalities of teaching in many contexts.

Finally, and perhaps most significantly, a fundamental reservation can be made with respect to the practical realisation of the experiential emphasis on message focus. Message focus has the goal of centring learners' attention on the language as a means of communication rather than simply as a code in its own right. The pedagogical realisation of this principle, however, depends on one factor more than any other, namely that students can identify with the task of message conveyance, in other words, whether the message has personal meaningfulness to them. If this is not the case, the risk of an empty form of language practice is high. This essential personal meaningfulness cannot, however, be guaranteed by materials or tasks alone, no matter how well produced or apparently motivating they may appear to be. It derives rather from the degree to which materials and tasks fit in with the learners' identity, interests, and concerns, both within the classroom and in the broader context of their life and aspirations. What constitutes a personally meaningful 'experience' of the language depends on various aspects of context, of which the learners' habitual modes of study, their contact with and attitudes to the TL, and their individual learning goals are just a few. The practical appropriateness of an experiential approach to learning therefore needs to be assessed holistically, within the framework of learners' broader experience of the language and of the learning process.

Have you as a teacher felt any reservations about the effectiveness of an experiential approach to learning?

- What are these reservations?
- Do they relate to the product of learning, or to students' interaction with experientially oriented learning activities?
- Can you find an example in your experience as a teacher or learner in which an experiential approach to learning proved problematic in one way or another?
- What was the source of the tensions in question?

## 4.3 Analytical learning

The experiential approach involves the attempt to introduce into a formal context features of naturalistic learning. This has undeniably enriched the range of options which are available to both teachers and students. It would, however, be naive to imagine that naturalistic learning occurs simply by osmosis. In addition to exposure to the TL and the possibility of using this language for communicative purposes, it calls for the explicit will to learn as well as the more or less conscious use of various strategies for analysing ambient data into meaningful units for comprehension, assimilation, and use. Furthermore, in the case of adolescent and adult learners at least, their socialisation, education and/or professional involvement call upon them to develop and make active use of a range of cognitive skills, i.e. the ability to analyse situations, to decide upon a course of action, and to plan the implementation of decisions. It would therefore be strange if these skills could not be put to good use in the learning of languages. This idea is well expressed by 'Derek', one of the learners interviewed by Stevick:

> Some people seem to think we should learn a foreign language as adults the same way we learned our native language when we were children. But we have to learn languages more in the way we learn other things as adults, and there is more method and more system. We do have mental files and we do have indexes. Why deprive a person of these skills? Let them use them in learning language! (1989: 64)

As these remarks suggest, it does not seem unreasonable to assume that students should be able to make productive use of the full range of their cognitive skills – including their analytical skills – in their language learning. In other words, they should be able to apply their ability to analyse data and to reflect on their choices within the context of their language study as they do in other aspects of their life.

### 4.3.1 The rationale for analytical learning

The first impression one has on encountering a new language is that of an incomprehensible and somewhat mysterious stream of sounds or signs on a page: how, one wonders, can anyone make sense of all of this? Over time, however, regularities emerge as the learner acquires the ability to negotiate a path through the system of the language. An experiential view of learning emphasises the role of exposure to and use of the language itself as means of promoting this process. Another view, which is considered here, suggests that language learning can involve the use of learners' analytical skills via activities which rest on the explicit study of the structural regularities and communicative patterns of the TL. An analytical approach to learning emphasises the explicit study of the TL as a linguistic and communicative system. This general type of learning can assume a variety of different forms. It is character-istic of the grammar–translation method (cf. Howatt, 1984), is found in the cognitive code approach (Carroll, 1966; Mueller, 1971), in various CALL exercises (Mishan, 2000), and in form-focused learning activities (cf. Doughty and Williams, 1998). It is also present in certain types of learner training or awareness raising activities involving the explicit analysis by learners of aspects of the TL or of their own language production.

An analytical view of learning posits that according explicit attention to the regularities of language and language use can play a positive role in learning. Each language manifests a number of structural regularities in areas such as grammar, lexis and phonology, and also with respect to the ways in which these elements are combined to communicate messages. The question, therefore, is not whether languages have structural regularities or not, but whether and in which way explicit attention to such regularities can facilitate the learning of the language. An analytical approach to learning rests on a more or less marked degree of part practice, i.e. isolating parts of the whole for explicit study and learning, even if its ultimate goal remains the development of learners' ability to put these parts together for integrated, holistic use. At least two main considerations lend support to an analytical approach to learning.

First, in terms of learning in general, the isolation and practice of sub-parts of a target skill is a fairly common phenomenon. Driving a car and playing a musical instrument, to take just two examples, are both integrative activities that involve the simultaneous use of a variety of sub-skills. In both cases, however, it is usual for people to practise sub-parts of the skill before they attempt to put them together integratively. (Immediate integrative practice of a musical instrument can be hard on the ear, and the same approach to driving a car can have rather more drastic consequences.) Furthermore, the use of analytical skills is part and parcel of everyday life, whether it be a carpenter taking measurements and selecting the correct form of wood before initiating construction, or an entrepreneur drawing up a business plan and cash flow forecasts before launching a company. In general terms at least, it would therefore seem surprising if these same skills could not play at least some role in language learning.

Second, explicit identification of regularities in a language has advantages which Johnson (1996: 83) refers to as 'generativity' and 'economy'. Mastering a regularity in a language gives learners access to the generative potential of this regularity in new circumstances. For example, once a learner has mastered the use of a certain tense or lexical structure, this is then available for use in new contexts not experienced by the learner to that point in time. In this way, having explicit access to a discrete set of rules which account for a substantial amount of language use is economical in terms of memory space and the storage of information. Explicit presentation or discovery of the structural regularities of a language can therefore represent a short-cut to mastery of this language and support learners' ability to manipulate these regularities for communicative purposes.

Analytical approaches to learning may be seen as being located on a cline between deduction and induction. The difference between the two rests primarily with the locus of control of the work of analysis. In a deductive approach, the main work of analysis is carried out by the 'knower', generally the teacher or materials writer. This usually means that a given regularity in the language is presented to learners as representing an accurate representation of one aspect of the TL system. Learners are then asked to work on tasks or exercises which manifest the target regularity in tightly controlled contexts of use. The inductive approach operates differently: instead of the regularity being presented in a 'pre-packed' form, students are required to derive the regularity themselves from a sample of language data provided.

The distinction between deductive and inductive learning activities is not, however, a black and white one. The data from which students are asked to derive a given regularity can be more or less transparent, and the task instructions can provide them with greater or lesser support. An inductive learning task may, for example, throw students into a whole edition of a newspaper and require them to identify instances of a certain structural regularity with no more guidance than that. Alternatively, the task may be based on closely controlled input data which points to the target regularity in a fairly transparent manner. Inductive learning engages students' cognitive skills in a problem-solving mode by requiring them to work out for themselves an aspect of the TL system. The rationale for inductive as opposed to deductive learning is that the process of working out the target regularity gives it greater prominence in students' minds.

---

What are your own views on the role and value of analytical modes of learning, and what role do they play in your teaching?

- In your experience either as a teacher or as a learner, have you found that analytical forms of learning have been given too much or too little importance?
- Have you ever encountered tensions between your own views of analytical learning and those of your students?
- Analyse your answers and compare them with those of other teachers.

---

### 4.3.2 From knowledge to skill

Johnson (1996) distinguishes between two sorts of knowledge of language: declarative and procedural. These can be seen as corresponding respectively to 'knowing that' and 'knowing how'. Analytical learning serves primarily to enhance declarative knowledge, and specifically students' knowledge of the structural regularities of the language. The main criticism of analytical learning is that declarative knowledge does not necessarily feed through to the ability to use a language for communicative purposes. In other words, someone may have a good knowledge of the structural regularities of a language without being able to make use of the language with the spontaneity and fluency which are required in normal communicative situations. Indeed, this was the main criticism of analytical approaches to learning in the early days of CLT, namely that they portrayed language learning as an accumulation of items of knowledge about the language rather than as the process of developing the ability to use this language for communicative purposes.

It is true that knowledge of the regularities of a language does not necessarily feed through to the ability to use this language fluently for communicative purposes. At the same time, explicit knowledge about the language can facilitate the learning process, as well as its communicative use, especially at more advanced levels. For this reason, the role of analytical learning needs to be evaluated less in terms of general principle than with respect to what the language and the broader language learning experience means to students as they are at a given point in their learning career.

One point which is relevant in this respect are the expectations about learning in general and of language learning in particular which students bring with them to the classroom. Another issue is the way they influence how students perceive and interact with the activities in which they are asked to engage. For example, if an approach to language learning differs radically from the mode of learning to which students are accustomed, they may find it difficult to relate to the learning procedures involved in a way that is meaningful personally. Furthermore, they may not have had the opportunity to develop the individual learning strategies or group-level collaborative skills which the approach in question calls for (cf. Kinsella, 1996). Anderson cites the comments of a Chinese teacher which are relevant in this respect.

> The [foreign experts] cannot accept the obvious fact that Chinese students learn better if they can learn in their own way: start with rote memorization, grammar rules, sentence construction and then worry about conversation and shades of meaning, not the other way round . . . Chinese students learn to read, write, speak, and then comprehend aurally in exactly the reverse order stressed by Western pedagogy. The emphasis on grammar means students tend to neglect comprehension, but can easily construct very good sentences. It seems inexcusably formalistic to most foreign language teachers. But in our experience, these students speak English more fluently after four years of study than their counterparts in the US speak Chinese.
>
> (1993: 474)

What is described here is a typically analytical form of learning based on part practice leading up, over time, to integrated language use. In this respect, it should be noted that the Chinese teacher cited by Anderson does not seem to question fluent and integrative language use as an ultimate goal, but simply points out that traditions in certain environments go about attaining this goal in different ways. There may, indeed, be good reason for adopting a holistic, communicatively oriented form of learning if students are learning the language for fairly immediate pragmatic use. If, on the other hand, the language is being learned for more or less distant uses, there may be no pressing need in pragmatic terms for students to develop active communicative skills en route. They have the time to develop these skills in their own preferred way, even if this involves a more analytically oriented form of learning.

The fundamental question is therefore which approach to learning is likely to have greater long-term effectiveness with respect to the learning time available, and also the greatest meaningfulness for students within the context of the learning process itself. Experiential learning accords most importance to skill development whereas analytical learning emphasises knowledge development. Neither can be viewed as 'the best' in abstract terms. Choices relating to these two approaches to learning therefore need to take account of the way in which the type of learning activities entailed interact with the specificities of each learning context in both pragmatic and also in attitudinal terms. In other words, it is necessary to evaluate these options in terms of the dynamic interaction between learning procedure, on the one hand, and learner expectations and goals, on the other.

---

With respect to one or more courses you are familiar with, analyse the relative balance of experiential and analytical modes of learning.

- Does this balance satisfy you, or do you feel it could be improved?
- How would you justify this balance with respect to the level of the students concerned, their learning goals, their cultural background, or the institutional context of learning, or any other factors you consider relevant?

---

## 4.4 Habit formation: Developing automaticity

I would like to start this section with a brief personal anecdote. Soon after arriving in Belgium, I realised that on leaving my apartment (often in a somewhat hurried manner in order not to be late for a class or meeting) I was getting something wrong in the way in which I greeted my neighbours. They would say 'Bonjour Monsieur' or 'Bonjour Monsieur Tudor'. For my part, I continued to say simply 'Bonjour'. I was told that the latter is less polite, and so resolved to add 'Monsieur' or 'Madame' to my normal greeting. And yet, day after day, I simply said 'Bonjour'. With time and explicit attention, however, I developed the habit of adding the required ending to my greeting, and felt a certain satisfaction at having brought this bit of my use of French closer to the accepted norms of usage. This change, however, did not simply happen: it required explicit attention until it became habitual.

This short anecdote is itself fairly minor, but it relates to one of the many aspects of what Widdowson (1978) refers to as 'the whole complex business of communication'. The point of the anecdote is that certain aspects of communication require both the knowledge that a certain language form is to be used and the ability to use this form in a fluent or automatic manner. Johnson (1996: 89) uses the term 'automatization' to refer to this process and suggests that it forms a bridge between declarative and procedural knowledge, i.e. between knowledge about a language and the ability to use the language fluently for communicative purposes. The automatisation of linguistic responses is thus part of the development of a rounded and fluent command of a language.

### 4.4.1 Habit formation as a comprehensive theory of learning

Automatisation of linguistic competence involves a degree of habit formation. Few people would currently consider habit formation as offering a full theory of language learning, although this has not always been the case: for a relatively brief period, a vision of learning wholly based on habit formation held the high ground in language teaching. The approach in question was audiolingualism, which was developed initially during the Second World War in response to the sudden need to train large numbers of US service personnel to operate in a variety of languages. It was developed further in the 1950s and enjoyed considerable prestige into the 1960s. No discussion of the role of automatisation or habit formation in language learning can therefore ignore audiolingualism.

Audiolingualism rests on two main sets of assumptions. One derives from structural linguistics and views language learning as a process involving mastery of the building blocks of the language system from phonemes and morphemes upwards to word, phrase, and sentence level. Language is therefore seen as a structured linguistic system which is organised hierarchically and which can be presented for learning purposes in a clear and internally coherent manner. The other set of assumptions derives from behavioural psychology and views learning, including language learning, as the creation of conditioned responses to stimuli. Viewed from these combined perspectives, learning a language involves the acquisition of a set of verbal stimulus–response associations. The meeting of these two lines of thought gave rise to an approach to language teaching which seemed to offer the possibility of establishing an objective and scientifically grounded approach to language teaching.

The audiolingual method establishes a strict hierarchy of skills – listening, speaking, reading, and writing – which are to be developed in that order. It also accords considerable importance to accuracy in pronunciation and in the manipulation of grammatical structures: accurate mastery of the component forms of the language is thus given priority over fluency of spontaneous speech. In terms of learning activities, audiolingualism involves detailed study of highly controlled segments of language coupled with intensive practice of the same elements. This generally takes place around selected structures in isolation and then in dialogue form in order to provide some context for the use of the relevant structures. Drilling plays a major role in audiolingualism, whether in the classroom or in the language labora-tory. The goal of audiolingual teaching is a thorough command of a carefully selected and graded set of structures so that these can be used by learners in a confident and automatic manner in response to the requirements of pre-defined interactive situations.

Although audiolingualism exercised a considerable influence on the practice of language teaching during the 1950s and 1960s, a number of fundamental questions were soon raised. To begin with, Chomsky's (1957, 1959, 1965) view of language as a generative system seriously undermined the view of language as conditioned verbal response. Chomsky suggested that a certain number of innate deep rules allow us to generate a vast range of linguistic utterances, including utterances we have never encountered previously. Chomsky's ideas therefore under-mined the theoretical bases of audiolingualism. In addition to this, with the development of communicative language teaching, the code-based and teacher-centred nature of audiolingual instruction came to be seen as a straightjacket which allowed little scope for the personalisation of learning content. Furthermore, doubts were expressed about the prac-tical effectiveness of audiolingual teaching. Specifically, many students found that they had difficulty in transferring their language skills from the tightly controlled practice of the classroom or language laboratory into normal communicative use. Moreover, many students reacted negatively to the learning activities found in the method, and in particular the emphasis on drilling, which were often perceived as arduous and stressful.

As a result of the questioning of the theoretical bases of audiolingu-alism as well as the practical discontent expressed with respect to both the effectiveness and the palatability of the method, audiolingualism would today find relatively few defenders as a comprehensive theory of language learning in its own right. This does not, however, mean that the idea of automatisation or habit formation should be thrown out. There is reason for exploring their role, if only as one among other forms of learning which can contribute to the development of fluency in language use.

## 4.4.2 A constructive role for habit formation

Communicative competence in a language involves the ability to understand and produce novel and potentially unpredictable instances of language, and this cannot be attained merely by habit formation. Nevertheless, fluent language use involves a variety of sub-skills and some of these do, in part at least, rest on a degree of predictability and habitual response. It is frequently the absence of such predictable elements which marks off even a proficient non-native speaker from a native speaker. This suggests that there is good reason for examining those aspects of language which are more predictable and which might usefully be made the object of an approach to learning based on automatisation of response, albeit as part of the long-term goal of spontaneous communicative fluency. In this respect, it may be helpful to distinguish between formulaic language use and what could be referred to as scaffolding language.

Certain aspects of language use such as greetings, basic interactional exchanges and conversational routines are fairly predictable, either in terms of what people say or in terms of what would be considered as acceptable verbal behaviour in the relevant situations. Native speakers of English respond to the phatic greeting 'Hello. How are you?' in a variety of ways depending on the context and on how well they know the interlocutor; e.g. 'Fine. And you?', 'Can't complain', 'You know me!' are just a few instances from the wide repertoire of native speakers of English. A learner at less than advanced level cannot realistically be expected to react with this degree of flexibility, and having a small number of acceptable response types such as 'Very well, thank you' or 'Not too good, today' can be very helpful in dealing with simple interactive situations in a manner which facilitates communication and, thus, opens up the opportunity for further interaction and learning. Helping learners to master simple interactive patterns of this nature can thus be a great assistance in their learning and use of a language.

Something similar applies to scaffolding elements, namely more or less set pieces of language which can be used to structure parts of utterances. Examples are phrases such as 'I'm not sure whether . . .', 'Could you tell me how / when . . .?', 'The real problem here is . . .'. The conscious learning and automatisation of a bank of elements of this nature can facilitate the structuring of utterances and in this way free the learner's mental attention for more context-specific and meaning-bearing aspects of interaction. Indeed, such elements are a part of the discourse structuring repertoire of native speakers which allows them to construct discourse in a smooth manner. Creating structured practice in elements of this nature involves identifying potentially high use aspects of the TL and focusing teaching on these as an aid to smoother comprehension and production of discourse.

One justification for a degree of habit-formation based learning is thus that it can help learners develop more fluency and communicative confidence by helping them to be able to use more predictable or high yield language elements without conscious reflection or planning. Another is that it can help students to acquire a more solid mastery of details of the language system which may easily be missed in spoken input and which can also be overlooked in production. Finding a balance between accuracy and fluency is a recurrent tension in language teaching. Traditional grammar-based instruction focused on accuracy at the expense of communicative fluency, and audiolingualism has a similar focus on the accurate use of language form at the expense of the development of the ability to use forms within the framework of spontaneous communicative exchange. Equally well, however, experiential approaches to learning sometimes fail to accord sufficient attention to language form, with the result that students can too easily fossilise into a fluent but inaccurate and limiting type of language use. A degree of form-focused learning geared to the automatic production either of frequent structures or of potentially difficult phonetic combinations can remedy this deficiency and thus play a role in the development of a rounded communicative ability.

One problem in this respect is that some of the learning activities associated with habit-formation based approaches, drill work in particular, are sometimes unpopular. 'Mindless parroting' is one not too uncommon way of describing audiolingual style drilling, and if this is the way in which drill activities are perceived by students, there is good reason to doubt their potential usefulness. More constructive perspectives exist (cf. Stevick, 1989: 26–27), but it is clear that the pain–gain ratio of such activities can be evaluated in very different ways by different learners.

One point that can usefully be borne in mind in this respect is that the classroom and the learning process itself have their own dynamics and therefore their own situation-internal authenticity. Focusing on resolving code-internal ambiguities and acquiring the ability to use aspects of the language smoothly and confidently can therefore be an authentic activity for learners as part of the broader goal of acquiring fluency in this language, especially if such activities are presented to learners clearly as one mode of learning alongside others. In this light, habit-based learning activities may be seen as pre-communicative activities which have the goal of preparing students for subsequent communicative uses of the language. The learning procedures involved may not be 'meaning-oriented' in the communicative sense, but they can well be 'meaningful' as part of the learning process and as one step in the development of communicative fluency.

Stevick (1989: 74) cites an interesting remark by 'Derek' which is relevant in this respect: 'If you cannot learn to say what you want to say, then learn to want to say what you can say.' This is a pragmatic response of learners who know that, at a given point in their learning of a language, they simply do not have the resources to express the ideas that they would naturally wish to express. If, however, they think their way into the language that they do have, they can, in a sense, appropriate this language for themselves and add it to their expressive resources, thus moving closer to the goal of spontaneous personal communication. Here we are looking at what could be called 'learning process-internal authenticity', and the ability of learners to find meaningfulness in the deliberate accumulation of resources for future use. Within such a perspective, learning activities involving a degree of habit formation can potentially play a productive role within the wider goal of developing communicative fluency.

---

Learning activities geared around automatisation of language use do not receive a great deal of attention in current discussions of methodology.

- How would you as a teacher analyse the positive and negative aspects of this approach to teaching and learning?
- What role do such activities play in your teaching?
- Do you feel that they could play a stronger role? If so, in which way and with respect to which aspects of the language?

---

## 4.5 The role of affect

The three visions of learning surveyed above relate to the process of language learning as such. In other words, they rest on hypotheses as to how students can explore and practise the TL, and all learning programmes must incorporate choices on this level. Language learning does not, however, operate mechanistically. Students are individuals whose interaction with learning activities is influenced by a variety of cognitive, psychological, and experiential factors, and these factors give rise to a certain affective interaction with the learning process. As practising teachers know, if students enter the classroom with a positive affective predisposition to the language or to the learning process, there is a good chance that productive learning can be achieved, whatever the practical conditions of learning and teaching, or the methodology used. If such a predisposition does not exist, teaching and learning are likely to be an uphill struggle for all concerned. Affect cannot therefore be ignored in any serious consideration of language learning (for an overview of perspectives on the role of affect, cf. Arnold, 1999).

However, the question of how affect can be integrated into a vision of language learning and operationalised in terms of teaching and learning procedures is by no means straightforward. Indeed, there is a growing realisation that the affective involvement of learners is a complex phenomenon which cannot be easily predicted or pre-planned. On the one hand, affect is an omnipresent phenomenon which relates to students' attitudes to and involvement in learning activities: in this light, positive affect cannot be seen as the reserve of any one approach to learning. On the other hand, certain approaches take the fostering of positive affective involvement as a methodological principle in its own right. This section therefore looks at some of the ways in which our profession has attempted to accommodate the affective dimension of language learning. First, it considers certain methodological perspectives which accord a specific role to affect. Then it considers the concept of affect in broader terms, with reference to the range of factors that can contribute to the development of a positive affective involvement of students in the learning process.

### 4.5.1 Affect as an explicit methodological variable

It is the humanistic movement which, in the recent history of language teaching at least, has accorded the most explicit role to the development of positive affect in language learning. In its early days, the humanistic movement painted a rather black vision of traditional education as information-centred, dehumanising, alienating and irrelevant to the real needs of students (cf. Moskovitz, 1978). In response to these perceived failures of traditional approaches to education, humanistic language teaching accorded a central role in language learning to the development of a positive affective relationship between the learner and the learning material, and warm and supportive interpersonal relationships in the classroom itself.

The first of these goals involves a marked preference for learning activities with a positive affective dimension. Such activities relate to topics which have emotional relevance to the learner, and particularly those which are likely to create positive emotional associations. Humanistic language teaching also favours activities which tap into learners' creative or imaginative potential, such as the use of drama, poetry, or imagination-based activities. (As we will see below, a number of these activity types have found their way into mainstream CLT.) The second aspect of the humanistic approach relates to the type of affective relations which are developed in the classroom, both between teacher and students and also among students themselves. This is one of the more characteristic features of humanistic language teaching. Its goal is to create warm, supportive, and trusting relationships in the classroom, with the idea that this will make students feel valued and at ease, and thus better able (or 'freer' in affective terms) to discover and develop their personal learning agendas in and via the TL.

There has been much debate on humanistic language teaching (cf. Brumfit, 1982; Appel, 1989; Atkinson, 1989), especially with respect to the question of classroom relations. There can, however, be little doubt that the humanistic emphasis on the role of affect has contributed considerably to the awareness of the role of this variable in language teaching well beyond the frontiers of the humanistic movement itself.

Another voice which has influenced the debate on the role of affect is that of Krashen (1982, 1985), and his distinction between learning and acquisition has influenced thinking on language teaching in a number of ways. He portrays 'learning' in rather black terms (reminiscent of the humanistic condemnation of 'traditional' approaches to education) as a mechanical and forced activity which is unlikely to take root in learners' minds and lead to productive language use. He therefore favours the term 'acquisition', but crucially maintains that this process is dependent upon what he refers to as the 'affective filter'. This, for Krashen, is an aspect of students' learning system which filters out input that has no affective meaningfulness for them, but which can also make learners receptive to learning if the input they are exposed to is pleasant or relevant to them in affective terms. In essence, Krashen maintains that we do not learn well if the learning process runs against the grain, and that what does or does not run against the grain relates significantly to the affective involvement of the learner with learning material and tasks. In pedagogical terms, this implies that input material, and also the tasks which students are asked to perform on this material, has to be selected not simply on linguistic criteria, but also with respect to the affective interaction between the learner and the material or tasks in question. Here again, then, affect assumes an explicit role in pedagogical planning.

Both the humanistic movement and the ideas of Krashen have had an influence on the somewhat heterogeneous phenomenon of mainstream CLT. In this respect, however, it is helpful to distinguish between what could be referred to as 'hard' and 'soft' CLT. Hard CLT is manifested most clearly in LSP and involves the establishment of learning goals which are derived from an analysis of the uses to which learners will have to put the language. Within this framework of reference, it is pedagogically coherent to link learning activities closely to the learners' target uses of the language. Learning by doing has a strong pragmatic justification: learners are involved in developing the skills they will require in given situations of use, which means that classroom learning activities can serve as direct skill training in the relevant areas of use. In such a context, creating a close link between learning activities and the pragmatic needs students have in the language can also have a strong motivational value, and in this way can generate a positive affective involvement in the learning process.

Such a close linking of learning activities and target uses of the language is not possible when the uses to which learners will have to put the language are distant or uncertain, and may have little perceived relevance to students. It is fairly obvious, however, that a great deal of language teaching is conducted in precisely such circumstances. The relevant authorities or possibly the students themselves have decided that knowledge of a language is likely to be of use to them at some stage in the future, without it being possible to specify precisely the reasons for which they are learning the language. Within such a context, what is learned may well be of less importance than ensuring that something is learned, and maintenance of student interest and involvement plays a key role in the pursuit of this goal. In view of the increased amount of language learning worldwide, it is probably fair to say that this is one of the main concerns in current language teaching methodology, namely to create learning procedures and a learning climate which are inherently motivating so as to foster and maintain student interest and involvement in the learning process.

This type of learning scenario has given rise to what could be called soft CLT, i.e. an approach to language learning which takes general communicative ability (more often than not defined around spoken skills) as a learning goal, and which pursues this goal by means of an experiential approach to learning supported by materials and activities which are designed to have a high degree of inherent interest. Considerations relating to motivation or, in broader terms, to students' affective involvement in the learning process, have therefore combined with the experiential view of learning looked at in Section 4.2 to produce what is arguably the currently dominant paradigm in language teaching. Thus, what is our dominant motivation when we set up learning activities which engage students in the viewing of a video on a topic of current interest and involve discussion or opinion-exchange activities on the topic in question? Is it that we feel that learning is best promoted by contact with and use of the language (i.e. the experiential view of language learning as such)? Or do we feel that this type of activity is likely to engage student interest and thus maintain their involvement in the learning process itself (i.e. an affectively-oriented view of the learning process)? There is, of course, no reason why the two should not coincide, but it is helpful to look carefully at the real reason why choices are made. My own feeling is that a large part of current CLT – which rests in theoretical terms on an experiential view of learning – is in reality strongly influenced by considerations relating to the engagement and maintenance of student motivation in the learning process, i.e. to factors which are primarily of an affective nature. Current CLT would thus emerge as a combination of experiential and affectively-based visions of learning.

---

If you have taught in a situation which corresponds to what was described as soft CLT, analyse the approach to teaching and learning which was adopted. Pay particular attention to the nature and goals of learning activities and materials.

- Were they designed primarily to foster an experiential form of learning or to enhance students' affective involvement in the learning process? (The two may merge, but try nevertheless to identify the primary goal.)
- How did the students react to the activities in question?
- What was your own evaluation of the approach adopted?

---

### 4.5.2 The diversity of affect

The perspectives on affect considered above are valid and can contribute to fostering a positive involvement of students in the learning process. It is, however, important to distinguish between general principle and the manner in which this is realised in a given context. Positive affective relations, which are explicitly promoted in humanistic language teaching, are certainly conducive to learning, but what is experienced as positive is likely to vary from one individual and one culture to another. It is therefore risky to earmark affect as being synonymous with any one type of interpersonal relation: humanistic classroom relations, for example, may be experienced as warm and supportive by one person or cultural group, but as intrusive and inappropriate by another. Something similar applies to the approach to motivation which is found in soft CLT. Lots of colour, variety, and activity may be perceived as stimulating by some students, but as confusing and lacking in structure by others. Thus, while the role of affect is certainly important in language learning, caution is required so as not to restrict it to any one of its possible manifestations. The subject is a vast one, and here I consider it by looking at just a few ideas which might stimulate reflection on certain aspects of what positive affect in language learning may entail.

One obvious source of positive affective involvement derives from students feeling that the activities in which they are engaged, not to mention the objectives which they are pursuing, are relevant to their life goals and concerns. This may be linked to the relevance of a given course to students' professional or educational needs, as one often finds in LSP teaching. It may also relate to the role which success in a given course has within the framework of students' educational career, whether the course content has a tangible link to any future pragmatic needs or not.

Another source of positive affective involvement is internal to the learning process and relates to the positive affective associations which can arise out of the process of learning itself. This can involve students seeing, for example, how a given role-play will help them to cope better with their use of the telephone the next day at work, if it is in these terms that their learning goals are defined. It may also relate to their ability to pass an external examination which requires them to demonstrate mastery of a given range of structures. Alternatively, it may relate simply to the satisfaction of having mastered a given element of the language with confidence as they progress through their set coursebook, e.g. the feeling that they have mastered 'Unit 9', whatever Unit 9 may involve. This derives from students' ability to see where they are going and to have a sense of achievement within the learning process itself. This is probably a very important ingredient of positive affective involvement.

A related source of positive involvement is for students to feel that they are accepted and valued as they are, and that they have something to contribute to the learning process as manifested in the learning tasks on which they are asked to work. Thus, if students enjoy working on problems alone and figuring out the rules of the language system, is there a chance for them to use these skills? If other students are able to memorise lists of words and expressions, do they have the chance to use this skill? The same applies for students who have a good ear for the spoken language and can imitate a foreign accent successfully, or for those who are skilled at negotiating their way through even limited language resources. The presence of a learning environment which validates as wide as possible a range of learning skills will by the same token be validating what a large number of students bring with them to the learning process, and this is a powerful source of positive affective involvement. What the learning activities are may be less important in affective terms than their power to validate the contribution individual students can make to their own learning.

The social context of learning can also play an important affective role, especially the feeling of being part of a shared learning endeavour, and this is not limited to classroom-internal factors. For example, if students' family or social group accord status to learning the TL, whatever happens in the classroom is likely to be bestowed with an aura of prestige and a sense of being worthwhile. It can also arise out of a certain type of relationship with fellow students, whether this relationship is explicitly supportive or has a competitive element to it. In either case, however, the nature of the 'sharing' of the endeavour has to be understood in the terms of the students themselves and of their own culture. In this respect, it is important to remember that no one set of cultural values is right for everyone: the feeling of sharing a learning endeavour can thus take many forms, and should not be prejudged from any one set of cultural values or interpersonal norms.

The idea of sharing the endeavour of learning also includes consideration of the role of the teacher, even if this may seem to contradict certain points made above. It is an observable fact that virtually all methods or approaches to language teaching have achieved positive results with more or less large numbers of students, and it is unlikely that all these students' spontaneous learning preferences will have fitted in neatly with the approach or method in question. There may be a number of reasons for this phenomenon, but one – and probably not the least important – is the role of the teacher. This need not be seen as the teacher 'making' a method work in a coercive manner, but can rather be seen as certain teacher traits combining with learner expectations to create constructive learning dynamics. Like laughter, enthusiasm and commitment tend to be contagious; therefore, the effect which teacher enthusiasm and commitment can have on student learning should not be underestimated. In this respect, it should be borne in mind that most students probably enter the language classroom with a belief that the teacher has something to offer them and that, if they 'play the game', they are likely to get something useful out of the experience. If these expectations are met in the sense that the teacher shows professionalism, appears to know what he or she is doing, and also demonstrates a genuine commitment to the students as individuals, the result can contribute significantly to the creation of a positive affective climate for learning.

Affect, then, is a complex and multifaceted phenomenon. That it plays an important and perhaps even a decisive role in learning can hardly be doubted. The way in which it precisely operates within a given situation is, however, by no means easy to determine. It arises out of the dynamic interplay of what students bring with them to the classroom (not just as language learners but also as individuals), the methodology and materials that are presented to them, how these fit in with their preferences and goal structures and, last but by no means least, the human relations which exist in the classroom both among students and between students and the teacher.

---

This section highlights two main points. The first is that affect plays a very important role in language learning, and the second is that the sources of positive affective involvement are varied.

- Working with one or more colleagues, brainstorm the various factors which you have found to contribute to a positive affective involvement of students in the learning process.
- What does this reveal about the nature of affect in language teaching?
- If any common ground emerges, what is it?

---

## 4.6 Overview

The four visions of learning surveyed in this chapter account for a substantial part of the methodological landscape within which teachers have to make decisions about the organisation of learning activities. As was the case in Chapter 3 with respect to language, each of the four visions of learning surveyed here contains a valid insight into what language learning can mean to a greater or smaller number of students as well as to other participants in the teaching–learning process. Furthermore, with the exception of habit formation (which few people would currently see as offering a comprehensive account of language learning), each of these visions of learning can serve as a basis for structuring a learning programme, either in their 'pure' form or in combination with others.

This inevitably raises the question of the basis on which decisions relating to the pedagogical organisation of learning activities should be made. This question, although fundamental for all language educators, does not lend itself to simple or straightforward answers. One point is that such decisions cannot be made on the basis of abstract principle or the inner logic of a given methodological perspective alone. This constitutes one side of the equation, and pedagogical decision-making clearly calls for careful consideration of the potential of a given approach to contribute to effective learning of the TL. In addition to this, however, attention has to be paid to the context within which the approach in question is to be realised, the meaning which it can assume for participants and, on this basis, the way in which it influences the dynamics of teaching and learning.

As was suggested in Section 1.5, context has two main components. The first relates to the pragmatic conditions of teaching and learning such as class size, the availability of learning resources, the influence of other agents (sponsors, educational authorities, etc.), and the agendas which these agents set for language learning. The second component of context is mental and arises out of the attitudes and expectations of the students concerned. In this respect, it needs to be recalled that language learning is a mental process and that it will only be effective if it assumes personal meaningfulness for students. Students can be asked to perform, or even be coerced into performing, certain learning-oriented activities, but these activities lead to effective learning only if they fit meaningfully into the mental frameworks which the students bring with them to the learning process. A given methodological approach can contribute to and support the creation of personal meaningfulness but cannot guarantee it. The vision of learning expressed in methodology is thus one element in the dynamics of classroom teaching and learning; it is not a magic wand.

# 5 Visions of the classroom

## 5.1 The many meanings of the classroom

At first sight, the concept of the classroom might not seem to be one that calls for a great deal of explanation. Indeed, some people might even question whether the term 'concept' is appropriate: Isn't the classroom simply a 'place' where students meet to learn a language? In a sense, this is the case. One difficulty, however, is that, as we have seen in Chapters 3 and 4, neither language nor learning are uncontroversial concepts. For this reason, differing perspectives on the nature of the classroom can arise, if only because what 'learning a language' entails can be understood and therefore approached in differing ways.

In addition to this, the classroom is a social as well as a pedagogical reality. Thus, while the official role of the classroom is pedagogical, the way in which this role is understood and defined is influenced by a variety of social agents: the management of a teaching institution, sponsors or parents, and various other political or social stakeholders. The vision that these various actors have of the classroom and the agendas which they wish to see pursued within it are significant constituents of the context within which teaching and learning are conducted. These expectations influence the way in which teachers and students interact with one another, with the decisions of social and institutional actors, and also with teaching procedures and materials. The classroom is therefore anything but a simple, uncontroversial concept and can have different meanings for the various actors who, in one way or another, have an interest in what takes place within it. Van Lier makes this point as follows.

> The classroom is not a world unto itself. The participants (teachers and learners) arrive at the event with certain ideas as to what is a 'proper' lesson, and in their actions and interaction they will strive to implement these ideas. In addition the society at large and the institution the classroom is part of have certain

> expectations and demands which exert influence on the way the
> classroom turns out. (1988: 179)

For this reason, it is necessary to look carefully at the way in which students, teachers and other participants perceive the classroom and the meaning which classroom learning has for them, not just with respect to language learning in a narrow sense of the term, but also within the broader framework of their value system and goal structures.

With this in mind, this chapter looks at four visions of the classroom, some of which will pick up on elements dealt with in Chapters 3 and 4, namely visions of language and of learning. The chapter also situates these elements in the broader context of the classroom in its function as both a pedagogical and a social reality. The goal of this chapter is to provide teachers with a few categories around which they can analyse the visions of the classroom with which they and other participants are working, and thus to explore the ways in which the interaction of these (possibly differing) perceptions contributes to the classroom dynamics.

## 5.2 The classroom as a controlled learning environment

The most traditional and arguably the most widespread vision of the language classroom is that of a controlled learning environment, namely a place where students work on the language according to a carefully designed learning programme under the supervision and guidance of a trained teacher. This vision of the classroom rests on a certain number of assumptions, whether or not these assumptions are explicitly formulated. The first is that there is a clear plan of what will be done in pedagogical terms and also with respect to the nature of learning which will result. The second is that the relevant learning plan will be realised by means of clearly structured teaching materials and learning activities. The third is that the teacher, who is the person most directly responsible for the realisation of the plan, will come equipped with a set of pedagogical skills that will allow him or her to realise the plan by means of an expert manipulation of methodological procedures relating to factors such as the presentation of TL material and the organisation of students' participation.

In this vision, then, the classroom is a controlled learning environment. Its purpose is to enable students to learn the language by the creation of conditions in which language learning can be undertaken in a structured manner. Methodology plays a central role in this vision of the classroom: methodology is the means by which the learning plan is realised, and provides the pedagogical structure within which students work on and practise the TL. The teacher, too, plays an important role, but this role is mediated through methodology. A good teacher is therefore one who can breathe life into methodological procedures in pursuit of the learning objectives set out in the curriculum. The students' role is also defined to a large degree by the methodology being used. It is the methodology and the learning activities that it generates which define the nature of students' participation in the classroom: their participation is therefore channelled through the assumptions about the nature of language and of language learning found in the methodology being used.

This view of the classroom is close to what Breen (1986) refers to as the classroom as an 'experimental laboratory'. It is the place where a certain vision of language and of language learning is realised by means of carefully planned pedagogical procedures with the expectation that, if this is done on cue, a more or less predictable set of learning outcomes will result. It is also linked to what Nunan (1989) describes as the curriculum as 'statement of intent': the curriculum sets out objectives, and the classroom is the place where these objectives are pursued in a controlled and focused manner. On the one hand, as most practising teachers know, this vision of the classroom is somewhat simplistic as it cannot be assumed that the plan will translate smoothly into reality. On the other hand, however, some degree of planning is essential in any educational endeavour, and even the 'designless design' of task-based learning remains a design, albeit a loosely defined one. Furthermore this vision of the classroom underpins much educational planning and is present in the expectations of a substantial number of participants.

### 5.2.1 Frameworks of control

The key element in the vision of the classroom as a controlled learning environment is that a set of methodological procedures are set in place with the goal of enabling students to achieve a pre-specified set of learning objectives. This clearly rests on the hypothesis that the use of a given set of teaching–learning procedures can lead in a fairly predictable manner to a specifiable set of learning outcomes. In order for this to happen, there must logically be a close control of the samples of the TL to which students are exposed and of the learning activities in which students engage; hence the idea of a learning environment that is controlled.

This vision of the classroom is often associated with code-based visions of language and with analytical and habit-formation based visions of learning, and there are some fairly obvious reasons for this.

The vision of language as a structured linguistic system allows for the prior isolation and sequencing of specific sub-parts of this system for learning purposes (to a greater degree than, for example, a vision of language as self-expression). Indeed, one of the advantages of a code-based perspective on language is precisely that it facilitates a pre-planned approach to the setting of objectives and preparation of materials: the language is a system which exists 'out there' and this system lends itself to analysis and pedagogical presentation. Furthermore, analytical and habit-formation based visions of learning allow for detailed pre-planning of learning activities to a greater extent than those which emphasise individual experience of the language and the negotiation of possibly unpredictable ideas and meanings.

The vision of the classroom as a controlled learning environment is not, however, the reserve of code-based visions of language or of analytical and habit-formation based visions of learning. The same underlying vision of the classroom is found in other approaches to teaching, including certain humanistic methods. Indeed, the very concept of 'method' implies a clearly defined vision of learning and is therefore likely to give rise to closely pre-specified teaching and learning activities. To take just two examples, both Community Language Learning and the Silent Way (for succinct surveys, cf. Stevick, 1990: 71–99, 101–130) rest on the use of closely defined teaching and learning procedures, and the roles which students are meant to play in the classroom are defined with great precision. A classroom in which one of these methods is used is therefore, in principle, as controlled a learning environment as one in which the audiolingual method is being used, even if the specific teaching techniques employed are very different.

CLT is a very broad church which has served as the meeting place for a wide range of different methodological insights and procedures. What Johnson (1982) refers to as the 'in at the deep end' communicative strategy is just one version of CLT, and many others exist which cater for a close control over both teaching and learning activities. Furthermore, as we see in Section 5.3 below, the communicative classroom has its own logic and works with its own vision of learning and, thereby, of the role that the classroom has to play in the learning process. Thus, although mainstream CLT generally tolerates a more flexible link between learning activities and projected learning outcomes than some other approaches, it would be naive to assume that the mainstream CLT classroom takes 'anything goes' as its operating principle, even if it may define intended learning outcomes in different terms from more traditional code-based approaches.

Although the approaches or methods mentioned above differ from one another in terms of the specific methodological procedures they use, they all rest on the view of the classroom as a place in which a certain number of hypotheses about language learning are realised by means of the controlled application of a particular array of teaching–learning activities. This explains the central role that methodology plays in the vision of the classroom as a controlled learning environment, since it is methodology which provides the framework within which the intended control of learning is channelled. It thereby allocates a specific role to the teacher as the person who has the task of manipulating the relevant teaching–learning procedures so as to orient student learning in the right direction. A controlled learning environment therefore also implies a controlled teaching environment.

The vision of the classroom as a controlled learning environment is attractive in a number of ways. It suggests that objectives can be set, methodology selected, materials prepared, and teachers trained to exploit them in a clear, rational manner. If all participants, students included of course, play their appointed role on cue, then a fairly predictable set of learning outcomes should result. This way of seeing language teaching rests on a positivistic perspective on teaching, and is understandably popular with planning authorities. It also corresponds to the way in which many non-specialists see language teaching and the role which the classroom has to play in the activity. It is thus a vision of the classroom which few teachers will fail to meet in their working lives, even if the reality of this vision may be less obvious to them in their day-to-day experience of their own classrooms.

---

Have you encountered the vision of the classroom as a controlled learning environment (whether it was referred to in these terms or not) during your training, in your interaction with students or colleagues, or in a course that you have taught?

- What is your evaluation of this way of seeing classroom teaching and learning?
- Does it correspond to your experience of teaching?
- If not, indicate why and in which ways?

---

### 5.2.2 Control in context

The vision of the classroom outlined above rests on a number of generally implicit assumptions. These are, in essence, that the plan of learning established by the course designer or teacher, and the vision of the learning process present in methodology will feed through in a fairly direct manner to student learning. The research surveyed in Chapter 1 indicates that this assumption is somewhat simplistic. To begin with, research on learner differences has shown that learners' psychological, cognitive and experiential characteristics may cause them to perceive methodological principles in different ways. In other words, what students are experiencing in a given class may not correspond to what the teacher or course designer assumes they are experiencing. Block (1996), for example, describes a study in which teacher intentions in and learner perceptions of a lesson are compared, and suggests that what we as teachers assume to be happening in a given class may not correspond to what our students are perceiving in the same class. In addition to this, there are the differing visions of the nature both of language and of learning which have been surveyed in Chapters 3 and 4, and it cannot be assumed that the vision of either which underpins the approach adopted in a given classroom will necessarily coincide with those of the learners involved.

For these reasons, a strong view of the classroom as a controlled learning environment is somewhat difficult to maintain in practice. It may be possible to speak of a controlled teaching environment to the degree that teacher actions and the activities that learners are asked to engage in can be controlled to a certain degree (although this can vary considerably from one context to another). Whether it is possible to assume that there will be a linear relationship between these actions and what precisely is learned is less certain. An explicit teaching agenda may well exist, but whether this will coincide with the learning agenda of a given class of students is another matter entirely.

These observations might seem rather disheartening. The task of course designers, materials writers and teachers is to set up conditions in which learning has at least a reasonable chance of occurring. The growing awareness of the non-linearity of the relationship between pedagogical action, on the one hand, and learning, on the other, does not, however, mean that all the complex structure of course design, methodological reflection, and teacher training has to be thrown out of the window with the remark that since it may not achieve its goals, it might as well be dropped.

The classroom, as was pointed out above, is a social institution to which many people look for guidance and support in the learning process, and this is by no means unreasonable. Furthermore, in terms of the practical organisation of teaching activities, course designers and teachers need at least to have something to work from. Although each group of students is something new, teachers cannot enter the classroom empty handed: they need a starting point, and students probably expect them to have one. Thus, while a strong version of the classroom as a controlled learning environment may not be tenable, a weak version of the same concept is both tenable and, in fact, probably necessary. From this perspective, the presence of a clear plan may be seen not as an ultimatum or a dogma to be pursued for its own sake, but as a starting point for a local negotiation of classroom realities. The plan thus becomes an element in the dynamics of teaching and learning.

As a social as well as a pedagogical reality, the pedagogical role of the classroom is defined in terms which are specific to the culture in which it is located. Students will therefore come to the classroom with certain expectations as to what a good classroom should be, and of the role the teacher should play within it. Some cultures – whether ethnic or institutional – may expect a more 'open' or 'democratic' type of classroom, i.e. one which leaves greater scope for student input and one in which teachers manifest their pedagogical concern for students in an individual manner. Other cultures may expect a more 'authoritative' approach with a stronger degree of prior decision-making as to the content and mode of learning, possibly with the teacher as a more directive figure of authority. In most cases, however, students enter the classroom expecting the teacher to have something solid to offer them in terms of professional knowledge and experience of language learning options. Thus, whether students come from a more democratic-based or a more authority-based culture, they are likely to expect at least a convinced and professionally competent 'negotiating stance' from teachers and the educational institution which they represent.

The question of the degree of control which is exercised on classroom learning therefore has to take account of a number of considerations. To begin with, realism is called for with respect to the practical need for sufficient structure and advance planning to make teaching manageable on a day-to-day basis. In addition to this, attention has to be given to a range of attitudinal factors, and particularly to the expectations which students have of the role of the teacher and of the classroom. This is because factors of this nature play a significant role in supporting students' affective involvement in the learning process. Such factors can vary considerably from one context to another. Thus, a course structure which operates with a strong view of pedagogical control can generate negative reactions from students who are used to a more open or relaxed approach, and vice versa. For this reason, the question of control in teaching and learning needs to be evaluated locally, in terms of the meaning which the classroom and classroom learning have for the various participants present in a given setting.

A distinction was made above between strong and weak versions of the vision of the classroom as a controlled learning environment.

- Which is closer to your experience of teaching?
- How do you react to the idea of pedagogical planning as a negotiating stance?
- Around which aspects of teaching do you feel you do the most 'negotiating' with students?
- Does this vary from one group of students to another? If so, in which ways?

## 5.3 The communicative classroom

The 1960s and 1970s witnessed a number of changes in society which led to a re-thinking of the goals of language teaching and learning, and thereby of the role which the classroom was meant to play in the teaching–learning process. First, the growth in international exchanges led to an increase in the demand for language teaching and greater concern with the development of practically relevant communicative skills. The vision of the language as a linguistic system thus came to be challenged by visions of language as a means of communication and of self-expression. This led to consideration of the way in which the classroom could best support the furtherance of the new set of goals which were being set for language teaching. In addition to this, there were calls for more learner-centred and democratic forms of classroom interaction in which learners' needs and preferences were given greater attention in educational planning. These trends may be seen in the move towards more experiential forms of learning and a greater concern with the role of students' affective involvement in the learning process.

The challenge was thus to make the language classroom 'a place of communication' in which a significant role is attributed to communicative language use as a means of learning. This involved an attempt to break down the dichotomy between the classroom and the 'real world' by making the classroom itself a place of communication and of communicatively-based learning. Indeed, creating conditions in which this view of the classroom can become a reality has been one of the main concerns of methodological reflection in language teaching over the intervening period of time. It is by no means easy to identify unambiguously the various strands of thought and methodological exploration which have arisen from the pursuit of this goal. It is, however, possible to identify two main lines of exploration in the attempt to rethink the role of the classroom in language learning. The first involves the rethinking of classroom learning itself so that it can better prepare students for language use outside of the classroom, i.e. to increase the relevance of classroom learning with respect to learners' future uses of the language. The second involves the exploration of the communicative potential of the classroom itself. The two are not wholly unrelated; nor, however, are they wholly synonymous. They are examined below in terms of the distinction between 'the classroom for communication' and 'the classroom as communication'.

## 5.3.1 The classroom for communication

A major criticism made in the 1960s and 1970s of the then current approaches to language teaching was that they provided students with knowledge of the TL, but not necessarily with the ability to use this language for communicative purposes. In other words, traditional approaches did not present language as a communicative tool and provided inadequate practice in the integrated use of the language for communicative purposes. The increased need for pragmatic language skills led to a demand that a stronger link be created between classroom learning and communicative language use, with the goal of making the classroom a meaningful preparation for 'real-world' communication. The intention was thus to reinforce the link between classroom learning and the situations in which students would be expected to use the language.

The language teaching profession responded to these new demands in two related ways. The first was to set up course design structures which were better able to accommodate communicatively-oriented learning goals. This involved the development of needs analysis procedures designed to identify learners' target needs (e.g. Munby, 1978), and functionally-oriented approaches to course design (e.g. Wilkins, 1976; Finocchiaro and Brumfit, 1983). The second involved the development of what came to be called 'communicative methodology' (Brumfit, 1984a), which favoured activities with a direct link with authentic language use for communicative purposes. This included the methodological principles discussed in Section 4.2.1, namely message focus, an emphasis on holistic practice, the use of authentic materials and of collaborative modes of learning, and the development of students' communication strategies.

The rationale for this new emphasis in classroom methodology derived from a number of the ideas surveyed in Chapters 3 and 4. One is the vision of language as a means of achieving communicative goals in interactive situations, and another links in with the vision of language as self-expression. In other words, these emerging views of language altered what was seen to be the object of study in the classroom: no longer the language as a code, but rather language as a means of achieving pragmatic goals or of personal expression. It was also linked to the experiential view of learning, which emphasises language use not simply as a goal but also as a means of learning.

The intention behind these changes in the way in which classroom learning was conceptualised was to create conditions within the classroom that would give rise to genuine communication among students. The classroom would, therefore, become a place of communication which would allow students to practise the communicative skills that they would need to use outside the classroom in real interactive situations. The goal was thus to strengthen the link between the classroom and the situations in which students would have to use the language. Within this perspective, the classroom was seen as a springboard for communication in real communicative situations: communication in the classroom was thus a preparation for communicative language use outside the classroom.

The intellectual climate in which the communicative movement developed was strongly positivistic: students needed to have certain skills in the language and the language teaching profession went about creating conditions in the classroom which would make it possible to develop the target skills in a coherent manner. In certain contexts, especially in LSP situations where students have clearly identifiable learning goals, the idea of the classroom as a preparation for communication can function in a fairly unproblematic manner. Frequently, however, the situation is less simple.

To begin with, communication itself is a complex undertaking and real communication is generally linked closely to a given situation in both pragmatic and interpersonal terms. For this reason, it can be more difficult than it might appear at first sight to set up within the classroom conditions which fully replicate the realities of communication as they manifest themselves in a particular situation. Second, and crucially, the successful realisation of an experiential approach to learning depends on genuine student involvement in the relevant learning activities. In other words, for 'experience' of the language to lead to learning, this experience needs to have some personal meaningfulness for the learner, and tasks or materials alone cannot guarantee this. Personal meaningfulness arises out of the interaction between tasks and materials, on the one hand, and learners' interests, attitudes, and expectations, on the other. For this reason, the pursuit of communicative meaningfulness needs to take account of attitudinal and affective factors as well as the objective relevance of learning content.

These considerations imply that the value of the classroom as a preparation for communication in real-world situations depends strongly on the subjective reality which classroom learning has for students in the here-and-now of their lives, within but also outside of the classroom. If students can perceive a clear link between the communicative activities being practised in the classroom and the situations in which they will or may have to use the language, there is a good chance that the ideal of the communicative classroom as a preparation for language use outside of the classroom will become a reality. If, on the other hand, students cannot easily create this link, there is reason to doubt the communicative authenticity of the activities in question, and thus their potential for generating meaningful learning.

---

Look at the way in which the vision of the classroom as a preparation for communication has manifested itself in your experience as a teacher.

- Profile a group of students with whom the vision of the class-room as a preparation for future language use has struck a chord and given rise to genuine learner involvement.
- Do the same with a group where this perspective has been less successful.
- Compare the differences between the two.

(N.B. You may find it useful to undertake this task with other colleagues in order to pool your experiences and what they have taught you.)

---

### 5.3.2 *The classroom as communication*

A distinction was made in Section 4.5.1 between hard and soft CLT, the former corresponding to LSP and the latter to general CLT. The difference between the two relates to the precision with which students' future uses of the language can be defined. In hard CLT it is generally possible to identify target uses of the language with at least a reasonable degree of accuracy; hence the 'specific' in languages for specific purposes (LSP). In soft CLT this is not always possible, other than in terms of likely possible uses. Indeed, soft CLT often rests on a policy decision to prepare a potentiality rather than on a requirement to respond to immediate pragmatic needs. This creates a situation which can be problematic in terms of a view of the classroom as a preparation for communication. One question relates to the choice of the communicative skills that are to be developed. Another relates to the meaningfulness that these skills are likely to have for students, and the effects that a lack of perceived relevance can have on student learning. As suggested above, tensions can arise if the communicative meaningfulness of the classroom has to be defined with respect to classroom-external uses of the language which may be difficult to predict in advance, which may or may not materialise, and which may have little relevance to students' present life and concerns.

In addition to this, a distinction is often made between the classroom and the 'real world'. This distinction relates to a functional view of the classroom as a place where knowledge and skills are developed for use at some stage in the future. With respect to language learning, this means that the language skills which are developed in the classroom are designed to facilitate language use in the communicative situations that students will or may encounter at some future stage in their professional, academic, or personal lives. This is, of course, a perfectly reasonable way of seeing the ultimate purpose of the classroom. We should not, however, forget that the classroom itself is part of the real world of students in the here-and-now of their life as individuals and social actors. Communication, then, is not just something which happens 'out there', but also a process which occurs within the social environment which we call the classroom. Van Lier makes the following remarks in this respect.

> The classroom does not provide the same motives for communicating as participating in the outside world does. The preponderance of information-exchange activities which we find in applications of the communicative approach tend to transform classroom communication into a rather narrowly focused enterprise. I suggest that this is largely so because we have failed to consider the communication potential of the classroom *itself*, and the authentic resources for interaction it has to offer.
>
> (1988: 29–30)

Van Lier here points to the rich communicative potential of the classroom itself, not just as a preparation for 'somewhere else', but as a social reality in its own right with its own communicative dynamics. Exploiting this potential for learning involves exploring the meaning which the classroom has for students and the communicative dynamics which it can generate. This, in turn, involves looking into the subjective reality the classroom has for students in the here-and-now of their lives.

One powerful source of communication is the learning process itself, and this relates to what was described in Section 4.5.2 as learning-process internal motivation. For students operating in an LSP context, for example, this may involve exploring the demands of their target situations of use and developing their ability to operate in these situations. For other students, the communicative potential of the class-room may lie in the resolution of difficulties with the language code, or in the preparation of a project with other students, as one finds in more recent developments of CLT such as the process syllabus or task-based learning (Section 4.2.1). In such cases, authentic communication may not necessarily revolve around direct preparation for future communicative tasks, but arises out of the nature of the classroom as a place of learning and of related goal-oriented interaction among teachers and learners. In other words, the classroom as a place of language learning is a source of a very real form of communicative dynamics; the class-room is thus a communicative reality in its own right.

Another potentially rich source of communicative dynamism in the classroom may be the role of the classroom as a social entity in its own right. This can manifest itself in terms of the development of explicitly social relations with other students. The classroom can also be a place where students can express their personal concerns or problems. In the case of immigrant learners of a language, for example, the language classroom can provide students with a context in which they are able to share their feelings of culture shock or confusion with others who are likely to be feeling something similar. While such learners would certainly need language support with respect to their pragmatic language needs, their more personal concerns, and their desire to share these with others may in fact be the richest and most meaningful communicative agendas which they bring with them to the classroom (cf. Cummings, 1996).

In many cases, the goals of the classroom are defined projectively, in terms of what it offers to students with respect to their future use of the language. This is a perfectly valid perspective, but it does not guarantee that these future uses will necessarily be the most meaningful source of communication within the classroom itself. The idea of the communicative classroom clearly calls for an attentive analysis of the uses which students will or may have to make of the language. It also, however, calls for the exploration of what the classroom means to students in the here-and-now of their daily lives, and of how this can contribute to the development of meaningful communicative dynamics.

With respect to a few classrooms you know well, either as a teacher or as a student, assess what is (or was) the richest source of communicative dynamics for the students concerned. Does this relate to the development of language skills for future use, to aspects of the learning process itself, to the classroom as a social entity in its own right, to a combination of these, or to other factors?

- How far was this communicative potential channelled for learning purposes?
- If you feel that this potential could have been better exploited, which strategies would you adopt in order to achieve this goal?

## 5.4 The classroom as a school of autonomy

This vision of the classroom is linked to the concepts of learner autonomy, self-direction, and learner empowerment. Together with the goal of increasing the communicative relevance and authenticity of classroom learning, interest in learner autonomy has been one of the main focal points of methodological reflection in recent decades. Furthermore, concern with learner autonomy has given rise to developments in the area of independent or self-directed study which have expanded what is meant by 'the classroom' to include language study conducted in self-access centres or other independent learning facilities. The vision of the classroom as a school of autonomy therefore needs to include learning conducted in such facilities as well as in more traditional classroom settings.

Two very basic principles underpin interest in learner autonomy. The first is that language learners are thinking human beings who bring with them to the classroom a variety of knowledge, experience, and insights which can allow them to play an active role in their language learning. In other words, language learners have the potential to be active agents in and co-authors (Pennycook, 1997) of their learning. The second idea is that the active engagement of learners' human potential can enrich the learning process itself and help students to develop independent learning skills which they will be able to transfer to their subsequent learning and use of language. In other words, it can provide them with skills that go beyond a specific body of language knowledge or set of communicative abilities, and can thus empower them both as language learners and language users.

Interest in learner autonomy raises a number of questions about the role that the teacher and the classroom have to play in promoting autonomy and empowerment. Some writing on learner autonomy portrays the classroom as a dark, oppressive place from which students need to be 'liberated'. In this view, one cannot help wondering whether the teacher's main contribution to learner autonomy would simply be to tell students to go away and get on with things themselves in a 'free' manner. There is, however, a broad consensus that the classroom and the teacher can play a valuable role in helping students to develop their potential for autonomous learning (Nunan, 1997; Tudor, 1997). This gives rise to the view of the classroom as a school of autonomy, i.e. as a place where learners not only learn the language as such but also learn how to learn.

The concept of learner autonomy is a very attractive one for a number of reasons, not least because it opens up the possibility of providing classroom learning with a genuine source of communicative meaningfulness (cf. Section 5.3.2) by exploiting what Van Lier (1988: 30) calls the communication potential of the classroom itself. A major focus of the language classroom is, after all, for students to learn the language (however this is defined), and the attempt to develop learner autonomy can make this endeavour the focal point for a genuine exchange of views and insights between teacher and learners and also among learners themselves. In other words, the vision of the classroom as a school of autonomy can support the practical realisation of the vision of the communicative classroom by providing an explicit and learning process-internal communicative goal to classroom interaction.

The concept of autonomy is, however, a complex one. What, in fact, does it mean for a learner to be 'autonomous'? The literature on learner autonomy is by no means unambiguous on the subject, and a number of analyses of autonomy exist (e.g. Benson, 1997; Pennycook, 1997; Sinclair, 1997; Usuki, 1999). Furthermore, learner autonomy and thus the vision of the classroom as a school of autonomy has implications which go beyond pedagogy in a narrow or technical sense of the term. Indeed, by seeking to change traditional teacher–learner roles, the objective of learner autonomy has implications of a social and thereby also of an ideological nature.

Usuki (1999) identifies two emphases in the use of the term autonomy which are relevant in this respect. One is what she refers to as the 'psychological' definition of autonomy, which focuses relatively more on the learner as an individual within the process of language learning itself. The other is what she refers to as the 'political' definition of autonomy: this includes the psychological definition but goes further to embrace critical evaluation of broader social, political, and ideological issues relating to language, the learning process, or aspects of the educational and political system within which teaching is organised. The first, or psychological view, portrays autonomy principally as a means of facilitating language learning, which one could call 'autonomy for language learning'. The other more political view emphasises the broader implications of autonomy with respect to students' interaction with society, which one could call 'language learning for autonomy'.

These two views of autonomy are, of course, related. The ability to reflect critically on even fairly technical aspects of language learning can lead on to critical reflection on broader issues of language learning and use, while this broader level of concern needs to rest on the ability to reflect critically on many detailed aspects of both language learning and language use. Nevertheless, Usuki's distinction is a real one with respect to the way in which the goals of autonomy are defined and pursued in the classroom. It will be used as a framework for the rest of this section.

## 5.4.1 The psychological perspective

As pointed out above, the psychological perspective on autonomy focuses on learners primarily in terms of their role as such, i.e. individuals who are involved in the process of language study. In this light, the goal is to help learners assume a more active and participatory role in their language study. This process has many stages and can assume a variety of forms depending on factors such as the general educational background and language learning experience of the students involved, their age, their motivation, and their expectations with respect to the learning process.

The development of learner autonomy may be seen as having two main components or stages: learner training and learner involvement (Tudor, 1996). The goal of learner training is to help learners to get into and to negotiate a path through the learning process in an informed and self-directive manner. Learner training activities therefore involve an initiation into language learning strategies and procedures (as examples of learner training courses, cf. Ellis and Sinclair, 1989; Willing, 1989). A first step, however, relates to learners' attitudes to and interaction with the learning process. Learners need to be helped to see that they can play an active and self-directive role in their learning, and that they need not view their role as merely following someone else's (probably the teacher's) directions. It also involves persuading students to assume this role. The two elements are equally important. Awareness of one's potential is one step towards autonomy, but this has to go hand in hand with the willingness to exploit this potential actively. The latter can assume the form of the explicit negotiation of a learning contract between teacher and students or a more implicit agreement between the two parties to adopt a participatory approach to teaching and learning. On this basis, it is then possible to work at raising learners' awareness of the various aspects of the learning process and gradually to initiate their active involvement in it.

If restricted to personal study or interaction with teacher-selected material and activities, learner training can serve a useful, even if restricted, function in empowering language learners. The inner logic of the concept of autonomy would, however, suggest that it should also give learners the chance to make real decisions about the content and organisation of their language study programme. This is the stage at which learner training merges into learner involvement.

There are many different ways in which learners can be 'involved' in shaping their learning programme. One area which offers considerable scope for learner involvement is that of goal-setting. This is probably most obvious in the case of adult learners who have direct experience of their target situations of use, and who can use this to inform goal-setting itself, as well as the selection of learning materials and the establishment of performance criteria (cf. Tudor, 1996). In such cases, which are more characteristic of LSP settings, it is feasible to envisage a high degree of learner involvement in course development. A similar principle can apply in other learning contexts, too. Even if teachers and students have to work with a pre-set syllabus or coursebook, students can develop their own individual or class lists of vocabulary which can then be used as the learning goal for at least part of their study programme and possibly also for purposes of evaluation. Furthermore, if students or teachers subscribe to a view of language as self-expression (Section 3.4), then learner involvement in the choice of topics, materials, and language resources is probably the only coherent approach to goal-setting.

Another potential area for learner involvement is that of methodology; this is not about what learners are to learn but how they are to go about learning. In this respect it needs to be borne in mind that teachers may generally be assumed to have a fuller vision of language learning options than learners and are thus likely to have more to contribute in terms of knowledge of the options available. Teachers thus have their own specialist knowledge to contribute to the negotiation of methodology, even if the relevant methodological choices need to take account of the learners' own preferences and insights into their learning needs. Possibly for this reason, the idea of materials adaptation (Clarke, 1989; Nunan, 1997) is likely to play an important role in the negotiation of methodology, as it allows learners to make a personal contribution to this aspect of their learning while at the same time developing their understanding of the learning options available to them. This point shows that learner involvement generally remains a shared under-taking which engages the professional experience and knowledge of the teacher and also the insights and emerging self-directiveness of the learners.

The pursuit of learner autonomy can influence teacher–students relations and thus classroom dynamics in a significant manner. Even in its psychological sense, the concept of learner autonomy has social implications and is thus likely to be interpreted by students in the light of their own sociocultural and educational traditions. Consequently, the precise way in which the promotion of learner autonomy influences classroom dynamics is strongly influenced by the attitudes and expecta-tions of the students concerned (cf. Riley, 1988; Ho and Crookall, 1995; Littlewood, 1999).

---

The psychological perspective on autonomy finds expression in an increasing number of ways in teaching materials and programmes.

- In which forms have you encountered it in your own teaching experience?
- How has it influenced the nature of your classroom interaction with students?
- How far have you gone with one or another group of students along the path from learner training to learner involvement?
- Is the notion of learner autonomy central to your teaching goals or is it subsidiary to another vision of the classroom and its goals?

---

## 5.4.2 The political perspective

The psychological perspective on learner autonomy – by using class time to develop learners' insights into the learning process and thus help them to develop their self-directive skills – has a clear and educationally valid rationale. An obvious question which arises with respect to the concepts of learner autonomy and learner empowerment, however, is how far they can or should be taken. If learner autonomy is viewed simply as a means of enhancing language learning in a narrow sense of the term, it can be integrated into conventional top-down learning structures without too many difficulties. If, however, autonomy is seen as having the broader educational goal of empowerment (cf. Freire, 1970), it can enter into conflict with established social structures at both institutional and political levels.

A truly autonomous learner may, for example, develop sufficient insight into language learning and use to evaluate and call into question virtually any of the assumptions about language, learning, or the classroom which are put forward by teachers, materials writers, or educational authorities. Such a learner may, for example, reject a functionally based syllabus as being narrowly utilitarian and designed only to produce trained workers for the capitalist system. Another autonomous learner may reject the whole notion of autonomy as being a manifestation of Western individualism and prefer a more teacher-centred approach based around knowledge transmission. Yet another may reject the political choices which have led to them learning one language as opposed to another which they believe to have more cultural relevance to them as members of their local community. A coherent approach to learner autonomy must either take these and many other possibilities on board or be sufficiently honest to state clearly how far the concept of learner involvement is to be pursued within the framework of a given programme.

The idea of learner autonomy can also enter into conflict with the hierarchical structures that are in place in a given educational and social context. When learner autonomy moves beyond what Usuki calls its psychological sense, it has implications for educational planning and the practical organisation of learning programmes in areas such as materials production, evaluation, and comparability of results. Learner autonomy is an educational concept and for this reason will sooner or later have social implications which go beyond the individual classroom and the relationship which exists between a given teacher and group of learners. It cannot therefore be value-neutral in social terms, and is therefore likely to interact with various aspects of the social context in which teaching and learning are conducted. Benson (1997: 32), however, points out that what he calls the 'critical' dimension to autonomy will be more or less 'politically charged' in different contexts. Nevertheless, by its essentially educational nature, the concept of the classroom as a school of autonomy has social implications which relate to fundamental aspects of the organisation of language education. Indeed, Benson (1997) is strongly critical of the approach to autonomy found in mainstream language teaching practice which, in his opinion, has assimilated the notion of autonomy into the dominant positivistic and technical perspective on the nature and goals of language teaching. This, in Benson's analysis, has emptied the concept of its real potential for both educational and social empowerment.

The concept of the classroom as a school of autonomy in its political interpretation has potentially wide-ranging social implications for students and teachers, and also for other participants. For some, it can be a place of liberation and the freeing of human potential. For others it can be a Pandora's box of unpredictability and dissent. Is the classroom a place where students learn to learn more effectively within a framework of goals set up by others? Or is it a place where students learn to understand and participate critically in the discourses of others, including those 'others' who are responsible for setting up and maintaining the system within which the students are working?

---

The political perspective on autonomy has received considerable attention in theoretical writing on language teaching in recent years. For some teachers it is a fundamental component of language education. For others it may seem far removed from the day-to-day realities of teaching and more a matter of politics than language teaching.

- What is your own perspective on it?
- What role does the political perspective on autonomy play in your own teaching, and which aspects of language learning does it relate to?

---

## 5.5 The classroom as socialisation

As was pointed out at the start of this chapter, the classroom is both a social and a pedagogical entity, and the two merge in a variety of ways. In other words, there is often a strong social rationale for students being in the classroom, and this rationale can influence a variety of factors such as which language is on the curriculum, the terms in which goals are defined, or the manner in which learning is to be organised. To begin with, most students are learning a language for reasons which, in a more or less direct way, have a social origin. For example, the political authorities of a country may decide that knowledge of a given language can strengthen the country's ability to compete in the global economy, or may view the learning of certain languages as a means of reinforcing national cohesion or the country's ability to cooperate with neighbours or allies. Decisions of this nature then filter down through the many organs of society to find expression in the curricula of educational institutions and in the requirements of employers. In this way, knowledge of a language can become a condition for access to further education or employment in certain sectors of economic life. Factors of this nature can exert a significant influence on which language or languages are learned, and also on the way in which learning goals are defined.

In addition to this, education has social goals which go beyond the accumulation of a discrete body of knowledge or skills, and these goals frequently relate to the inculcation of the belief and value systems of the society in question. The classroom is thus a social institution which, in the eyes of various social actors, is expected to serve a purpose in the development of a certain type of citizenship. The classroom – and the language classroom is no exception – is thus a place where agendas of a social nature are pursued in addition to or by means of the learning of a language. There is nothing inherently insidious about this. These points need to be borne in mind, however, if we wish to understand what takes place in the classroom and if we wish to understand the meaning which apparently technical methodological choices can assume for students, teachers, and a variety of other actors. One reason for bearing these points in mind is that these choices can be the expression of a hidden social agenda which goes well beyond language learning as such.

The social aspect of language teaching and learning should not, however, be viewed in a static or stereotypical manner. Cultures and societies are dynamic entities which evolve over time and which frequently contain a variety of different belief and value systems. These value systems reflect the perspectives of the various socioeconomic or sociocultural groupings within the culture or society in question. Classrooms are therefore likely to reflect the core belief and value systems of a society as they stand at a given point in time. They will also reflect the dialectic which exists among different groups within this society. This can give rise to disagreements about both the nature and the goals of language teaching, disagreements which frequently centre on aspects of methodology. Discussion of the relative merits of a specific methodological choice – group work as opposed to full class teaching, to take just one example – may thus occult a much more profound and ideologically charged debate which turns on questions of personal freedom and the locus of control in society at large. Furthermore, debates of this nature are not limited to academic or political circles. They also take place in a more or less explicit manner in the classroom itself, and thus become part of the day-to-day dynamics of teaching and learning in the classroom.

The social dimension of language education and the role which the classroom plays or is intended to play in students' socialisation is very complex. In this section it will be looked at from two angles. The first is that of 'imposed socialisation', which relates to the way in which the pedagogical choices of actors physically external to the classroom reflect and seek to perpetuate a certain set of beliefs and values of a social nature. The second is that of 'emergent socialisation', which relates to the way in which classroom participants develop their own set of norms and thus their own form of self-organising socialisation.

## 5.5.1 Imposed socialisation

No educational decision is unmarked, and even apparently 'innocent' or technical choices are rooted in a certain vision of society and of social life. Furthermore, education, including language education, often has the explicit goal of socialising students into a given culture and social system. It is virtually inevitable, then, that what takes place within the classroom is influenced by the belief and value systems of the society in which the classroom is situated and of which it is part. All societies have their own belief and value systems and seek to express and perpetuate these systems in their various social institutions. Indeed, Waldrop (1992: 214) cites researcher Chris Langton as describing beliefs as the 'genes' of culture, i.e. those elements by which a culture is transmitted from one generation to another.

The vision of the classroom as socialisation therefore makes us move beyond a technical view of methodology to explore the social meaning which methodological choices have for students and for other participants in language education. All methodological choices rest on certain assumptions about the nature of language and of language learning, and also of the role that the classroom is meant to play in the process. Such assumptions often reflect conceptions of social organisation which go beyond language learning in a narrow sense of the term. Nunan makes this point by remarking that:

> Any educational decision . . . is a highly political one. Any learning endeavour will be carried out within a particular socio-political and educational context in which certain rules and procedures will be in force. The most important of these will be implicit. They will not be found in statements of educational policy or curriculum frameworks. However, they will reveal themselves to the sensitive observer through the actions of the participants in the educational system. The hidden culture of an educational system or institution will manifest itself as much by what does not happen as what does happen. The culturally aware observer will ask: Why is there no group work in these classrooms? Why do students never ask questions? How is it that the teacher only asks lower order factual questions?
>
> (1997: 195–196)

The answer to these questions is often to be sought in the social norms of the society in question, and in the social agenda which is being

pursued in the classroom and which underpins the various methodological choices made. Evaluating such choices without consideration of
their social basis (however hidden this may be) is thus unlikely to yield
an in-depth understanding of precisely what these choices mean to the
participants involved. When a certain methodological choice is made
we therefore need to look beyond its officially stated rationale in terms
of language learning. We need to do this in order to appreciate its social
rationale within the relevant context and the way in which it reflects the
agenda being pursued by the agents responsible for its selection. The
hidden agenda of education can and frequently does express itself both
in what is taught and also in how this is taught.

In a study of a reform of English language education in Japan,
LoCastro (1996) makes the following remarks about educational
systems and, specifically, about some of the sociocultural values which
underpin education in Japan.

> It may be argued that educational systems all over the world
> exist for the purpose of maintaining the *status quo* and for
> teaching obedience to and acceptance of the power structures
> present in a particular society. The socialisation of learners,
> with the goal of training them into becoming productive, law-
> abiding citizens, may be the not-so-hidden agenda of formal
> education.
>
> The particular manifestations of this hidden curriculum in
> Japan still show the impact of Confucian influences from China.
> Formal education is for the general good, with a strong de-
> emphasis on individualism. (1996: 47–48)

LoCastro suggests that this manifests itself in classroom behaviours and
interactional patterns which serve to create an ethos of group solidarity,
respect for authority, and 'an ideology of Japaneseness characterised by
submission to the existing socio-political order' (1996: 48).

LoCastro then goes on to analyse the implications that the proposed
changes would be likely to have on modes of classroom learning and
interaction. Her main point is that the reform in question would have a
significant effect on the whole network of social and interpersonal
behaviours in the classroom to which both students and teachers are
accustomed. What might therefore be seen as a fairly technical change
in classroom methodology can thus have repercussions of a far more
wide-ranging nature. LoCastro (1996: 54–55) points out that the
reform in question is part of a broader debate in Japanese society. The
educational authorities responsible for the change fall into the camp of
the 'modernisers', and therefore it may be assumed that they would not
be unhappy with the broader social implications of the changes in

English language education. She also, however, describes the new courses as 'vaguely written, unclear documents' (1996: 54), and ascribes this to caution on the part of their authors with respect to how far and how fast they feel the relevant changes can take place. The proposed change in English language teaching thus reflects a dialectic in Japanese society while also being a potential bearer of change in this society.

The socially embedded nature of both the educational practices and the attempts at reform described by LoCastro are not of course specific to Japan, and similar stories could be told in other countries. The bashing of 'woolly-minded liberal education' and the rallying call of 'back to basics' which characterised much political rhetoric in the United Kingdom of the early 1990s is one case in point. Indeed, the underlying system of values which would have found expression in the educational manifestation of the proposed return to 'basics' was the same that underpinned parallel changes in many aspects of social and labour legislation of the period. No matter how value-neutral or apolitical teachers may wish to be, it can be difficult for them to avoid playing a more or less conscious role in the socialisation of their students. It is therefore necessary to be attentive to the way in which the more or less hidden social agenda which underpins methodological choices can influence students' interaction with these choices and thus the dynamics of teaching and learning in the classroom.

---

Have you encountered what was referred to above as imposed socialisation in your teaching experience?

- How has this manifested itself? In coursebooks or other teaching materials, in the way in which learning goals are defined, in aspects of recommended classroom interaction, or possibly in other aspects of teaching and learning?
- Has this ever proved problematic to you as a teacher or an individual?
- Have your students ever shown resistances to aspects of language teaching which can be attributable to factors of this nature?
- Analyse the origins of the resistances in question and your own reaction to them.

---

### 5.5.2 Emergent socialisation

The points made above point to the influence which various social actors can exert not just on language learning in the narrow sense of the term, but also on the way in which language teaching procedures influence students' broader socialisation. This influence is very real, and it would be naive to underestimate the role it plays. It plays a role by way of various means such as prescribed curricula and coursebooks, entry examinations, notions of best practice in teaching and materials development, and so on down the line to decisions regarding, for example, the establishment (or not) of independent learning facilities, and even the types of seating chosen for language classrooms. (What message do neat rows of desks carefully screwed to the floor communicate about the nature of classroom interaction?) These many factors contribute significantly to the context within which language teaching is lived out in the classroom.

However, while the imposed social agenda serves to shape the context within which students and teachers meet and interact, it does not necessarily operate in a linear manner. Each classroom develops its own dynamics, and although the individuals present in it are inevitably influenced in many ways by the context within which they are operating, the way in which they go about working out their own modus vivendi is unique to each classroom. The social reality which emerges in the classroom is thus complex and potentially unpredictable. On the one hand, it is influenced by the broader context in which the classroom is situated; this includes the official agenda being pursued in a more or less explicit manner by the relevant political or educational authorities. On the other hand, however, the interactive dynamics which emerge in each classroom give rise to a social reality which is specific to that classroom, and which pulls participants in a certain direction. In other words, each classroom develops its own rules and thus its own form of socialisation around which individual participants, including the teacher, have to negotiate their specific role and identity.

The question of classroom socialisation therefore needs to be seen as operating from the inside out as well as from the outside in. It is for this reason that teachers have to learn to tune in on the 'rules' which operate in each specific classroom, which includes what can or cannot be done or asked of the students. In part, this involves the attempt to understand what students bring with them to the classroom in terms of their attitudes, expectations, and goals, which need in the first instance to be understood in terms of the inner logic of the students themselves. In addition, it calls for the exploration of the dynamic interaction between these factors and the methodological choices which the teacher adopts (or is required to adopt) with respect to language, learning, or the classroom itself. Much can be imposed from 'the outside', but the reality of classroom teaching emerges from the meaning which the classroom and the methodological choices that are enacted in it assume for participants. This is always a local phenomenon.

---

Select a specific class which you know either as a teacher or as a learner and try to identify the 'rules' which operated in it. (N.B. These 'rules' may not have been official ones, and may never have been formulated explicitly by any of the participants.)

- What were the rules in question and which aspects of participants' behaviour did they relate to? (In this respect, you may find it useful to focus on one specific event or classroom ritual.)
- How far did these rules coincide with the official agenda of classroom interaction which was operant in the institution in question?
- Now select two classes you have taught in the past; an 'easy' one and a 'difficult' one. Compare the nature of the classroom relations which operated in each and then try to identify why one was 'easy' and the other 'difficult'.
- What does this suggest to you about the social dimension of language teaching?

---

## 5.6 Overview

Of the four visions of the classroom discussed in this chapter, the first two – namely that of the classroom as a controlled learning environment and the communicative classroom – are explicitly methodological in the sense that both relate directly to language learning. The vision of the classroom as a school of autonomy in its psychological sense also relates directly to the enhancement of the language learning process as such; the political perspective on autonomy, however, embraces considerations of a social and ideological nature which include but which also go beyond language learning in the traditional sense of the term. The vision of the classroom as socialisation, on the other hand, has little to do with language learning as such, and is linked to the role which the classroom can play in the broader process of socialisation. This may involve the will of a given social group to inculcate a certain set of social attitudes and values in the population (what is referred to above as imposed socialisation), or to the creation by classroom participants themselves of a certain shared social reality (what is referred to as emergent socialisation).

As is the case with respect to the concepts of language and of learning, then, the classroom itself is by no means a simple or uncontroversial phenomenon. There are at least two sets of reasons for this. In the first place, the classroom is the place where a certain methodology is enacted. In other words, it involves pedagogical decisions based on a certain perspective on the nature of language and of language learning, and these decisions have a significant influence on the role which is attributed to the classroom in the learning process. In addition to this, the classroom is a social reality which is influenced by a variety of participants and the social agendas which these participants wish to pursue within it. Classroom realities therefore emerge dynamically from the interaction of the beliefs, expectations and goals of the various participants involved more or less directly in teaching and learning.

One point that needs to be borne in mind with respect to the vision of the classroom as socialisation is that this perspective is rarely explicitly stated. Educational authorities, for example, very rarely formulate in explicit terms the social agenda which underpins a given language teaching programme. Nor do students necessarily negotiate their own mode of social interaction in the classroom in explicitly social terms. More often than not, this dimension of classroom life is negotiated around the surface script of language teaching and learning, what we generally refer to as methodology. For this reason, language educators need to be aware of the possibly varied origins of students' and other participants' attitudes to methodological choices. Does, for example, a group of students' resistance to group work, explicit grammar study, or the use of a certain type of textual material arise 'simply' out of student reservations regarding the vision of language or of learning present in these activities? Or do the activities in question activate reactions of a deeper and more socially based nature, such that the students are reacting less to a certain mode of language study than to the social message which they feel to underlie these activities?

In order to understand what takes places in our classrooms, we therefore need to explore what the classroom means to participants in both pedagogical and social terms and, indeed, with respect to the way in which the two interact with one another. Tensions or disagreements which manifest themselves with respect to apparently methodological factors may, in fact, arise out of tensions between the ways in which students or other participants interpret social aspects of the classroom and the role which it is meant to play in students' lives. It is perhaps for this reason that educational 'crises' tend to be more frequent at times of social change when the various participants in the educational process are having to rethink the nature and goals of education and of the role which institutions such as the classroom are meant to play in the broader endeavour of education. On the one hand, such factors may seem far removed from a naive view of what teaching a language involves. In reality, however, they are crucial if one wishes to understand the dynamics of classroom teaching and learning and thus be in a position to react in a meaningful and contextually appropriate manner.

# 6 Methodology and context

## 6.1 Putting methodology in its place

In Chapters 3–5 it has been suggested that while methodological choices relating to the presentation of the TL, the organisation of learning activities, or with respect to the role of the classroom itself influence classroom dynamics, they do not necessarily do so in a linear manner. Specifically, it has been suggested that the pedagogical reality which methodology assumes in the classroom derives not just from the inner logic or theoretical potential of the methodology in question, but also from the meaning which it assumes for students and teachers. And this, the local meaning of methodology, is intimately linked to context. In other words, the passage of methodology from theoretical principle to pedagogical reality is highly context dependent.

This implies that pedagogical choices need to take account of two sets of factors. One is the theoretical potential of a certain approach or set of methodological procedures to promote learning. The other is the context in which methodology is used and within which students interpret and interact with the methodology in question. The pedagogical reality of methodology – i.e. the reality which it assumes in real classrooms – arises out of the interaction of these two factors. We cannot therefore assume that methodology as theoretical principle corresponds to methodology as pedagogical reality. This is because the latter arises dynamically out of the way in which methodology is interpreted and lived out by participants, and that is context specific.

A realistic and sustainable approach to pedagogical planning needs therefore to take account of the inner logic or theoretical potential of methodology, but also of the context in which teaching and learning are to be conducted. This involves consideration of the practical conditions in which teaching is to be conducted as well as of the attitudes and expectations of the participants with respect to teaching and learning. This perspective on pedagogical planning is related to the distinction made in Chapter 1 between the technological and ecological perspectives on language teaching. The technological perspective is strongly positivistic and posits or, at least, operates as if a fairly linear relationship exists between methodological principle and pedagogical reality. The ecological perspective, on the other hand, views situations holistically, and in terms of the concerns, values, goals, and expectations of the participants directly involved in them. From this perspective, methodology does contribute to classroom realities, but it does so dynamically, in interaction with various aspects of context.

Chapters 3–5 have been organised around established professional categories of methodological choice with discussion of the meaning which these choices can assume for participants (principally students) in the light of various aspects of context. The present chapter focuses specifically on the interaction between methodology and context. This interaction is inevitably a local one: a given methodological approach interacting with the specifics of one particular context. For this reason, the chapter includes an analysis of two case studies in order to allow for a close analysis of the context in question and thereby of the meaning which methodological choices assume for participants within this context. The details of the two case studies examined may differ in varying degrees from those of other contexts. The goal, however, is to explore methodology in context and thus to raise some of the questions which need to be addressed in assessing the contextual appropriacy of methodological options.

## 6.2 Exploring context

Both pragmatic and mental components of context need to be taken into consideration in pedagogical planning. The pragmatic component of context is generally more accessible to analysis than the mental component. The factors which can play a role in shaping the pragmatic context of teaching and learning include class size, the availability of teaching–learning resources, the hierarchical and decision-making structures in place, levels and orientation of teacher education, and teacher salaries. Analysing factors of this nature can provide a variety of insights into the feasibility of certain methodological options. To take just one example, if teaching is conducted in an overcrowded auditorium, certain forms of group work may be problematic or, at least, may need to be approached in a different manner from that which is feasible with small groups of students in a classroom which has easily moveable seating (cf. Okoye, 1994).

The mental component of context can be more difficult and also more time-consuming to investigate (cf. Chapter 7), but it is no less important than the pragmatic component. Potentially relevant aspects of mental context include the belief and value system of the target society, its educational traditions and practices, and the approach to language teaching current in the society in question. They also include the learning strategies and modes of study which students habitually use. In this respect, it may be necessary to complement analysis of the traditions of teaching and learning current in the society as a whole with an analysis of the practices and ethos of teaching and learning specific to the target institution and student population.

Although in investigative terms it is useful to distinguish between the pragmatic and mental components of context, in practice the two merge in a variety of ways. We therefore need to study the interaction between pragmatic and mental context and thus to explore context holistically as emerging from the interaction of a variety of both pragmatic and mental factors. Good material conditions, for example, are not in themselves a guarantee of effective and harmonious teaching. Nevertheless, they can facilitate experimentation with novel methodological procedures or allow an extension of the learning opportunities made available to students. If such measures are perceived to be successful, all participants can feel encouraged to make a further investment of time and energy, and thus to initiate a virtuous cycle of experimentation and engagement. The opposite can also occur. Poor material conditions can put a variety of obstacles in the path of innovation, and this in turn can generate a feeling of discouragement and of being trapped by circumstance, which can lead to a downward cycle of demotivation among both teachers and students (cf. Fortez, 1997). In both cases we witness a dynamic interaction between the material conditions of teaching and participants' attitudes to and their affective involvement in the teaching–learning process. Educational planning must clearly take account of factors of this nature: not only what the material conditions of teaching in a given setting are, but also the influence which these conditions have on participants' attitudes to and affective involvement in the teaching–learning process.

According a central role to context implies that pedagogical planning is inevitably a local affair. General principles of the type found in some writing on methodology can certainly provide insights into the teaching–learning process and can open up potentially useful avenues of exploration. It cannot, however, be assumed that any one methodological principle will be appropriate to the details of a specific setting. It is perhaps for this reason that increasing importance is being accorded to case studies as a means of exploring language teaching (Stake, 1980; Easton, 1982; Yin, 1994; Richards, 1998; Wallace, 1999). All case studies are idiosyncratic to the extent that they relate to the specifics of one teaching situation. Nevertheless, by focusing on the details of language teaching as it is lived out in a particular context, case studies can bring to light the dynamic interaction between participants and context. In this way they can provide more relevant insights into the specific realities of teaching and learning than methodological generalisation. The details of the situation in question may be what Freeman (1996: 91) describes as 'messy', but it is precisely in the untidiness or 'messiness' of local detail that teaching and learning are lived out in real classrooms.

The two case studies that are examined in this chapter both relate to situations which may be seen as problematic in one way or another, and this reflects a deliberate choice on my behalf. Instances of best practice can provide both inspiration and guidelines for positive intervention. There are, however, reasons for supplementing instances of best practice or 'success' with others which are problematic or which may even be seen as 'failures' (cf. Hall, 1997). The first is that language teaching does not always work out on cue. Too exclusive a diet of success stories can seem to invalidate the efforts of many language educators to achieve constructive goals in situations in which the cards seem to be stacked against them being able to emulate the best practice of others. For many language educators throughout the world a little is sometimes a lot, and the study of problematic situations can bring this out more clearly than instances where theoretical principle appears to translate fairly smoothly into practice.

Second, and more fundamentally, problematic situations or even 'failure' can bring out more clearly the complex interaction of factors which are involved in all language teaching situations. One potential pitfall in exploring 'success' is the temptation to assume that it is the official agenda – which is often embodied in methodology – that is directly responsible for the observed success, and therefore not to look further into the dynamic interaction between this official agenda and the context in which it is realised. When difficulties arise, however, we may be more willing to analyse the complex interaction of methodology and context. Furthermore, the presence of tensions or mismatches can give greater prominence to those factors which play a decisive role in the harmonious realisation of language teaching. In other words, difficulties or even failures can teach us more about the reality of language teaching than easy and unanalysed success.

In your experience of teaching, have you encountered situations in which aspects of context impacted on your methodological choices? Specifically, did you find it necessary to rethink aspects of your teaching in response to aspects of the pragmatic or mental context in which you were working?

- What were the factors in question, and in which way did they influence your approach to teaching?
- What is your reaction to the remark made above that 'failure' merits study to at least the same degree as 'success'?
- Has the study of 'failure' figured in your own professional education?

## 6.3 The force of circumstance

It has been suggested in the previous chapters that considerable diversity exists among students, teachers, and other participants with respect to the nature and goals of language teaching, and that this contributes significantly to the mental context in which language teaching is lived out. There is also great diversity with respect to the practical conditions in which teaching and learning are conducted. At one extreme we find schools and language centres which work with groups of 10–12 students or fewer, enjoy easy access to well-qualified teachers and to teaching materials, have good material resources, and may be able to offer students a self-access centre or CALL facilities. At the other extreme there are teaching settings where classes of 100 plus students are the norm, where the only resource may be a textbook shared by 10 or more students, or a blackboard with a more or less reliable source of chalk, and where teachers may need to have a second job in order to survive financially.

Both types of situation are part of the landscape of language teaching worldwide, and both need therefore to be accommodated inclusively in our understanding of what language teaching is and how it is lived out. In other words, we cannot take the well-resourced setting as the norm and view others in deficit terms or as departures from this norm. Nor, indeed, can it be assumed that what is appropriate in a well-resourced (and frequently an Anglo-Saxon) setting is also appropriate in other contexts with a few more or less technical adjustments. Material factors exert a direct and potentially significant influence on aspects of classroom methodology; they also interact with other aspects of context in a complex manner. If we wish to understand the dynamics of teaching and learning as lived out in a given setting, we therefore need to explore both pragmatic and mental aspects of context, and also the way in which the two interact.

One material factor which has received explicit attention in language teaching is that of class size, and in particular teaching in large classes (cf. Coleman, 1989). This section focuses on a case study involving large classes in Pakistan (Shamim, 1996a). The rationale for the inclusion of the study in this chapter is not, however, to focus on the problems posed by large class teaching as such. The study is used rather with two broader goals in mind. The first is to explore the classroom dynamics which arise out of classroom participants' reactions to difficult material conditions: in this case, large class size. Large class size is therefore taken as one aspect of context, and as the focal point for the development of a certain set of classroom dynamics. The second is to raise the question of where reform or innovation might best be initiated, and the meaning which such change could have for participants within but also beyond the language classroom as such.

### 6.3.1 The setting: Large classes in Pakistan

The data on which the study (Shamim, 1996a) is based were gathered in six state secondary schools in Karachi. In total, 232 English classes taught by 27 different teachers were observed. Furthermore, 20 teachers and 21 groups of three to five students from the wider observational corpus were subsequently interviewed by the author of the study. The classes observed were representative of state schools in urban areas like Karachi, with classes ranging from 45 to 100 plus students. The author of the study describes these classes as 'overcrowded', noting that the seating arrangements were based on two-person desks which were frequently occupied by three students at a time. The classrooms were mainly teacher-fronted and Shamim gives three reasons for this.

1. The teachers' lack of awareness and/or feelings of insecurity in using other types of classroom organisation.
2. The effect of culture, whereby the teacher is traditionally seen as an authority figure and is given proper respect for his or her age and superior knowledge.
3. The view of teaching/learning that is prevalent in the community where teaching is viewed as transmission of knowledge. (Shamim, 1996a: 124)

Shamim also points out that the overcrowding of the classes often made it difficult for teachers to move around among the desks, with the result that they remained 'tied' to their traditional place at the front of the class. Shamim reports that the classrooms on which the study was based typically manifested four main features: an active teacher and passive learners, teachers having low proficiency in the TL, the presence of a set syllabus and textbook that had to be completed for exam purposes, and limited time. On the first point, namely the 'active teacher', it needs to be pointed out that teacher activity was generally concentrated at the front of the class and entailed a very traditional form of 'activity', with the teacher as the source and dispenser of knowledge.

These practical factors – especially teacher-centred lessons and thus the advantage for students, as we see below, of being close to the teacher and the blackboard – created a situation in which the front of the classroom assumed the status of a privileged learning area, the 'action zone' in Shamim's words. The study looks at the power of attraction which this zone had on students and thus on their classroom behaviours, as well as on the attitudes of students and of teachers to the students who were in or out of the action zone.

### 6.3.2 The 'action zone': Opportunity, attitude, and aspiration

The favoured status of the 'action zone' formed by the front rows of the class in learning terms results from a number of both practical and attitudinal factors, and contributes to the interactive dynamics around which the study revolves. It is therefore crucial to understand what the 'action zone' meant to participants and thus the dynamics to which it gave rise. This is approached under three headings: opportunity, attitude, and aspiration.

### 1 Opportunity

The classrooms in the study had six rows of double seat desks which were often occupied by three rather than the intended two students. The first three rows were generally perceived as being the front of the class and the fifth and sixth as the back, with the fourth row being perceived differently from one class to another as either the front or the back. Given the physical layout of the classes, frequent overcrowding, and the generally teacher-centred approach to teaching and learning, the front rows offered a number of learning advantages. To begin with, students in these rows were better able to hear what teachers said and see what they wrote on the board, two basic enabling conditions for learning in the teacher-centred mode of teaching operant in the classrooms in question. In addition to this, being in the front rows allowed for more teacher supervision and monitoring. Students in this area had to pay more attention because they were more directly under the teacher's eye and were thus less likely to be distracted by chatting peers. They could also have their work checked more easily by the teacher. In all, then, the front rows offered a number of clear practical advantages for students wishing to work on their English.

## 2 Attitude

In addition to these practical factors, a number of attitudinal factors also intervened, and Shamim observed different patterns of interaction between teachers and students in the front as opposed to the back rows. For example, students in the front rows were more frequently nominated to read a text aloud or to answer the teacher's questions. Teachers also asked different types of questions of students in the front as opposed to the back of the class: students in the front were asked more difficult questions (on the assumption that they would be better able to answer them) whereas the questions asked of students in the back rows more often had the role of attention maintenance or discipline. Furthermore, teachers waited longer for students in the front row to provide answers. This, too, was an indication of teachers' higher expectations with respect to students in the front rows, either in terms of their abilities or at least the seriousness of their attempts to answer the question. Indeed, Shamim notes that teachers considered the students in the back rows to be 'dull' or 'lazy' (1996a: 131) compared with those in the front.

These factors led to the creation of two classes within the same classroom. One was made up of the front rows, which was assumed to comprise clever or at least motivated students, and the other was made up of the back rows, where teacher expectations were lower regarding both ability and diligence. Indeed, Shamim observes one extreme case of a teacher who had a good pedagogical reputation in her school: 'She had sixty-five students in her class. However, she was really teaching a class of only eight students – the monitors who sat in the front row' (1996a: 129).

Not surprisingly, similar attitudes and expectations existed among the students themselves. Students who sat in the front rows considered students at the back to be 'careless', to 'have a lower ability level', as 'lacking in confidence', as talkative, or as guilty of doing other work (e.g. homework they had not done in time for another class) during the lessons (1996a: 132–133). A consensus thus emerged between teachers and students which established a qualitative distinction between students in the front as opposed to the back rows.

## 3 Aspiration

As a result of the practical and attitudinal factors mentioned above, the front of the class was a desirable place to be in learning terms. It offered practical advantages in terms of the possibility to follow the lesson, more monitoring by the teacher, and also placed students in a more supportive and encouraging learning environment. For students anxious to learn, the front rows therefore became an object of aspiration. In this respect, it is important to look at the reasons for which students came to find themselves in or out of the 'action zone' constituted by the front rows of the class. Most teachers initially allocated places to students on rational criteria such as height, with the taller students being seated at the back of the class to facilitate their being able to see the board. This arrangement, however, quickly broke down and was replaced by a self-organising principle among the students themselves which teachers had little power to oppose. This involved students coming in early for class and staking their claim to a certain place by leaving their school bag there, a custom (or informal rule) whose force was not questioned by other students. Furthermore, if students staked their claim to a given place early in the year, they had at least some right to keep it unless they failed to renew the claim regularly, e.g. by coming late too often. These arrangements were not, however, immutable, and Shamim reports that there was tough competition among students for a place in the action zone. She continues by remarking that: 'Although many students would like to sit in the front, not all are willing to make the extra effort involved in getting the front seats' (1996a: 127).

The advantages of the front rows thus gave rise to a self-organising dynamic among students in the classroom. This recalls what Arthur (1989, 1990) refers to as 'increasing returns', i.e. the way in which an initial advantage (in this case, getting a place in the front rows) leads to further advantage and gain. Shamim puts this in terms of the rich (i.e. the students who made the initial effort to get a place in the favoured learning zone) getting richer, while the poor (i.e. those who lacked the will to make the initial effort) get poorer.

> The students who are already highly motivated (or who have a strong personality) choose to sit at the front. Further, the students in the front, by virtue of their being in the action zone, get increased opportunities for learning in the classroom. As a result, their classroom performance is better than that of students who are seated in the back, and their level of motivation is higher. (1996a: 138)

Shamim also points out that sitting at the back did not necessarily have a negative effect on highly motivated students, even though these students had to make more effort to learn, and also that they tried to move towards the front as and when the opportunity presented itself.

## 6.3.3 Analysis

Other than describing the approach to teaching adopted in the classrooms studied as 'traditional' and teacher-centred, Shamim does not enter into a detailed description of the methodological procedures used. In view of the presence of a set syllabus and textbook which had to be covered for the students' examination, the official vision of these classrooms would probably correspond to what was described in Section 5.2 as the classroom as a controlled learning environment. In reality, the picture that Shamim paints is a rather Darwinian one, with individuals competing with one another to gain access to limited resources, with the resources in question being opportunities to learn. Within this system, those who made the initial effort to avail themselves more of these resources by staking their claim to a place in the front rows prospered, whereas the others did not, or did so less well, at least. This inevitably recalls Darwin's notion of the survival of the fittest. Thus, far from being a 'rational', controlled learning environment in the normal pedagogical sense of the term, what we are confronted with here is a self-organising system as described in complexity theory, with the 'system' arising out of a combination of practical circumstances (specifically, class size) and the way in which teachers and students react to these circumstances and to one another.

The dominant vision of language would seem to be code-based, and that of teaching largely analytical, with the teacher playing a strongly directive role as source of knowledge and correction. These are most relevant in the present study in that they place the object of learning (the code) and its mode of presentation (as knowledge held by the teacher) in a certain physical location, namely the front of the class, i.e. a place whose accessibility depended a great deal on students' physical location in the classroom. Shamim points out that although the students were reasonably well motivated to learn English, the language had little immediate relevance to them outside of the classroom. Consequently, the best, and possibly the only way in which they could channel their motivation was by making the most of the classroom learning opportunities available. These opportunities, however, were located at the front of the classroom, which brings us back to the role of students' positioning with respect to the front of the class.

### 6.3.4 Discussion

Few observers would consider the situation described by Shamim to be satisfactory. The question therefore arises as to how it could be altered in order to offer all students better access to learning opportunities. Shamim suggests that one of the causes of the classroom behaviours she observed was the teachers' lack of awareness of modes of classroom organisation other than the teacher-centred approach which prevailed and which, almost by definition, invested the action zone of the first few rows with its status as a privileged learning area. One implication is therefore that if the teachers came to be aware of different modes of teaching and of classroom management – albeit in terms of alternative means of exploiting the recommended textbook – student learning could be delocalised away from the exclusive and often inaccessible front rows. One practical outcome of the study would thus be to highlight the need for teacher training in terms of teaching procedures and classroom management.

One strategy might therefore turn on methodological innovation realised by teacher education. In itself, this would appear to be a logical approach to adopt, and I do not wish to question the value of such a measure. I would, however, like to raise a number of questions as to the meaning which methodological changes geared towards a more inclusive approach to classroom teaching could have for teachers and for students in the broader context of their life and educational experience.

Shamim makes a number of observations about the teachers which are relevant to understanding their role and behaviours, and also how they might react to change. She notes that most teachers in the schools in question were female, and that teaching was often seen as a secondary activity to their social roles as wife, mother, and daughter-in-law. It was a 'comfortable' profession which allowed women to supplement family income while still having enough time for their domestic responsibilities. Teaching was poorly paid and male teachers often had a second job. In addition, most teachers had low proficiency in English and many taught the language out of necessity rather than choice. The author also says that the B.Ed. programme which the teachers in the study had followed had an out-of-date syllabus and that English was not a popular subject.

Other than the question of the outdated B.Ed. which had been followed by the teachers, none of these considerations seem to be directly pedagogical in nature. Nevertheless, they are potentially relevant to the teachers' willingness to adopt change. To begin with, a change in pedagogy and classroom management would involve re-thinking established habits of behaviour and, initially at least, more preparation. Then, in the crowded classrooms described, a more inter-ventional form of pedagogy would almost certainly be more energy-consuming. In other words, from the teachers' point of view, a change in classroom methodology could make their job more demanding and thus leave them with less time and energy for their family commitments and/or second job. Thus, if teachers' salaries and the social status of teaching remained unchanged, it is not certain that increased pedago-gical awareness alone would alter the situation radically. In this respect, Markee's (1997: 59) concept of 'relative advantage' needs to be borne in mind: 'if potential users perceive an innovation to be relatively advanta-geous to them, they are more likely to adopt it than one they judge to be financially, professionally, or personally disadvantageous to them' (1997: 60). In essence, then, what would be the relative advantage to teachers of adopting a more active and interventional style of teaching in the broader context of their lives and priorities?

Another point which needs to be considered are student reactions to a change in classroom interaction. In this respect, it should be remem-bered that the teachers did attempt to arrange seating on the basis of height at the start of courses, but that this attempt met student resistance and was abandoned. One question therefore is how far students would be prepared to change in their classroom behaviours (Shamim, 1996b; Slembrouck, 2000). Shamim does not state whether the front row phenomenon was characteristic of students' behaviour in their other classes, i.e. whether it was part of their broader educational experience. If it was, however, it would be even more difficult to get them to change the habit in their English classes alone. This point relates to the students' habitual modes of behaviour in their education as a whole, and the understandable tendency for students to look for the familiar in their modes of learning and classroom interaction. Innova-tion in the language classroom therefore needs to be evaluated in the light of the students' educational experience and culture as a whole. In other words, consideration of methodological change needs to take account of the compatibility of a given innovation with the expectations and habitual modes of study which students bring with them to the classroom.

In this respect, it needs to be borne in mind that the classroom behaviours described by Shamim were constructed jointly by both teachers and students. The teacher-centred style of teaching in operation certainly contributed to the creation of the front-row phenomenon. It should not be forgotten, however, that the students themselves sup-ported this phenomenon, for example by 'overruling' the teachers' initial attempt to organise seating on the basis of height. Indeed, the students seem to play a powerful role in the creation of the classroom dynamics described: they had their own rules and conventions of behaviour, even if these rules benefited some students more than the others, and they showed little willingness to give these rules up at their teachers' request. Indeed, on one reading, Shamim's study might be seen as indicating that teachers had relatively little control over their classes, and yet Shamim nowhere describes disorder. The system in place was thus 'approved' and, indeed, supported by the students themselves.

These remarks are not intended to discourage constructive intervention. The intention is simply to point to the complexity of effecting educational change in a system which operates on the basis of its own internal set of rules. The remarks also bring out the importance of considering the question of classroom innovation within the broader context of participants' lives. For the teachers in Shamim's study, this relates to the cost–benefit ratio of adopting a more active and energy-consuming mode of teaching. For students, it relates to the habits and modes of behaviour which they have developed in other aspects of their educational experience. And for both groups, it might involve their willingness to accept changes in their broader educational culture and modes of classroom interaction.

Pedagogical reform therefore has to be planned within the overall context created by such factors. Apparently rational responses may prove ineffective if they are based on assumptions other than those of the participants involved in a given setting, or if they fail to take account of the full complexity of the context within which they are to be implemented. Educational change and innovation are always context specific and need therefore to take account of the various aspects of the situation in question.

---

Shamim's study points to the significant influence which material factors (class size, but possibly also the social status of teaching as a profession) can exert on classroom realities. From your own experience as a teacher or learner, analyse a situation in which material factors have impacted negatively on aspects of teaching and learning.

- What were the factors in question, and in which way did they influence the behaviours of teachers and/or students?
- What possibilities do you see of improving the situation other than by changing the material conditions themselves?

---

## 6.4 Conflicting rationalities

At the start of this chapter it was suggested that the reality which methodology assumes in the classroom depends on the meaning which it has for participants, and that this in turn is dependent on various aspects of context. If a given methodology fits in with participants' beliefs and expectations about language learning and is compatible with other aspects of context, then there is a good chance that it will contribute constructively to learning, and that methodology as pedagogical reality will correspond fairly closely to methodology as theoretical principle. The converse is also true. Thus, if there is a mismatch between the assumptions about language or of learning on which the methodology is based and the attitudes and expectations of participants, than the reality which the methodology assumes in the classroom may differ considerably from its theoretical form. In either case, then, we witness a dynamic interaction between methodology and context. The success of a given methodology does not, therefore, arise out of the methodology itself, but rather from its potential to engage participants', and in the first instance students' active participation in the learning process.

Context, however, results from a variety of both pragmatic and mental factors, as well as the dynamic interaction between the two. The case study which is examined in this section (Canagarajah, 1993; cf. also Canagarajah, 1999) illustrates this point well. The specifics of the study relate to the tensions which arose in one Sri Lankan classroom around the use of a certain coursebook. In more general terms, however, the study points to the multifaceted nature of context, and how various contextual factors influence learners' interaction with methodology. The study cannot be said to have a particularly happy ending. However, precisely because of the many tensions it brings to light, the study provides a good insight into the range and complexity of factors which intervene in students' interaction with methodology.

### 6.4.1 A coursebook and its context of use

This study (Canagarajah, 1993) describes a mismatch between an established approach to language teaching as manifested in a certain coursebook and the learning preferences and cultural identity of a group of learners of English in Sri Lanka. The study shows how an established methodological approach may fail to fit in harmoniously with a given context. In this way, it reminds us that it is unsafe to assume that 'accepted practice' is equally acceptable to all participants in all contexts. Specifically, the study shows how an 'imported' methodology can fail to take root in a particular context. The methodological approach discussed in this study arises from the assumptions about language and language learning which are manifested in a certain coursebook. In addition to the question of the mismatch between methodology and context, Canagarajah's study shows that very many different factors intervene in the creation of classroom dynamics. The classroom, in other words, is not a place where students operate 'simply' as language learners in a disincarnate, value-free manner, but is an integral part of students' lives which can only be fully understood in these terms.

The study relates to the learning of English by a group of 22 Tamil Sri Lankan university students in their first year of Arts and Humanities at the University of Jaffna over one academic year. The students were following an obligatory general English course as a result of them having failed an initial placement test in English. For this reason, they had to take the general English course in question and obtain a good mark (a B grade in the first sitting) in another examination in order to be eligible for admission to their second year of studies and have access to the ESP courses which were part of the specialised options they would take in subsequent years. In other words, their English course was not simply a course but also a barrier the students had to surmount in order to pursue their university studies.

Canagarajah, who was the class teacher of the students in his study, provides information on the socioeconomic background of the students which is relevant in a number of ways. Most of the 22 students in the class were from disadvantaged socioeconomic backgrounds, something which in Sri Lankan society is often associated with limited levels of competence in English. Specifically, good levels of competence in English, including spoken fluency and 'correct' pronunciation, are associated with Sri Lanka's socioeconomic elite, a group to which the students did not belong. It therefore needs to be borne in mind that the students were not in a very comfortable position at the start of the course. Their prior schooling, for socioeconomic reasons beyond their own control, had not prepared them well for the English language requirements of university study, and the course they were following was crucial for them to be able to pursue their university studies. Furthermore, they were studying a language which was socially marked in their home culture, and their difficulties in English were, in a sense, a reminder of their disadvantaged status in Sri Lankan society. This having been said, Canagarajah observes that the students' initial attitudes to English were favourable, and that they had good levels of motivation, seeing English as important and useful in terms of its role in education and with respect to their future job prospects.

## 6.4.2 Coursebook and methodology

The course which the students were following was organised around a coursebook, American Kernel Lessons (*AKL*): Intermediate (O'Neill, Kingbury, Yeadon, and Cornelius, 1978). Canagarajah expresses certain reservations regarding the use of a single coursebook for the course, but says that the decision to use *AKL* resulted from pragmatic and, in particular, financial reasons. The practical conditions of teaching in Sri Lanka made it very difficult for teachers to gain access to a range of materials or to prepare and reproduce their own courses. Mainstream coursebooks were, however, made available and replaced periodically by aid agencies. Canagarajah remarks that coursebooks thus constituted a less than ideal but nonetheless a practically useful response to the need for teaching materials in difficult circumstances.

*AKL* is aimed at intermediate level learners, focuses strongly on the tense system of English, and makes use of a variety of learning activities organised primarily in grammatical terms but with a strong situational component. The coursebook is divided into units, each of which has the following components. Part A introduces the target grammatical item of the unit via a set of situations accompanied by visuals. Part B introduces the grammatical element more overtly and provides pattern practice. Part C contains a serialised detective story which introduces new vocabulary and provides reading and listening comprehension. Part D caters for role-playing and provides grammar revision exercises, while Part E involves guided composition. The coursebook thus manifests a fairly mainstream ELT approach and, although *AKL* appeared in 1978, many of its features recur in more recent ELT coursebooks.

Canagarajah makes certain points about the nature of the situations used in *AKL* which are relevant to understanding the students' reactions to it. One is that the conversations in *AKL* are goal oriented whereas Canagarajah suggests that 'Tamil discourse values the "digression" and indirection typical of oral communities' (1993: 609). Another relates to the value system found in the situations, and in this respect Canagarajah observes that in the situations contained in *AKL* upward social mobility and consumerism, the work ethic and the routine of factory life are positively connotated, whereas strikes and demonstrations, and the lifestyle of African Americans are not. In other words, there was an implicit social agenda in the coursebook which did not coincide with the value system, social experience, and aspirations of the students.

## 6.4.3 Student reactions

The students showed initially good levels of motivation for learning English. Canagarajah reports that attendance was 94 per cent for most of the first two months of the course, but fell to 50 per cent until the eighth month, this drop in attendance being accompanied by various forms of student discontent in class. Attendance rose again to 90 per cent from the eighth month, when the students' examination was approaching, with students demanding practice exams and focused examination preparation. Faced with these reactions, Canagarajah realised that something was not working, and the study revolves largely around his attempt to understand students' reactions to the course and, in particular, to the approach to language learning found in the course-book, *AKL*. Canagarajah derived data from two main sources. The first were the observations and field notes he made during the course, backed up by an analysis of the glosses and drawings made by students in their coursebooks. The second were a pre-course questionnaire relating to the students' attitudes to English, and one-to-one interviews with students at the end of the course prior to the examination. The problems Canagarajah identified clustered around three main areas: the place of grammar, the nature of the learning activities, and the cultural content of the coursebook.

## 1 The place of grammar

A substantial cause of student discontent was the relative importance given to grammar learning in the course. Specifically, the students wanted more explicit grammatical instruction, which in their eyes meant the provision of abstract grammatical rules, grammatical para-digms, and charts which they could study and learn as products or content.

Student preferences in this area manifested themselves in a number of ways. Canagarajah notes that the students often skipped activity-oriented classes but attended classes which dealt with the more overtly grammatical elements of the coursebook (cf. the breakdown of course-book components given above). As mentioned above, student atten-dance fell off dramatically from the second month of the course. Canagarajah discovered, however, that from this period a number of students had been following extra classes (for which they had to pay) given by private teachers who used Indian and Sri Lankan coursebooks and who adopted a very 'traditional' grammatically based approach to teaching. The students thus actively sought out the kind of grammar teaching they felt they were not getting in class. Furthermore, even within *AKL*-based classes Canagarajah observes that students tended to 'filter out' grammar and vocabulary from 'supposedly interesting conversations' (1993: 617). In other words, they recycled *AKL* input into their own preferred view of language and of learning. The post-course interviews conducted by Canagarajah with the students revealed that they were reasonably happy with the more explicitly grammatical parts of *AKL*, although most felt that *AKL* should be replaced by a more grammar-based coursebook, that grammar should be given primacy in the course, that grammar should be taught first, and that time should not be 'wasted' on skills and activities. These student reactions reveal a perspective on language as the code and as content, as opposed to language as a skill and a means of communication.

## 2 The nature of the learning activities

The students also manifested discontent with some of the learning activities employed in the course. For example, the students were reluctant to participate in the role-play or conversation activities found in *AKL*. They also showed resistance to engaging in collaborative learning activities, and tried to shift classroom interactive patterns towards a teacher-centred format. One instance of this is that students rearranged into neat rows the desks that Canagarajah had put in a circle before the class began. Canagarajah suggests that the students were looking for a product-oriented and teacher-centred mode of learning, an approach which was held in high esteem in the students' own culture and to which they were accustomed from their previous educational experience.

## 3 The cultural content of the coursebook

Canagarajah reports on two apparently contradictory reactions of students to the cultural content of *AKL*. During the course itself, the students manifested resistance to the cultural content of the coursebook. This was manifested in at least two ways. One was the nature of students' comments and drawings in their coursebooks, which Canagarajah interprets as an attempt to 'localise' the scenes shown (e.g. by drawing in Sri Lankan clothing on the characters) or as indicative of a negative affective reaction to the scenes and cultural norms portrayed. Another was the students' reluctance to participate in role-play and conversation activities. Canagarajah observes that in these activities the students 'uttered their parts in a flat reading intonation when they were supposed to dramatize the dialogue in front of the class' and that they found it 'funny' or 'unbecoming of them' to attempt to bring the dialogues to life. He goes on to comment: 'It soon became apparent that the discourse behind these dialogues was itself so alien to these students that they had difficulty entering into the roles specified' (1993: 617). Students thus felt a credibility gap when it came to stepping into the roles of characters in *AKL*, or even with the attempt to suspend their disbelief and use the relevant activities for intonation or pronunciation practice.

After the course, however, the students showed a somewhat different reaction to the cultural content of *AKL*. Their attitude at this stage was fairly relaxed, and even interested, albeit in a detached manner. Canagarajah explains this change in two ways. The first is that the students converted culture, or cultural knowledge at least, into a 'product', i.e. something to be studied and learned for its information value and stored in memory for possible future use. This is a strategy similar to that which they adopted with respect to the language itself. This strategy, however, became difficult to use when the students had to assimilate verbally aspects of this culture in role-play or conversation activities. In other words, as long as the TL culture could be viewed in a detached manner, it had a certain interest value for students, but became problematic when they were asked to step into this culture (albeit verbally) and were no longer able to view it from a safe distance as interested observers.

Canagarajah suggests that the students' interaction with the cultural content of *AKL*, and thus with the coursebook's role-play or conversation activities, was not related exclusively to the foreign TL culture but also had links with aspects of Sri Lankan society. Canagarajah reports that 'correct' English is seen as the hallmark of the privileged elite, and his interpretation of students' reticence about spoken activities is that they felt uneasy about using their own 'sub-standard' English even within the context of the classroom. (Canagarajah notes, for example, that students said they would not object to using English with a foreigner, but would hesitate to do so with another Sri Lankan.) This may have caused inhibitions among the students, and may also have made them feel that they did not want to break ranks by approximating towards a form of English which is associated with Sri Lankans from a more privileged social background than that of their fellow students. The question of identity with respect to use of the TL thus related not only to the source TL culture as such, but also to the social connotations of English usage within Sri Lankan society itself. The students were therefore reacting not only as learners of a foreign language but also as users of a language in a society within which this language is socially marked.

### 6.4.4 Analysis

This study reveals a number of significant mismatches between the approach to language learning embodied in a fairly mainstream coursebook and the attitudes and expectations of one group of students. In other words, a mainstream methodology did not fit very harmoniously at all into one context. The various factors which contributed to this mismatch are not, however, easy to disentangle from one another.

The underlying vision of language found in *AKL* was that of the language as a linguistic system, and this would seem to correspond fairly well with the vision held by the students themselves. The main organisational principle of *AKL* is grammatical structure, and the students did not have any major objection to this, even if they looked for a more explicit or formal presentation of grammar than was given in *AKL* overall. The students' objections to *AKL* do not therefore seem to have arisen out of disagreement with the vision of language on which the coursebook was based, even if there were differences of emphasis between *AKL* and what the students expected from a language course.

The real problem with respect to the vision of language found in *AKL* is to be sought in the cultural supports via which the language is presented. Specifically, the coursebook presented a mainstream view of the TL culture around a set of values with which the students could not identify. In other words, although the underlying vision of language in *AKL* was essentially that of the language as a code, the code was presented in a culturally marked manner and conveyed a value system which was alien to the students both in terms of their day-to-day experience of the world and also with respect to their own value system and cultural norms. Here we return to the points made in Section 3.5, namely that the exemplification of language can rarely be value neutral. Paradoxically, the attempt of the authors of *AKL* to make their text interesting and informative in cultural terms had precisely the opposite effect with the students in question, as a result of it being loaded with cultural values and associations with which the students neither could nor wished to identify.

Problems also arose with aspects of the learning process itself. In this respect, a serious mismatch became apparent between the coursebook and the teacher, on the one hand, and students, on the other. The students worked with an approach to learning which was based largely on analytical learning, memorisation, and the storing of factual information for future use. *AKL* offered some scope for this mode of learning, but also integrated other approaches which students patently had difficulty in accepting. The students appreciated and accepted the elements with which they felt at home: the remaining elements were either adapted to the students' accustomed mode of learning or, in the case of those which did not lend themselves to this approach, were simply rejected.

There was thus a mismatch between the approach to learning adopted in *AKL* and that to which the students were accustomed and with which they felt at ease. The students were primed for a strongly analytical form of learning and reacted negatively to the more experiential modes of learning present in *AKL*. This, however, was complicated by the fact that precisely those experiential forms of learning to which the students were less accustomed were also linked to elements of the TL culture with which they had difficulties in identifying. Problems relating to mode of learning were thus linked with problems regarding the cultural content of the target learning material, and also with questions of students' identity within their own culture. There were thus real problems in terms of the compatibility between the students' vision of learning and that found in *AKL*. These problems were, however, compounded by a variety of other considerations relating to the students' identity with respect to the image of the TL culture presented in the coursebook, and also in terms of the role which this language played within their own community.

The vision of the classroom with which the various participants were operating was also a cause of tensions. In the eyes of the authors of *AKL*, the classroom was intended to be a strategy rich environment capable of accommodating a variety of learning styles and preferences. The teacher, Canagarajah, seems to have viewed the classroom in experiential terms, as a place where students were meant to use and explore the language as a worthwhile learning experience in its own right. What, however, did the classroom mean for the students, and what were they seeking to find in and derive from it? Why, in fact, were they in the English class at all, and what did it represent to them in the context of their life and aspirations? One answer to these questions is that the students had failed an entrance examination in English and had to succeed in another examination in order to be able to pursue their university studies, something which (for fairly obvious reasons) had a considerable pragmatic relevance for them and for their families. A major instrumental objective in the students attending the English course was thus to prepare themselves for the examination on which so much of their future depended.

Canagarajah makes the following remark about the students' motivation:

> Seeing little possibility of relating what they learned to their
> sociocultural background, students saw little meaning for the

course other than the formal, academic one of acting through the examination and satisfying the English requirements of the institution. (1993: 617)

What Canagarajah describes as something 'formal' and 'academic' was, of course, a pressing pragmatic reality to students from disadvantaged backgrounds for whom university education (which would be denied to them were they not to pass their English exam) had a major pragmatic relevance. This inevitably raises the question of the correspondence between classes based on *AKL* and the demands of the examination. Specifically, did students' attendance of classes help them to succeed in their end of year examination? In other words, was there a mismatch between one aspect of context (the students' examination) and another (*AKL*)? Canagarajah does not address this point, but it is likely to have played a crucial role in students' interaction with *AKL*. A significant factor in the case study discussed in Chapter 3 (Tudor, 2000) related to students' ability to see a clear link between classroom learning activities and the demands of their final examination. A central element of the programme reform adopted consequently involved making this link stronger and more transparent.

The coursebook operated with a vision of the classroom as a strategically varied and culturally engaging place of language learning. The teacher had another vision: that of the classroom as a place for integrated experiential learning. The students, on the other hand, seem to have been working with another still: a vision that involved learning a foreign language and learning about the foreign culture, but also, and perhaps primarily, as a place for preparing for an important life event, i.e. their English examination. These varying visions of the role of the classroom do not seem to have come together very happily, which is perhaps not surprising.

### 6.4.5 Discussion

Canagarajah's case study is an almost classic case of conflicting rationalities. For this very reason, it offers a good basis for analysing the not always happily reconciled expectations and goals which can meet in the language classroom and which underpin classroom dynamics.

The central participants in the case study are *AKL*, the teacher, and the students. *AKL* is a professionally prepared coursebook that makes an attempt to accommodate a variety of learning styles, but which is aimed at a very broad audience and cannot realistically be expected to fit in seamlessly with the specificities of each learning context. Furthermore, it has a socially marked manner of portraying the TL culture which could be unproblematic or even motivating for some students, but which had the opposite effect in this study, as the social values in question conflicted with those of the students concerned. Then there are the attitudes and philosophy of the teacher and author of the study, Canagarajah, who was trying to help his students discover a sense of personal and educational meaningfulness in their language study. However, as a result of the decisions of the aid agencies who donated and therefore, in practice, imposed *AKL*, he found himself having to do this by means of a coursebook which conflicted on a number of counts with the expectations and cultural values of the students concerned.

Then we have students themselves, who brought with them to the classroom their culturally based views of language and of learning. They also brought to the classroom their social and political attitudes with respect to the TL culture as represented in *AKL* and also with respect to the social connotations of the TL within their own society. In addition to this, the students had to pass their English examination in order to pursue their university studies, and they do not appear to have perceived *AKL*-based classes as particularly relevant in helping them to achieve this goal. This raises the question of the compatibility of the vision of language learning promoted by *AKL* and that on which the students' examination was based, and thus introduces another set of participants, namely the persons responsible for the students' end of year examination.

Canagarajah's study points to at least two aspects of the interaction between methodology and context. The first is that what takes place in the classroom is influenced by a wide range of factors and by the assumptions and actions of participants who may be physically far removed from the classroom itself: in this case, the authors and publishers of *AKL*, the aid agencies, and the persons responsible for the students' examination. All of these participants contributed more or less directly to the classroom dynamics described by Canagarajah. The second is that students do not interact with classroom realities, and specifically with methodology, 'simply' as language learners in a disincarnate sense of the term. For Canagarajah's students, the language classroom was anything but a value-free, sanitised learning environment. It was an integral part of their lives as individuals, as members of a given community, and also as young people wishing to make a success of their university studies. These factors all contributed to the context within which the students interacted with the methodological approach of *AKL*, and this interaction was not a terribly happy one.

Canagarajah's study describes the negative reactions of one group of learners to a certain coursebook. Have you encountered resistances or discontent with respect to a certain coursebook or methodological approach?

- If so, analyse the origins of these reactions. Did they relate to aspects of the coursebook or methodology in terms of learning procedures as such, or to factors linked to students' identity or aspirations beyond the classroom?
- Alternatively, perform the same task with respect to a coursebook or methodology which was well received by students.
- Compare your analysis with those of a few colleagues. What does this suggest about classroom teaching and learning?

## 6.5 Overview

The interaction between methodology and context is a complex one, and the two studies discussed in this chapter have raised only a few of the many issues on which this interaction can turn. It is, however, clear that methodology and context interact in a variety of ways, so that methodological choices cannot be made in abstraction of the context in which they are to be implemented.

The classroom behaviours described by Shamim emerged from various aspects of the context in question, particularly the teachers' habitual style of teaching, class size, and the students' own informal rules of classroom behaviour. Any attempt to effect change in the modes of classroom interaction observed would therefore interact with these aspects of context. It is also likely that it would interact with the teachers' evaluation of the cost–benefit ratio of them adopting a new and possibly more demanding role in the classroom.

One difference between Shamim's and Canagarajah's studies is that in the situation described by Shamim the classroom behaviours in question were emergent from context, and the question is how these behaviours might be changed. In Canagarajah's study we find a certain methodology (in the form of *AKL*) being imported into a situation as a result of the decisions of participants external to the situation itself. Specifically, Canagarajah's study points to the problems which can arise if there are mismatches between a given methodology and the context in which it is used. It also points to how complex a phenomenon context is. In addition to the students' culturally based attitudes to learning, aspects

155

of context which play a role in this study are the students' attitudes to the portrayal of the TL culture as found in the coursebook and also to the sociocultural connotations of the TL in their own culture. Yet another factor is the role which a pragmatically relevant examination played in shaping the students' expectations and learning priorities.

Both studies demonstrate that 'context' includes factors which go beyond the classroom as such. Exploring context and its influence on methodological decision-making can therefore involve consideration of factors which may not seem directly pedagogical in nature. Pedagogical choices therefore need to be evaluated in terms of the meaning which they can assume for students and teachers in the full context of their lives within but also beyond the classroom.

# 7 Exploiting local dynamics

## 7.1 The mental context of learning

Chapter 6 focused on the interaction between methodology and context, and it was suggested that classroom realities emerge dynamically from the interaction of classroom participants with methodology and with various aspects of context. In this way, the reality which a given methodology assumes in the classroom depends not only on the theoretical potential of the methodology in question, but also on the meaning which it assumes for participants. This means that a close study of context is essential to any attempt to understand classroom dynamics and also, of course, in pedagogical planning.

One aspect of context which merits particular attention are the educational traditions of the society in which students have been educated and socialised. The reason is that these traditions are very likely to influence what students expect to find in the language classroom, and how they interpret and interact with what is proposed to them by their teacher, in coursebooks, or other teaching–learning materials. The exploration of students' traditions of learning (their habitual mode of learning, favoured study strategies, and their general ethos of study and learning) can be helpful in a number of ways.

The first is that it can help teachers to better understand students' interaction with various methodological options, and thus to understand the meaning which these options have for students in the light of their habitual modes of learning and of classroom interaction. The second is that it can help to avoid ill-informed judgements of local practice by helping language educators from outside of the context in question to understand students' actions and behaviours in terms of the inner logic they have for the students in question. The third, and perhaps the most fundamental, reason is that the students' habitual mode of learning can provide positive guidelines for methodological intervention. The idea is that, by harnessing students' habitual approach to learning, it may be possible to develop an approach to learning to which students can relate in a more harmonious manner than would be the case if they are asked to adopt learning strategies or modes of classroom behaviour to which they are unaccustomed. In other words, local learning dynamics can serve as a source of guidance in the choice of methodology. This is a strategy which involves looking into the target context itself and not outside of it for guidance in methodological decision-making.

## 7.2 Cultures of learning

Cortazzi and Jin (1996) use the term 'culture of learning' to refer to the beliefs, attitudes, and expectations which underpin students' classroom behaviours and their interaction with the teaching–learning process.

> By the term 'culture of learning' we mean that much behaviour in language classrooms is set within taken-for-granted frameworks of expectations, attitudes, values and beliefs about what constitutes good learning, about how to teach or learn, whether and how to ask questions, what textbooks are for, and how language teaching relates to broader issues of the nature and purpose of education. (1996: 169)

Two points need to be made in this respect. The first is that students' culture of learning plays a powerful role in guiding their behaviours in the classroom as well as their evaluation of the actions and behaviours of other participants. The second is that participants may not be explicitly aware of the principles on which they are operating. Their culture of learning may thus constitute a powerful but potentially hidden agenda, one which underpins their actions, but which they may not have analysed explicitly. This can clearly give rise to misunderstandings in situations where participants from different cultural backgrounds are working together, as is frequently the case in ELT, whether in terms of large-scale teaching projects or in the case of individual teachers working in a cultural setting other than their own.

Cortazzi and Jin give an example of precisely one such misunderstanding with respect to Chinese students' use of memorisation as a learning strategy.

> Chinese students' undoubted achievement in acquiring an advanced knowledge of grammar or memorising many English words is seen by Western teachers as being primarily a negative factor: rather quaint, a misguided use of effort and a barrier to communication. A Chinese mastery through memory – which students say brings confidence and a feeling of success – is

commonly characterised by Westerners as 'parrot learning' and a 'burden'. This seems a one-sided judgement predicated on current Western conceptions of the overriding importance of oral interaction and learner-centredness. (1996: 186)

Cortazzi and Jin are here pointing to a case of how participants from one group can evaluate the learning behaviours of participants from another group judgementally because they are unable to see the inner logic of these behaviours and the role they can play in fostering a constructive and affectively meaningful approach to the activity of language learning.

This suggests that language educators need to be willing to explore students' habitual learning behaviours in terms of their own inner logic and of what these behaviours mean to students within the framework of their own culture of learning, and thus to avoid the temptation to evaluate these behaviours in a more or less judgemental manner against notions of best practice derived from their own educational culture. Or, to put this more constructively, an explicit exploration of students' culture of learning should be an integral component of pedagogical planning. This can allow for improved mutual understanding based on a constructive validation of students' existing educational practices, and can also provide direct input to the development of a locally meaningful approach to teaching and learning.

Achieving this goal calls, in the first instance, for an open and constructive analysis of students' culture of learning. It also, however, requires outside observers to undertake a parallel analysis of their own culture of learning and of the possibly unstated assumptions on which it rests. This in turn calls for the willingness to explore and validate different rationalities of learning (Section 2.2). Exploring the culture of learning which is operant in a given context is not, however, an easy undertaking. It calls for a study of the deeply rooted cultural and educational traditions of the target society, as well as of the way in which these interact with current socioeconomic and ideological trends. It also calls for the willingness to invest both the time and the effort which are required to understand students' behaviours in terms of the meaning which they have for them in the light of their own beliefs and assumptions. The exploration of local cultures of learning does not therefore fit easily into a quick-fix, technocratic approach to decision-making. Nevertheless, both in purely educational terms and with respect to the long-term cost of programme development, it is a crucial element in developing a locally meaningful and sustainable approach to teaching.

This chapter looks into the question of the role which students' local culture of learning can play as a guide to pedagogical planning. This is done by considering two case studies, each of which points to the usefulness of harnessing local learning dynamics. The first (Coleman, 1996a) shows how behaviours can be misunderstood if the culturally specific meaning they have for participants is not grasped. It also shows how – with relatively minor alterations – behaviours which, when viewed from one perspective, may seem 'problematic', can, when viewed in terms of their local meaning, offer rich scope for effective teaching and learning. The second, Kershaw (1997), makes a similar point, but also illustrates the type of ethnographic research which can be involved in forging an understanding of a culture of which one is not part. Both studies, however, reveal that the effort to tune in to local dynamics is not always straightforward. Coleman, for example, raises the fundamental question of how far, if at all, the outside observer – or 'expert' – has the right to intervene, even if it may be with the best intentions, in a situation which has its own rules and inner logic. And Kershaw is very honest about the significant effort which the discovery and the positive channelling of local dynamics can ask of the teacher. In both cases, then, the effort to understand and to make active use of local learning dynamics emerges as a key constituent of an ecological and locally meaningful approach to pedagogical decision-making. In neither case, however, is this an easy or even an uncontroversial option. Nevertheless, no language educator can afford to ignore this line of exploration or the effect which the development of a locally meaningful approach to language teaching can have upon the dynamics of class-room teaching and learning.

---

Have you ever encountered tensions or misunderstandings with students or colleagues which could be attributable to mismatches between your own and their culture of learning?

- If so, which aspects of teaching or learning did they relate to?
- How did you attempt to resolve the tensions or misunderstandings in question?
- What role did the study of different cultures of learning play in your teacher education?

---

## 7.3 Discovering the rules

The data on which Coleman's study is based were gathered during an intensive period of classroom observation in a major Indonesian state university over three academic years from 1981–1984. The study involved the observation of 28 different Indonesian lecturers of English teaching about 500 lessons. The total student population present at these lessons amounted to approximately 27,000, in classes of between 20 and 110 students, with an average of 54 students per class. Coleman combines his analysis of the lessons observed with discussion of participatory and interactional patterns in certain Indonesian cultural events and of the students' other learning activities in an attempt to interpret the lesson observation data in culture-internal terms.

Coleman points out that the classroom behaviours observed derive from one university over a specific period of time. They may not have prevailed in other Indonesian universities at the same period and may have changed in the university in question since that time. Nonetheless, given the very substantial amount of data gathered, the observations made may be seen as relating to a significant educational reality in its own right. The study offers the possibility of exploring how different the interpretation of objectively observable phenomena can be, depending on the values of the observer and on whether the phenomena in question are placed in their cultural context or not. Coleman himself expresses this in the following terms:

> What is to be done when apparently exotic behaviour is discovered in the language classroom, especially if both the teachers and the learners who are involved perceive their behaviour to be unexceptional? Should we be critical of this behaviour and try to bring about reforms, or should we attempt to make sense of what we find?                     (1996a: 64)

Another implication of this study is that most classroom behaviours are perceived to be more or less 'exotic' by one group of observers or another. Thus, no matter how 'rational' our own classroom behaviours may be according to our own conception of language education, they too will be embedded in our own culture and values. If we accept these behaviours uncritically, we therefore run the risk of not fully understanding what we ourselves are doing, why we are doing it, and how the behaviours in question fit in with the broader goals of education in our own societies.

### 7.3.1 Classroom behaviours observed

The basic format of the lessons observed by Coleman involved the teacher standing in front of the class on a raised platform or behind a lectern addressing the class, which was generally grouped tightly together at the front of the lecture hall.

## 1 Teacher actions

The first set of teacher actions observed by Coleman was a fairly 'traditional' formal explanation of grammatical points. Coleman observes that when this occurred student attention was well focused. With respect to one lesson, Coleman makes the following remarks about student response to the teacher's grammatical explanations.

> There is rapt attention when [the teacher] does the traditional English-teacher act of talking about grammar, but doing it in Bahasa Indonesia. The situation in the class fluctuated dramatically, then, between quiet attention and anarchic chaos.
>
> (1996a: 68)

As a rule, the teachers observed paid considerable attention to the explanation of grammatical points, whether these explanations were given in English or in Indonesian. In addition to grammatical explanation, Coleman observed teachers reading through the coursebook and asking basic information-oriented questions about the content of the coursebook, or suggesting which elements of the coursebook students should work on themselves. The teachers also asked for some fairly uncomplicated forms of student interaction with the coursebook material such as repeating segments of the text or dialogues.

These actions – grammatical explanation, information-based questions, and repetition tasks – are fairly traditional in language teaching terms, especially in large class teaching. Coleman observes, however, that they were not always carried out in a particularly accomplished pedagogical way. For example, some teachers spoke in a fairly inaudible manner, so that only the front few rows could hear clearly what the teacher was saying. Furthermore, the learner group as a whole seemed not to have a very clear overview of what specific aims there were. Few students had a copy of the coursebook from which the teacher was working, and the teachers seemed fairly unconcerned about the fact that students were coming and going in a rather chaotic manner. Also, attention levels fluctuated dramatically from one part of the lesson to another and from one part of the student body to another. Coleman points out that some teachers were able to retain students' attention, but the general impression is one of a lack among teachers of what are generally considered to be basic pedagogical and classroom management skills such as voice projection or the ability to monitor and retain student attention. In pedagogical terms the teacher actions, therefore, were not very sophisticated or even accomplished.

## 2 Student actions

Coleman's observations in this respect seem at first sight to be somewhat contradictory. On the one hand, student behaviours during classes appeared to be fairly chaotic. Students came and went with little apparent concern for the allotted class times; they chatted freely with one another and engaged in a variety of activities wholly unrelated to the English lesson (writing love poetry is one example cited). In other words, student behaviour could be interpreted as showing a serious lack of discipline or concern either with the goals of the lesson or with the teacher's attempt to conduct a respectable class. On the other hand, however, Coleman points to the presence of 'a harmonious relationship' (1996a: 69) between teachers and students, and no perception on either side that anything was out of place or not working as it should. In other words, the initial (or external) impression of disorder was not perceived by participants in these terms. Indeed, Coleman points out that despite their behaviour (i.e. behaviour which would in many contexts be viewed as undisciplined or disrespectful), the students showed great respect for their teachers.

This leaves us with an apparent paradox: behaviours which would be viewed as chaotic and undisciplined from the 'rational' perspective of the outside observer were not perceived in this way either by the teachers or by the students concerned. The question therefore arises as to what was going on and how this is to be interpreted. Had Coleman not sought to understand the meaning which the classroom behaviours had for the participants in their own terms, the response might have simply been to recommend 'corrective' measures. Such measures might include teacher training to help the teachers perform their tasks more 'effectively' and thereby to make better use of class time, as well as attempts to engage students more fully, or more attentively at least, in class activities. Some measures of this nature were taken and their results are discussed subsequently. For the moment, however, we follow Coleman's logic and trace his attempt to understand the meaning and origins of the behaviours observed within the context of Indonesian culture.

### 7.3.2 *Classroom behaviours in their cultural and educational context*

In his attempt to understand the classroom behaviours observed in terms of the meaning they had for the participants, Coleman looks at two aspects of the broader cultural and educational context in which they were situated, specifically two Indonesian cultural events, and then the other learning activities undertaken by students in parallel with their classes at university.

## 1 Aspects of Indonesian culture

Under this heading, Coleman (1996a: 74–76) discusses two aspects of Indonesian culture, the first being the performance of the Javanese *wayang kulit* or shadow puppets, and the second being the *sambutan* or public address given by a government official at public ceremonies.

In both cases, Coleman observes forms of participation which are close to those observed in the English classes. The shadow puppet shows – which occur as part of weddings, circumcisions, or other important family events – last all night and the audience is free to come and go as they like, to chat with one another during the performance, or even to have a nap. Coleman makes the observation that: 'For the Javanese, there is no paradox in paying deep respect to the performer and yet behaving in a "pleasantly chaotic" manner while he [or she] performs' (1996a: 77). The performance becomes a 'ritual ceremony' which contributes to creating 'a benevolent atmosphere in its vicinity' (1996a: 77). Something similar applies to the *sambutan*, which is delivered at ceremonies such as the opening of a public building or wedding receptions, and is given by persons whose status accords them public respect. Here, too, members of the audience often chat with one another and pay mixed levels of attention to what the speaker is saying.

In neither case, however, is the inattentive or apparently chaotic behaviour of the audience seen to be disrespectful or inappropriate. Such behaviour is accepted as normal and reflects neither on the quality of the puppet show nor on the status of the speaker at the *sambutan*. In other words, benevolent and respectful but nonetheless disorderly-appearing behaviour is a culturally accepted phenomenon as part of what Coleman sees as a certain type of social ritual. What Coleman is suggesting, in fact, is that participants in the English classroom (both teachers and students) may have been transferring into this setting patterns of behaviour which were familiar to them from other aspects of their cultural life and rituals. The English class, therefore, tends to assume a ritual function within the broader context of students' education and socialisation.

## 2 Other learning activities

The nature of the English classes described inevitably raises the question of how much learning of English did (or could) take place within them and, if the answer to this question is less than convincing, where precisely students engaged in the activity of learning the language. Coleman describes a number of independent study activities undertaken by students which make it possible to situate the function of the English classroom within students' broader educational endeavours, study habits, and socialisation.

The first activity mentioned by Coleman is the formation of informal study groups. These groups were constituted by students themselves around a student who was recognised by others as being strong in a given subject. They were most common in the period leading up to examinations and when an assignment was set. Coleman says that these study groups were 'probably [students'] most important learning procedure' (1996a: 79). These groups testify to students' self-directiveness and personal initiative, and also to their propensity for collaborative learning. (I recall a similar phenomenon from my own teaching experience in Libya, where students constituted comparable groups, again centred around students who were acknowledged to be particularly strong in a given area. In the case of my Libyan students, however, the strong student in the group would sometimes go to the subject lecturer and ask for additional explanations on aspects of the course which students found difficult or where they felt the need for extra input.)

Another parallel learning activity undertaken by students involved visiting lecturers at home. It was apparently not a rare event for students to visit their lecturers at home, and Coleman suggests that these visits served two purposes. One involved 'some conscious and deliberate teaching–learning of a subject' and the other was for students to have the opportunity to '"tune in" to the lecturer's wavelength' (1996a: 79) more closely than was possible in the classroom itself. This activity has parallels, albeit in a more informal and sociable manner, to the function played by tutorials in the UK or US education systems.

Another activity involved students seeking out opportunities to practise a skill. In some cases, these opportunities were arranged for them in a form such as chemistry laboratories, whereas with respect to English they had to be sought out by students themselves. Coleman reports that students went to 'extraordinary lengths to track down foreigners on whom they [could] practise their English' (1996a: 79).

Finally, students made use of small private language schools and small tutorial groups to carry out extra work on their English. A variety of learning options therefore existed outside the formal classroom setting, even if students needed to show personal initiative or make financial sacrifices to avail themselves of these opportunities.

### 7.3.3 Analysis

Coleman's analysis of the students' cultural background and their additional learning activities suggests that the rather chaotic classroom behaviours he observed may indeed have played a role within students' broader educational experience, and that this role was neither chaotic nor lacking in purpose. The real purpose of the students' classroom learning needs, however, to be sought in a broad interpretation of the concept of 'learning' and of the role which the classroom was meant to play in the process.

Within the English classes observed by Coleman, the operant visions of language and of learning do not emerge very strongly. The main vision of language is code-based, with a primary focus on grammar. There would seem to have been a fair degree of consensus between teachers and students on this, as indicated by the importance of grammatical explanation in teaching and students' 'rapt attention' when the teacher engaged in grammatical explanation. It is difficult to identify a clear vision of learning within the classes themselves, but the teaching–learning procedures described by Coleman point to a primarily analytical approach to learning within a code-based view of language. The type of learning activities in which students engaged outside of the classroom – i.e. in their study groups, when visiting their lecturers, or in private language schools – are not specified, but are likely to have mirrored that found in the classroom. The students' self-initiated seeking out of contacts with speakers of English, however, points to their realisation of the usefulness of a more experiential form of learning or, at least, of the need to complement a code-based and analytical form of learning with communicative practice. Furthermore, whatever the approach to the specifics of learning that took place in the informal study groups or on visits to their lecturers' homes, the global strategy adopted is a collaborative one which involves a good deal of personal initiative and self-direction. These factors bring us back to a consideration of the nature and role of the classroom in students' overall learning experience.

Were it not for the cultural background information provided by Coleman, one might be at a serious loss to find what precise role the classroom was meant to play in students' language learning. It was certainly not a high-powered and focused learning environment, but this does not mean that it did not have a role to play. To begin with, it allowed the lecturer to provide the students with at least general guidelines as to what they should be learning and where they should set their priorities, even if these were then tightened up further in study groups or on visits to the lecturers' homes. In addition to this, the classroom provided a social context in which students could establish the kind of contacts they would subsequently use for developing a more focused form of learning, including fellow students with whom to work in study groups and, of course, the lecturers themselves. The classroom was thus a launching pad for an approach to learning which was socially based, involving collaboration among students and more or less informal contacts with lecturers. Sullivan (1996) mentions similar patterns of behaviour in educational institutions in Vietnam, where classmates often become friends and sources of mutual support for life (something not wholly dissimilar to what we currently call networking). In this interpretation, the overarching purpose of the classrooms in Coleman's study is thus as an area of socialisation, as Coleman suggests:

> I am proposing, then, that at the time that these observations were made universities in Indonesia were providing an intensive training for future government officials. They were inculcating a highly developed sense of status and an awareness of the proprieties required for the maintenance of a stable society. The English lesson played its part in this long socialisation process.
>
> (1996a: 78)

In other words, English classes played a part in and contributed to the students' overall learning of English as a subject. They also, however, did this as one part of a much broader process of socialisation (cf. Section 5.5). The most important function of the classroom may thus have been one of socialisation into a certain section of Indonesian society.

## 7.3.4 Discussion

Coleman's study is instructive for anyone involved in education, but it is perhaps of particular relevance for teachers or language advisors working in cultures other than their own. In the first instance, it describes an attempt to look beyond a certain set of classroom behaviours with the goal of understanding the inner logic which underpins these behaviours for the participants involved. In this respect, Coleman's study shows that the behaviours in question had a clear and coherent role in the students' educational experience and, indeed, in their broader socialisation.

In addition to this, Coleman describes two attempts at reform or, to put this more clearly, to increase the explicit learning potential of classroom teaching and learning. One involved developing the teachers' repertoire of pedagogical skills so as to help them to exploit the learning potential of the classroom setting better. Coleman observes, however, that this was tried out but that it did not produce a long-term change: teachers 'constantly slipp[ed] back into the old ways, despite genuine efforts to "teach" more effectively' (1996a: 80). Coleman reports that this resulted in part from the students themselves not wanting to change, and pulling their teachers back by a sort of cultural magnetism to the familiar mode of classroom interaction.

The first attempt at reform operated according to fairly mainstream positivistic criteria, and was based on an outsider's analysis of the target situation: the observation of 'bad teaching' thus leading to 'remedial' actions designed to effect improvement. The second attempt, on the other hand, involved the integration into classroom teaching and learning of the collaborative modes of behaviour which characterised the students' habitual approach to learning. Specifically, it turned on the exploitation of students' willingness to move around and to work in small peer groups as part of a collaborative approach to learning. This worked quite well, and the teachers adapted to it easily, assuming 'consultative and inconspicuously managerial roles' (1996a: 81) in a relaxed manner. This initiative operated by importing into the class-room the type of participant roles and modes of interaction which teachers and students had previously practised outside the classroom. English lessons became 'highly interactive task-based events' with a lot of movement, exchange of information and language use' (1996a: 81). Coleman reports that '[r]ather to everyone's surprise, there was no difficulty in bringing about such a revolution in classroom behaviour' (1996a: 81). Furthermore, Coleman reports that the change was greeted with enthusiasm, and test results indicated that the students' classroom learning had improved in an objectively measurable manner.

Norris and Spencer (2000) describe a similar strategy involving the development of a cooperative and negotiative approach to course development in the same national setting, Indonesia. They attribute the success of the project significantly to the fact that the approach adopted exploited certain values fundamental to the students concerned, which include 'creating a sense of unity from diversity, harmony, cooperation, self-reliance and national esteem' (2000: 201). Norris and Spencer's study thus operated on the same principles as the second reform described by Coleman, namely channelling the students' own culture of learning and their spontaneous propensity to assume personal initiative and to collaborate harmoniously with their peers and with teachers to achieve a shared goal.

Coleman's study is relevant to the goals of this chapter in at least two ways. In the first instance, it shows how the meaning of apparently 'exotic' classroom behaviours can be sought in the exploration of the participants' traditions, values, and culture of learning. Second, it illustrates how these traditions can be channelled to generate a harmonious and locally meaningful approach to learning. In this sense we can see methodology as being emergent from rather than imposed upon context.

However, Coleman cautions against too hasty a desire to initiate 'reform'. In the situation described by Coleman, a system was already in place, and there was no perception by insiders of this system being problematic. The 'problem' was that aspects of this system – classroom teaching and learning procedures – did not correspond to mainstream methodological conceptions of effective teaching and learning. With this in mind, Coleman warns of the danger of outsiders 'subverting the lesson to our own ends', and carries on to say:

> I am beginning to suspect that the conventional patterns of behaviour which we encounter in an academic institution have valid functions within the 'ecosystem' of that particular academic culture, however exotic some of those behaviours may appear to the outsider. Although our attempts at reform may be admirably well intentioned, our missionary zeal to do away with behaviours which are apparently inappropriate may actually have unforeseen repercussions elsewhere in the academic ecosystem. (1996a: 81)

In this way, Coleman highlights the risks involved in 'reforming' aspects of an educational culture without fully understanding the meaning which they have for participants and the role they play within the educational system as a whole and, in particular, in students' educational socialisation.

This is clearly a fundamental question with respect to the idea of working with local learning dynamics. Exploiting students' spontaneous cultures of learning offers the possibility of creating a more locally meaningful approach to teaching and learning than importing a methodology to which students may not be accustomed or which conflicts with their habitual mode of learning. One question which inevitably arises in this respect, however, is when change should be considered to be relevant at all. There would seem to be two answers to this question. The first rests on the adage 'If it's not broken, then don't fix it'. In other words, if teaching and learning seem to be functioning effectively and harmoniously, there may in fact be no reason to intervene, even if the approach to teaching and learning in place does not correspond to the notions of best practice held by the outside observer. The second is that societies change, and this can give rise to demands or create tensions which traditional approaches to teaching and learning may not be able to accommodate easily. Holliday (1996), for example, points to a breakdown of traditional approaches to teaching in Egyptian universities under the pressure of increasing student numbers. He argues for a 'rationalised-traditional' methodology, one which is rooted in the participants' traditional culture of learning, but which explicitly accommodates input from external methodological insights. This approach rests on the idea of continuity in change, with the essential element of continuity being sought in the traditions, values, and culture of learning of the participants most directly involved in classroom teaching and learning.

Coleman's study looks at classroom behaviours which would be viewed as 'exotic' from the perspective of mainstream language teaching. 'Exotic', however, is a relative term. All too often, it involves 'othering', or the negative stereotyping of behaviours which are simply different or 'other' from our own (cf. Susser, 1998; Johnson, 1999; Kubota, 1999).

- Have you encountered a teaching situation which you found to be 'exotic' or difficult to understand in one way or another? How did the 'differences' in question manifest themselves in the classroom? Were you able to work from these differences to an understanding of the inner logic of the situation in question?
- Now take a look at your own educational background and the modes of classroom behaviour in which you grew up and were educated. Try to evaluate how these behaviours could be seen by someone from another culture. (You may find it helpful to ask students, colleagues, or friends from another culture to help you with this.)
- What does this suggest about the nature of 'otherness' in language education?

## 7.4 A study in educational ethnography

Coleman's study took as its starting point a teaching situation which was already in place, which was not perceived as problematic by the participants immediately involved in it, but which could be perceived as such from a 'rational' outsider's perspective. Reform was effected harmoniously by exploiting the learning dynamics which already existed among the students and teachers concerned. The reform may thus be seen as a case of continuity in change. The study surveyed in this section (Kershaw, 1997) has points in common with Coleman's (cf.

Section 7.3) in that it illustrates how students' underlying culture of learning can be used to underpin methodological intervention. It differs, however, in that Kershaw was faced with bridging a major sociocultural discontinuity between his students' traditional culture of learning and the demands of a society which was very different from that in which the students had been socialised. This was a challenge relating to the specifics of the situation in question, Papua New Guinea, as we see below.

Kershaw's study is a good illustration of the ethnographic type of research which can be required if one wishes to understand students' culture of learning and thus be in a position to develop a locally meaningful approach to teaching and learning. As we see below, this involved Kershaw exploring the belief and value system, and the traditions of learning in which his students were brought up and socialised. This allowed him to establish what he felt to be an approach to learning which was capable of channelling the students' culture of learning productively in response to the demands generated by a socio-cultural setting far removed from that in which the students had been socialised.

### 7.4.1 The business visit project

Kershaw describes a project organised at the Papua New Guinea University of Technology (Unitech) involving business visits by first-year students in the department of Accounting and Business Studies. The project was organised jointly by the department of Accounting and Business and the department of Language and Communication Studies. It involved close cooperation between the two departments in inte-grating the project as fully as possible into the students' academic programme. One reading of the study would be that it describes a 'progressive' pedagogical undertaking which shows a collaborative, experientially based approach to learning with a strong degree of learner self-direction. In other words, it could be taken as manifesting many features of what is seen as current best practice in language teaching. What makes the study of particular interest in this chapter is less what is done, than the sources of the approach to learning described and the meaning which it had for students in the context of their cultural background and acquired learning strategies. Specifically, Kershaw links this in with the traditional approach to learning that the students in question had developed as part of their socialisation in Papua New Guinea. I start by describing the project itself; I then look into the cultural background of the students and how this underpinned their interaction with the project.

In brief, the project described by Kershaw involved students arranging and conducting visits to commercial companies located in the vicinity of Unitech. During these visits, the students had to gather information on their host firms and then report back orally and in writing to their fellow students on what they had learned. The goal of the project was to stimulate communicative needs and thus to set up an agenda within which students had to develop the relevant proficiencies in the TL, English. The specific goal of the business visits project was to develop the type of language skills which students would need in order to conduct educational research and to interact in the business world. In terms of the status and role of the TL, Kershaw points out that English is the dominant language in Papua New Guinea, a country with 860 indigenous languages for a population of 4.2 million people. None of the indigenous languages are spoken by more than a quarter of a million people. Furthermore, the students' target domain of activity, namely the business sector, is largely Anglo-Saxon or, at least, English-speaking.

The project had six main stages, although Kershaw points out that the task was 'defined minimally and vaguely in order to give as much responsibility for shaping the project to the students as possible' (1997: 167). The first stage of the project was group formation, which involved students deciding on who should work with whom. Kershaw explains that a certain number of basic conditions had to be laid down regarding group composition, but also points out that after having given these conditions he withdrew to let students form the groups themselves. The next stage was visit targeting, namely deciding on the company where each group of students would try to arrange a visit. Then followed the practicalities of arranging the visit, a stage which involved students engaging in the various language activities required to arrange their visits, including the use of the telephone, and of faxes or standard business letters. The next stage – Stage 4 – involved peer feedback in the form of advice and tips on what counted most and on what should or should not be done from second-year students who had undertaken the business visits project the previous year. Kershaw points out that at this stage, too, he withdrew, to let the students share insights more freely. He also suggests that the advice of the older students was often taken more to heart than the same advice from the teaching staff.

Stage 5 was the visit itself, where students visited their chosen companies and tried to gather the information they needed for their project report and presentation. The face-to-face contact per visit varied from 40 minutes to 2.5 hours, with an average of 79 minutes. At this stage, too, the teacher withdrew in order to allow students to develop the activity themselves. Finally, Stage 6 consisted of oral and written feedback, where students presented the results of their visits to their fellow students by means of structured and coordinated group presentations. Kershaw points out that interest was high at this stage since all students were anxious to find out about companies which might one day be potential employers. This stage of the project was formally assessed.

## 7.4.2 Evaluation of the project

Kershaw offers a realistic and open analysis of the project in terms of a SWOT (Strengths, Weaknesses, Opportunities, and Threats) analysis (1997: 172). Some of his comments relate to aspects of the project which go beyond student learning per se and include factors such as staff stress and unevenness in visit quality. With respect to the learning gains of the project, however, Kershaw's analysis is very positive.

The first strength identified by Kershaw is authenticity. The students were involved in a project and used the TL with the teacher, with fellow students, and with various representatives of firms in order to achieve a tangible pragmatic goal. Furthermore, language skills were taught on a 'just-in-time' basis, i.e. they were taught at the stage of the project when they were needed. Thus, telephoning skills were taught when students were having to start making contact with firms, so that they had a clear pragmatic goal in front of them while working on the language input and practice tasks. Interestingly, Kershaw points out that this approach avoided any tension between fluency and accuracy since, by this stage of the project, students could see that an accurate, well-written letter would help them to arrange their visit. Learner autonomy and decision-making were another important learning gain, as the students had to organise a large amount of their work on their own such as arranging visits, conducting interviews, preparing their oral presentations, and so on. Another strength, problem-solving, derives from autonomy, as the students themselves had to deal with the frequent problems that arose in the course of arranging the project. Kershaw reports that the only area where students were looked after was transport, and this was for reasons of security should any students become stranded in dangerous areas. Task-driven inputs is another advantage which Kershaw mentions, and this relates to the policy of only teaching a language skill (just-in-time teaching) when the students would need to use it immediately. This is clearly linked to the idea of authenticity both of task and of language input, and Kershaw states that it had a positive effect on motivation. Experience of business culture is the last strength of the project mentioned, and this relates to the motivational effect of students having a glimpse of the world they were preparing to enter, and of doing this via the language they were studying.

Kershaw suggests that the project was successful, and that it was well received by and motivating for the students concerned. It might therefore seem possible to end the story here, and to conclude that a task-based approach involving collaboration among learners and a substantial degree of autonomy is a productive and motivating approach to learning. While this might not be an incorrect reading of Kershaw's study, it would however miss a number of key points, and in particular the way in which the project fitted in with the cultural background and socialisation of the students concerned. In other words, it would look at surface phenomena rather than the subjective or experiential reality these phenomena had for participants.

### 7.4.3 A culturally embedded methodology

In methodological terms, Kershaw centres his study on the question of meaningfulness within the target context, Papua New Guinea.

> Much of the art of teaching, of promoting learning and acquisition, depends on making what needs to be learned meaningful in order to make it memorable, creating a dynamic of interaction between the learner and the matter to be learned. And there lies the challenge in the different cultures of Papua New Guinea. (1997: 165)

In an attempt to illustrate this 'challenge' Kershaw cites the story of a technician at Unitech who had approached an expatriate lecturer for help with a life insurance form and who, under the rubric of *Any Dangerous Sports*, had entered 'tribal warfare, but only at weekends' (1997: 165). Kershaw provides this anecdote to illustrate what he describes as the 'bizarre juxtaposition of cultures' (1997: 165) existing in Papua New Guinea:

> Stone Age societies endure side by side with quite advanced western-style development, hence so many of the nation's problems of dislocation. The problem in implementing tertiary education in such circumstances is that so much of the knowledge which for the sake of development needs to be imparted is totally abstracted from the perspective of a Papua New Guinea student; book learning all too often seems like so much tedious and complicated make-believe. (1997: 166)

Educating students for the modern and largely Anglo-Saxon world of business when many of them come from a culture which is so different can therefore be nothing other than a challenge. This is a challenge that Kershaw sees as revolving significantly around the creation of personal meaningfulness in the learning process. Kershaw's study describes an attempt to realise precisely this form of cultural learning process, and thereby also of personal meaningfulness in that process. As was pointed out above, one reading of the study might indicate that this had been achieved by importing some 'advanced' Western methodological principles, namely task-based experiential learning and learner autonomy. What is significant about the study is that this methodology, rather than being imported, was a locally based phenomenon which reflects the traditional approach to learning in Papua New Guinea.

Kershaw points out that the traditional learning style in Papua New Guinea is experiential and collaborative in nature. The young acquire a wide range of skills relevant to their environment and needs in an experiential, hands-on manner, whether the object be the construction of a house, a suspension bridge, or a musical instrument. Furthermore, the learning process itself is collaborative in nature with the young working with and learning from the skills of others, generally members of their family or clan.

> By the time he reaches manhood, a Papua New Guinean male traditionally will have learned to build a house capable of withstanding some of the most rugged climatic conditions in the world; he will make and maintain deadly weaponry; he can construct traps for birds, bandicoot and boars; and, depending on his location, he may also build suspension bridges or ocean-going sailing vessels. He may well choose to make musical instruments, or carvings; he will surely know how to create impressive costumes for sing-sings. And all of this without opening a single book; none of Papua New Guinea's myriad languages has evolved a written system. He will have learned experientially, and invariably in collaboration with his kith and kin.
>                                                                       (1997: 166)

The task-based nature of the business visits project built on this learning tradition in at least two ways. The first was the concrete nature of the task itself, which involved achieving the practical goal of arranging a visit, gathering the relevant information, and communicating it to fellow students. The second was the shared, collaborative nature of the task. The students worked in groups, listened to the insights of the more experienced second-year students, and shared their own discoveries with their fellow students. In these ways, the business visits project allowed students to make active use of the ethos of learning and the learning strategies which they had acquired from their cultural background and their socialisation into their own culture. In addition to this, the task entailed a substantial degree of autonomous

decision-making and problem-solving by students working collabora-
tively as a self-supportive group, another characteristic feature of the
students' culturally based approach to learning.

These factors need to be borne in mind in understanding certain
aspects of the pedagogical organisation of the project described by
Kershaw. One was the minimal definition of the target task, which left
the students themselves with the responsibility of shaping the project as
a whole. This is a characteristic feature of the traditional approach to
project organisation in Papua New Guinea. Another was the withdrawal of the teacher during the group organisation phase and the
feedback session organised by the second-year students. In both cases,
the teacher's withdrawal from the classroom was intended to give
students the responsibility for sorting things out among themselves, as
their traditional approach to learning prepared them to do. Indeed, the
strongly autonomous and collaborative nature of the students' learning
culture meant that a key pedagogical skill for the teacher was to know
when not to intervene or, in certain cases, when to physically leave the
room in order to let students get on with things on their own.

In this respect, Kershaw openly acknowledges that the business visits
project created a great deal of work for the teachers involved, and came
to be a rather stressful experience as the penultimate stage – i.e. the
visits themselves – approached. The teachers' task in the project may
have seemed slight in terms of the traditional teacher role of imparting
knowledge or intervening energetically in activity organisation. Indeed,
as just pointed out, one factor which contributed to the success of the
project was for the teacher to know when not to intervene and thus to
give students the personal space to assume the responsibility for their
choices. This does not, however, mean that the teacher's task was an
easy one. The pedagogical intervention of the teachers in this study
revolved largely around the setting-up of enabling conditions within
which students could channel and make active use of their potential for
autonomous behaviour. This, however, was no simple task, as it
involved the re-creation within an institutional setting of the type of
practical challenge which the students' culturally based traditions of
learning prepared them well to deal with. The success of the project
described by Kershaw therefore rests on a combination of insightful
educational ethnography and skilful pedagogical management.

### 7.4.4 Analysis

This study fits in well with current notions of best practice in language
teaching. The vision of language is very clearly functional: language is a
means of achieving things, whether this be exchanging information and

insights with fellow students, writing letters or telephoning target firms, or presenting and discussing the information obtained during visits. Language is thus a means of achieving pragmatic goals within a variety of socio-professional or educational contexts. The vision of learning is equally unambiguous. Learning is strongly experiential, with students learning by doing, both within their project groups and with respect to the people they had to contact to arrange their visit. This did not exclude a degree of more explicit, analytical learning with respect to the teaching of specific language skills, but the latter was fully integrated into an experiential approach to learning.

The classroom in this study served a number of functions. From time to time, it served the traditional role as a place where students were provided with instruction in a given skill area, this being most marked in the just-in-time teaching of pragmatically relevant language skills. It was also the launching pad for the project, in that it was in the classroom that Kershaw established the ground rules of the project and monitored students' activities. It is important to remember in this respect, however, that Kershaw was careful to remove himself when he felt that this was necessary in order to allow students to organise activities and methods in their own way. The classroom in this study thus has strong traits of the classroom as a school of autonomy, in that the teacher's actions were designed to support an autonomous approach to learning among the students. In addition to this, the classroom also had many traits of the communicative classroom: it was the place where students shared their ideas in preparation for the project and also in the presentation sessions which followed completion of the visits. Furthermore, Kershaw comments that peer correction worked very effectively, which indicates that the students were involved in a rounded form of communicative exchange, not simply about the external mechanics of the project but also in terms of their efforts to achieve the linguistic goals that arose in as effective a manner as possible.

### 7.4.5 Discussion

The main point of interest in this study has already been highlighted, namely the value of looking into students' culturally based traditions of learning as a source of meaningfulness and a means of generating productive learning dynamics in the classroom, and so only two points are considered briefly here.

The first is that although this study points to the role of experiential learning as contributing to positive learning dynamics, it would be unwise to assume that this would be the case to the same degree in other contexts with students from different learning backgrounds and cultures.

Indeed, this would be to miss the central point of the study, which is precisely that the key to the success of the business visits project was that the methodology in question found its bases in the inner logic of the context itself. Specifically, the approach adopted by Kershaw was consonant with the collaborative, hands-on approach to learning with which students were familiar from their upbringing and socialisation in their own culture.

The second and main point, however, is that the students came to the course with a powerful set of learning strategies which rested on a task-based or problem-based mode of learning coupled with a predisposition to collaborative learning with group members and autonomous decision-making. A more teacher-directed academic approach would very likely have failed to activate and harness this learning potential. The approach described by Kershaw, however, did precisely this. Thus, meaningfulness was created by delving into the culturally based learning traditions of the students themselves and creating a bridge between the modern, westernised learning goals of the students at Unitech and their much older culturally embedded approach to learning. Kershaw makes this point in the following terms:

> Cross-cultural sensitivity suggests that solutions to challenges to a given culture should be sought from within that culture. Although Munby (1978) chooses to characterise traditional styles of learning as constraints ('traditional' clearly has negative connotations here), as Barron (1991) argues, they are an essential component of a cross-culturally appropriate ESP syllabus. Indeed they offer more in terms of opportunity than constraint. For example, I have never known peer correction to work as well in any other culture in which I have taught. (1997: 167)

---

Look at the cultural background and traditions of a group of students with which you are familiar and try to identify modes of learning, study habits, interactional patterns, etc. that could be used to promote language learning. These may be macro elements such as the hands-on and collaborative approach to learning described by Kershaw, or they may be micro elements such as the use of memorisation techniques, a liking of poetry or of word plays in everyday life, or an esteem for 'diligent hard work'.
Here are two pieces of advice to be used with this task:

- First, be open minded, and do not dismiss factors simply because they may not fit in with a given method, current approved practice, or your own preferences as a teacher or learner.

- Second, do not think too far ahead too soon: just observe learning habits in their own right and in terms of their own inner logic, and only then think of how they could be channelled to support the students' learning.

## 7.5 Overview

The last few decades have witnessed an intense period of methodological reflection and experimentation, and this has considerably increased the range of options available to teachers. There is, however, a growing acknowledgement that methodological decision-making needs to take account of context. In other words, methodological decision-making cannot rest on current notions of best practice alone, but needs to include consideration of the meaning which methodological choices have for the students and teachers working in a given setting. In this chapter it has been suggested that one aspect of context which merits particular attention in the choice of methodology is the culture of learning proper to the setting in question.

The studies surveyed in this chapter highlight the value of this strategy in two main ways. To begin with, Coleman's study shows how the exploration of students' (and teachers') culture of learning can help to avoid a mis-reading of classroom behaviours which, at first sight, may be perceived as ineffective by an outside observer. In this way, it can guard against a form of judgemental ethnocentricity and facilitate a better understanding between local actors and those from outside the target setting. In addition to this, both Coleman's and Kershaw's studies point to the positive effects of exploiting students' culturally based modes of learning in the language classroom. This may be seen in the second reform described by Coleman and in Kershaw's whole approach to the business visits project. In both cases we witness the positive effects of setting up a learning framework which allows students to make use of their habitual learning strategies and modes of interaction.

Exploring and exploiting students' culture of learning offers the possibility of creating learning structures which are inclusive of local perceptions. In this way, it can contribute to a more harmonious and locally meaningful approach to learning than one based on assumptions (albeit perfectly valid ones) arising from a cultural background different from that of local participants. This having been said, tuning in on local learning dynamics can be time-consuming, and can also call for changes in aspects of pedagogical planning. There is a fairly widespread belief among language educators that methodological answers are to be sought in the current canon of best practice and then 'implemented' in different situations: in other words, we tend to look outside of our situation for answers to challenges within this situation. An acknowledgement of the role of local learning dynamics does not undermine the value of reference to notions of best practice as a source of methodological insights and options. It does, however, suggest that this needs to be complemented by the study of local situations in their own terms. This offers the possibility of developing an approach to learning which is inclusive of the perceptions of local participants and thus of generating locally meaningful learning dynamics.

# 8 Negotiation in the classroom

## 8.1 Teaching as negotiation

It has been suggested on a number of occasions in the previous chapters that diversity is a fundamental feature of language teaching. In some settings, it is true, there is a high degree of consensus among students, teachers, educational authorities, materials writers, and other participants about both the nature and the goals of language teaching. This cannot, however, be taken as the norm, and the various participants involved more or less directly in language teaching often have differing conceptions of what language teaching is and how it should best be pursued. The classroom is thus a place where a variety of potentially differing perspectives on language teaching meet and interact. The nature of this interaction is a complex one, but it is fundamental to the dynamics of classroom teaching and learning. It will be looked at in this chapter in terms of the concept of 'negotiation', and it will be suggested that classroom teaching is strongly negotiative in nature.

A first point which needs to be made is that the term 'negotiation' as used in this chapter does not necessarily imply an explicit discussion of options in an open, 'rational' manner. This is, of course, one possibility, or one mode of negotiation, and it manifests itself in the trend towards learner-centredness (cf. Nunan, 1988; Clarke, 1991; Tudor, 1996) as well as in the development of explicitly negotiative approaches to course development and pedagogical decision-making (cf. Breen and Littlejohn, 2000). Sometimes, on the other hand, it is closer to what is described as accommodation (Giles *et al.*, 1991; Giles and Smith, 1979), or the generally unconscious adaptation by one (group of) individual(s) to the attitudes and norms of another. In still other cases, it can involve the more or less conscious use by one participant or group of participants of strategies likely to influence the behaviours of another in a certain direction.

The term negotiation will thus be used in this chapter in a broad sense. It can of course include the explicit negotiation of aspects of teaching and learning among students, teachers, or other participants. It also, however, includes the more indirect interactive strategies by which students and teachers attempt, in a more or less open, or even a more or less conscious manner to influence one another's behaviours. The latter form of negotiation rarely figures in what Nunan (1989: 9) refers to as the curriculum 'as a statement of intent', but is an integral part of what he refers to as the curriculum 'as reality' or 'what actually goes on from moment to moment in the language classroom'. It is therefore a fundamental component of the dynamics of classroom teaching and learning.

## 8.2 Negotiative dynamics

An explicitly negotiative approach to course development has the evident advantage of allowing for an open sharing of perceptions and goals among participants. Nevertheless, even if official channels for negotiation do not exist, a significant part of what takes place in classrooms rests on a form of negotiation, albeit an informal one.

This informal type of negotiation can manifest itself in many ways in the practicalities of teaching. A given teacher may, for example, feel able to allow students in one class to work in groups with minimal intervention on his or her behalf, confident that they will be getting on with productive learning activities without direct supervision. The reason for this may be that the students agree with the teacher's philosophy and goals, that they accept the teacher's authority as counsellor and therefore feel that doing what the teacher asks them to do is the best route to success, or because they spontaneously prefer to work in this manner. In another class, however, the same teacher may find it necessary to direct and monitor activities very closely, which may lead him or her to adopt a more highly pedagogised, discrete-point approach to teaching. This may be because the students have shown dissatisfaction with open-ended learning activities, or seem to lose concentration if they are left to themselves for very long. There can be a number of reasons for these reactions. One may be that a more directive approach to teaching corresponds to what the students expect, or they may not feel enough personal motivation for language learning to sustain their involvement independently over longer stretches of time. In both classes, however, we can speak of forms of negotiation in the sense that student attitudes and behaviours interact with teacher actions and decisions to create a certain set of classroom dynamics. Nothing may ever have been discussed explicitly in either class, but a certain modus vivendi will have emerged as the result of this implicit negotiation of the day-to-day realities of teaching and learning.

More or less explicit forms of negotiation exist at different levels of the educational hierarchy. A ministry of education can design a new language programme, fix specific goals, and recommend a given methodological approach or set of materials. The success of the programme in question will, however, depend on how open teachers and students are to the programme in question. If it departs too much from what they expect or are willing to accept, it may suffer the phenomena of tissue rejection or token adoption (Section 2.4). Educational planners and institutional authorities thus frequently need to 'negotiate' with the teachers responsible for programme realisation, whether this takes place in an open, officially sanctioned manner or not.

From the point of view of individual teachers, one frequent set of negotiative partners are their hierarchical superiors: ministries, institutional managers, etc. Another is 'the profession' in the sense of the general consensus at a given point in time of what constitutes methodological best practice, and which is conveyed by the materials which are available on the market or which underpins decision-makers' conceptions of how language teaching should best be approached. Then, of course, teachers have to deal with their students and how they view language and language learning, and students are by no means uninfluential actors in the creation of classroom dynamics. Teachers thus have to work in a context which is often shaped by a variety of more or less differing perceptions, goals, and priorities. And yet, if teaching is to lead to effective learning, teachers need to help their students find a sense of personal meaningfulness in the learning process. As Breen and Littlejohn point out:

> [The] teacher is at the centre of the negotiation process. Many teachers are obliged to mediate for their students a language syllabus or curriculum over the design of which they had little or no control.
> (2000: 27)

This level of negotiation is crucial to teaching and learning as lived out in real classrooms, and is an integral part of the curriculum as a living pedagogical reality. Unfortunately, it may have to take place behind the closed doors of the classroom, with teachers trying to help their students find a sense of personal meaningfulness in the learning goals or methodology decided upon by participants physically distant from the classroom itself. 'Making a programme work', which is how the teacher's task is often defined, may thus turn on the teacher's ability to negotiate with students a shared understanding of the nature of language, of learning and, indeed, of the role of the classroom itself. In this sense of the term, then, the negotiation with students of a shared understanding of the nature and goals of language teaching is a fundamental component of classroom dynamics and, indeed, of effective teaching.

This untidy and often 'unofficial' form of negotiation has manifested itself in some of the case studies reviewed in Chapters 6 and 7. In Shamim's study (Section 6.3), for example, we witness student resistance to the rational approach to seating initially attempted by their teachers. The front row phenomenon may thus be seen as an arrangement which was co-created by both students and teachers. In part it resulted from the pedagogical approach adopted by the teachers, but in part also from the students' preference for their own set of classroom rules. The teachers could, of course, have carried on insisting on the control of seating, but they gave up this effort in the face of student resistance to change. In Canagarajah's study (Section 6.4), too, we witness students trying actively to negotiate classroom learning with their teacher in their unwillingness to cooperate in certain learning activities or in their re-arranging of desks. Coleman (Section 7.3) observes a similar, although less tense, phenomenon with respect to the first attempt to reform the classroom behaviours of the teachers involved in his study. He points out that it was the students who were largely responsible for undermining the reform in question by pulling their teachers back towards habitual forms of classroom interaction. Indeed, a main point in Coleman's study is precisely that the teaching–learning behaviours he describes were constructed jointly and consensually by both teachers and students within the broader context of their culture and socialisation.

Such complex and not infrequently unofficial aspects of classroom teaching may not fit in easily with the elegant intellectual structures found in policy documents or methodology texts. They are, however, an integral part of the dynamics of teaching and learning as they are lived out in real classrooms. This chapter focuses explicitly on this aspect of teaching, namely on the way in which participants negotiate – in a more or less open manner – their classroom identities and behaviours. As in Chapters 6 and 7, this is done around two case studies. The first study (Duff and Uchida, 1997) is set in a language school in Japan, and highlights the role which student expectations and preferences can exert on the classroom behaviours of teachers. The second study (Uvin, 1996) shows a teacher and course designer in the USA involved in two simultaneous negotiations about the content and organisation of an in-service ESOL (English as a second or other language) course. One negotiation was conducted with the students following the course, and this led to the adoption of a collaborative approach to course development. The other negotiation was between the teacher and the numerous other participants who had a stake in the course, and who were therefore able to exert an influence on factors such as the terms in which course goals were defined and presented.

---

In your experience either as a teacher or as a student, have you encountered the informal type of classroom negotiation described above?

- What was the object of the negotiation in question?
- In which ways did the participants involved in the negotiation go about influencing one another's behaviours?
- How do you react to the idea of teaching as a 'negotiative' activity?

---

## 8.3 Negotiating classroom identities

This study (Duff and Uchida, 1997) looks at the interaction between four teachers and their students in a language school in Japan. The main focus of the study as described by Duff and Uchida is the way in which 'teachers' sociocultural identities, understandings, and practices [are] negotiated and transformed over time', and the factors which are associated with these changes (1997: 457). The perspective adopted on the study in this chapter is slightly different and relates to the way in which, in certain circumstances, teachers can be 'negotiated upon' by their students. Within the context of this chapter, Duff and Uchida's study is thus used to highlight the role that students can play in the negotiation of classroom realities and how they can negotiate their teachers' behaviours in a direction which corresponds more to their own conceptions of language teaching and learning, and the type of interpersonal relations which they wish to have in the classroom. It thus shows the importance of exploring what language learning means to students and how this influences their actions and interaction with the methodological and interpersonal choices of the teacher. The study also points to the influence which the ethos and goals of the institution in which teaching is being conducted can exercise on teacher behaviours, and in this way points to the multidirectional nature of negotiation in the classroom.

### 8.3.1 A language school and its ethos of learning

The study is located in a language school in Japan which the authors describe as 'a large, well-established, private educational institution in a medium-sized Japanese coastal city' (1997: 453) and to which they give the pseudonym of Kansai Cross-Cultural Institute, or KCCI. The data on which the study is based were gathered over a period of six months and included questionnaires, journal entries by the teachers involved, the recording of lessons, and a number of other ethnographically oriented research methods.

The KCCI is a language school which offers a variety of English courses such as communicative English, cross-cultural communication, business English, and preparation for study abroad, as well as courses in a number of other languages. The institution has a strong and explicit concern with promoting cross-cultural communication. The authors cite the description of the school's English conversation course as indicative of the ethos of language teaching in the institution, and thus of the conception of teaching and learning which underpinned the school's own actions and to which certain types of students were attracted.

> In our English conversation course, you will learn not only everyday conversation but also conversation skills that can be applied in your real life situations. All our class sizes are small so you can learn English in a relaxed atmosphere. Speak as much as you can and make as many mistakes as you want! In the beginning and intermediate levels, a Japanese teacher and an English native-speaker teacher team-teach . . . We believe that the pleasure of learning a new language is broadening your world view. In English courses such as [KCCI], the real-world materials from foreign countries, such as newspapers, magazines, and movies are used so that our students will be exposed to the cultures of English-speaking countries.          (1997: 459)

This course outline points to a strongly experiential view of language learning and the emphasis given to the affective component of learning, in particular with respect to the 'relaxed atmosphere' of learning and the emphasis on authentic materials and cross-cultural understanding. The authors also mention that end-of-term dinner parties:

> were common (even expected), and students who had been away were accustomed to bringing edible souvenirs to share in class, a sign of students' group membership and contentment with the course.          (1997: 469)

The element of sociability and friendship thus played an important role within the learning culture of the school and of its students.

## 8.3.2 Participant conceptions of teaching and learning

In any negotiative situation, it is crucial to identify the participants, or negotiative partners, involved, as well as their relative role and influence. The most evident groups of participants were the students and teachers, whose roles are looked at below. Another participant was the institution itself, with its own rationale of language teaching and learning, and the power it was able to exercise on the teachers both as employer and decision-maker, and also as protector of the attitudes of the students which it had attracted. This role does not receive explicit attention in Duff and Uchida's study, but it is reasonable to assume that the institution was present in the negotiation between students and teachers, even if it played this role discretely by means of tacit support for or disapproval of certain types of student attitudes and teacher behaviours.

A key group of participants were clearly the students themselves. The authors profile the student body as follows.

> The majority (70%) of adult students are women – wealthy housewives or single women in their late 20s or early 30s, who prefer to take morning classes. Evening students are more diverse in terms of gender, age, occupation, and sometimes ethnicity. As KCCI is relatively close to the main business district, many evening students work full time in the city. The evening classes are also popular among college students.
>
> (1997: 459)

The students thus had certain traits in common with respect to their socioeconomic background and their attitudes to learning English. The target language was something important to them, but few students appear to have had any very pressing pragmatic need to learn it. Learning English was thus a fairly relaxed affair which fitted into the students' social or recreative agendas more than into any clearly defined set of pragmatic needs.

Furthermore, it should be recalled that the students had made a choice to study English at the KCCI, as opposed to another of the fairly numerous language schools in the area. In other words, the KCCI can be assumed to have attracted a category of student who felt affinity with the relaxed, experientially based and 'fun' approach to learning promoted by the school. The students, therefore, were not an arbitrarily selected group of individuals, but rather a population that had opted in a more or less conscious manner for the approach to language learning which was publicised by the school (cf. the course description given earlier).

The other main group of participants are the teachers. Their personalities and attitudes to teaching are crucial to the study in that it is they who were the main object of the negotiation. It is therefore important to look at who the four teachers were and what they brought with them to the classroom, and thus to the negotiation of classroom realities in which they were to become involved.

## 1 Danny

Danny was an American in his late 20s. Duff and Uchida describe him in the following terms.

> Danny had a strong attachment to U.S. popular media and was a committed vegetarian, nonsmoker, feminist, and environment-alist . . . with a cultivated sense of humour and a dramatic flair . . . Danny believed that culture played a minimal role in communication and that all that mattered were 'politically correct' behavior and attitudes and a teaching environment rich in animated, spontaneous language use. (1997: 461)

Danny structured his teaching style around the popular US talk show format in which he played the role of the host, questioning, entertaining, and sometimes teasing his students. His students enjoyed the approach and adapted to his 'charismatic, exuberant, and often mischievous social/cultural role . . . as fun-seeking entertainer and social commentator as well as language educator' (1997: 461). Indeed, they went along with this role to the point of playing tricks on him, such as locking him out of the classroom or hiding his materials, which Danny enjoyed. In part, Danny's style of teaching may have been influenced by his own negative reactions to the more formal aspects of his own educational experience. He felt that learning English should be 'real, natural and engaging' with an emphasis on colloquial English (1997: 468). Danny had not been formally trained in ELT, but in the social sciences. He focused his teaching around popular US culture as regards both input materials and his own style of teaching and classroom personality, emphasising spontaneous, natural communication, colloquial spoken language, and a relaxed, fun atmosphere in the classroom.

## 2 Carol

Carol, too, was an American, but for reasons related to her own ethnic background and educational experience, she identified less spontaneously with mainstream US culture than Danny. For this reason, Carol felt less at ease with the role of teacher of US culture. This led her to avoid discussing her own sociopolitical and cultural beliefs with her students, which created a less close rapport than the students expected and wished to establish. She also adopted a different classroom personality to Danny.

> [Carol] resorted . . . to a rather formal, structured curriculum, in part to avoid the kind of self-disclosure and contrived intimacy that characterized many conversational EFL [English as a foreign language] classes with young foreign teachers . . . Carol also resisted the prevailing local expectation that EFL teachers should be entertainers and conveyers of Western (e.g. White, middle-class, Hollywood) cultural values and that classes should first and foremost be fun. (1997: 463)

Carol saw herself as a language teaching professional and wanted to realise this identity in the classroom by approaching her teaching in a structured, language-focused manner, without assuming the roles of confidante, personal advisor or entertainer which were expected of EFL teachers at the KCCI.

> A role that Carol believed English learners in Japan expect from their teachers – but that she did not want to assume fully – was that of guidance counsellor. She found that EFL programs such as KCCI attracted students with interpersonal difficulties, people looking both for a hobby and emotional support, for a safe haven in which to vent their frustrations and find companionship. (1997: 463)

This notion of the role of language learning, and thus of the language teacher, did not coincide with her own views and interpersonal preferences in the classroom.

## 3 Miki

Miki was a Japanese teacher from a privileged background who in addition to teaching was programme coordinator at the KCCI. She believed that 'interpersonal relationships are determined by individuals' personalities and values rather than culture per se' (1997: 464). In fact, she did not accept the goal of the school to:

> promote internationalization through the exchange of culture and 'having a good time in English'. Part of her ambiguity derived from her identity as a teacher of language, not culture. She viewed language learning as a legitimate end in itself, not necessarily a tool for the transmission of culture, values, and philosophy. (1997: 465)

In her own eyes, Miki was a 'linguistically oriented Japanese teacher' and felt that it was the role of the native-speaker teachers to provide the cultural input and jokes. Duff and Uchida suggest that Miki's background and education in a traditional Japanese school contributed to these attitudes. In certain respects, then, Miki's attitudes to language learning and to her role as language teacher were fairly close to Carol's. She did, however, feel that Japanese teachers were better able to assume the role of 'empathetic counsellor' with students than their native-speaker colleagues. Miki thus saw a difference in the roles of native-speaker and Japanese teachers within her students' learning. The role she allocated to herself within the process was that of language teacher in a more traditional, linguistically-oriented sense of the term. She also felt that, as someone who had herself gone through the process of learning English, she was well placed to advise the students on their learning.

## 4 Kimiko

Kimiko, too, was Japanese and had considerable teaching experience both at the KCCI and at other schools. She had had extensive experience of life outside of Japan and this had left her feeling alienated from mainstream Japanese culture.

> [Kimiko's] sense of adventure and independence differentiated her from her peers, yet she did not want to be viewed as either feminist or westernized, nor did she want to impose on her classes the U.S. and other values she had appropriated. She saw grappling with current world affairs and lifestyle issues, expressing opinions, and learning and accepting differences as integral parts of English language teaching and learning at KCCI. For Kimiko, the English classroom was a place for communication, and KCCI was a cross-cultural cocoon of sorts. For the students who were housewives, she felt, it was a place 'where they can release all their stress'; it thus served social, affective, and educational purposes. (1997: 466)

The authors observe that the classroom became a place of learning for both Kimiko and her students: it allowed Kimiko to reconnect with aspects of her own culture while she set herself the goal of raising her students' cross-cultural awareness. This reflected her belief that language and culture are inseparable. Like Miki, Kimiko saw the roles of Japanese and American teachers as complementary. For Kimiko, 'Japanese teachers could be good role models, and expatriates could offer students sociocultural knowledge that Japanese teachers lacked' (1997: 466–467).

These brief profiles show that the four teachers involved in the study were anything but 'simply' teachers. Each had his or her own views of the role the teacher should play, of the nature of language, and of the link between language and culture. These differences fed through to their classroom behaviours and the way in which they sought to promote learning. It is clear that their views of the nature of the classroom also differed. This is what each teacher brought with himself or herself to the classroom. What happened then, however, resulted from the way in which these attitudes interacted with the context in which they were working and, in particular, with the expectations of the students and of the school.

### 8.3.3 The negotiation

Duff and Uchida point to the ongoing nature of negotiation in the teachers' lives.

> The teachers were continuously negotiating the curriculum, the institution's expectations of them, their own teaching/learning preferences, and their comfort level in dealing with (cross-) cultural issues and materials.                                (1997: 469)

This manifested itself in a variety of ways, and the authors mention questions such as seating arrangements, use of audiovisual equipment and materials, organisation of lessons and activities, break-time behaviours, perspectives on various issues, and interpersonal conflicts. In other words, the form of negotiation in which the teachers were involved was far from neat and orderly. Indeed, it was something much more organic: a matter of individuals trying to shift behaviours and patterns of interaction in a direction which corresponded to their own perceptions of a situation, and to their sense of ease or satisfaction within this situation.

The students played a central role in this negotiative process. The authors describe the general direction in which students tried to move teachers' behaviours in the following terms: '. . . all four teachers had been pressured by their classes to create an entertaining, mind-broadening, nurturing, exciting classroom environment' (1997: 469). This was the dominant negotiative stance of the students, and the individual teachers responded to it in different ways and with differing degrees of ease depending on the attitudes which they brought with them to the classroom.

Danny was the teacher who appeared to fit in with the approach the students were looking for with the greatest ease. His extrovert, fun-oriented approach to teaching, and his preference for the use of popular

US cultural materials, fitted in well with what the students expected from an English class. The authors suggest that Danny may have become more reflective on himself as a result of being involved in the research project itself, but there is no mention of him altering his teaching style during the six months during which the study was conducted. This may be because his spontaneous approach to teaching corresponded to student expectations and for this reason was not seriously questioned.

The situation was less easy for Carol. Her fairly earnest approach to language learning with its focus on the language itself, as well as her more distant interpersonal relations and her lack of ease with the emphasis on 'fun' learning, gave rise to discontent among her students. Students became critical of Carol's more 'professional' approach to teaching and the methods she used. They manifested this discontent by actions such as arriving habitually very late for her classes. Duff and Uchida report a remark by Carol which indicates her personal reaction to her growing perception of the discrepancy between her preferred approach to teaching and that which the students were looking for.

> [When Michiko said that both her former teachers just played a lot of games,] I felt 'Oh shoot.' In this class, you know, I've been trying to do other things than just playing games. And I wonder if the kind of things I've been trying to do are just too far away from what the students want to do. (1997: 464)

Carol did move in the direction wished by the students, incorporating more discussion topics, role-plays, storytelling, brainstorming, and other interactive activities, and the authors say that this compromise seemed to work. The result from Carol's point of view, however, was less than ideal, and she remarked in her journal that it was pulling her away from 'what I love about language teaching, which is language' (1997: 464). Carol, then, did negotiate, but the result of her negotiation was more to her students' than to her own satisfaction.

Miki's experience was similar in certain respects to Carol's. Miki's students grew bored with the coursebook she was using and attendance fell off. In response to this, she, too, 'somewhat reluctantly' (1997: 465) included more games in her lessons.

> For example, the newfound communicative focus in [Miki's] teaching was evident in interactive pair work, the analysis of advertisements by students, trivia quizzes, and grammar games using dice. Nevertheless, she felt a lesson 'doesn't have to be a carnival all the way through', and continued to promote

grammatical accuracy through a variety of exercises and correction strategies (something she felt distinguished her approach and NSs' [native speakers']). (1997: 465)

Miki, then, experienced student resistance to her linguistically oriented approach to teaching and moved in the direction favoured by the students. She did, however, retain an underlying grammatical emphasis which reflected her own view of language learning and her own teaching preferences and priorities, even if she altered the relative emphasis between language learning per se and the more social or fun aspects of the learning process.

In the case of Kimiko, there are also signs of tensions and a shift in her teaching in the direction wished by the students. This may have been precipitated by the fact that she team-taught with Danny, so that students were able to compare her style of teaching directly with Danny's. Unlike Danny, Kimiko did not feel at ease with seeming to 'impose' US cultural values, whereas this (or at least a very spontaneous celebration of this culture and values) was apparently what the students were looking for. Compared with this student agenda, Kimiko's relativistic and internationalist perspective may have come across as disappointingly unspecific. She responded by adding a stronger cultural element to her teaching to satisfy students' interest in the sort of specifically US cultural input which they got from Danny. Kimiko also felt that the students had somewhat negative perceptions of Japanese teachers (herself, for example) as being 'too grammar-oriented, serious, organized, and humorless compared to foreign teachers like Danny' (1997: 467). There may be something in this, but Danny would probably be a hard act to follow for many teachers, Japanese or other. This points to the fact that students were not simply comparing their teachers against their own internalised set of learning preferences and learning goals, but also one against another.

In summary, then, all of the teachers in this study, with the apparent exception of Danny, felt themselves being pulled in a direction which was decided upon by the students and with which they individually did not necessarily feel at ease.

### 8.3.4 Analysis

One dominant set of perceptions emerges in this study, namely that of the students. As already suggested, however, the school recruited students who presumably felt attracted by its general philosophy and approach to language teaching, and thus constituted a group of learners with at least fairly similar attitudes to language learning. In addition to this, the school would probably have supported student demands which corresponded to its own ethos of teaching and learning. This section therefore looks at the perspective on language teaching found in the school and among its students, or at least those involved in the study.

The language was seen as a means of communication and interaction, of pursuing personal interests, and of establishing meaningful or at least pleasant contacts with other people. The students chose to study English as a subject of general interest, and in some cases as a free-time activity. It was thus an object of interest in its own right, and the most immediate communicative goal English served for the students was as the medium by which they pursued their social or interpersonal agendas within the classroom itself, with one another and with their teachers. For many students, then, language learning was at least in part an occasion for interaction and socialising with kindred spirits and interesting US or Japanese teachers. The communicative and self-expressive functions of language were thus realised primarily within the social setting of the language classroom itself, and this may have been a sufficient goal in its own right for at least a good number of the students.

The vision of learning is explicitly experiential – the language was to be learned by students engaging in language use and interaction (cf. the conversation course description given previously). Central to this approach are role-plays, interactive activities, games, and the use of a variety of engaging and colourful media inputs. Furthermore, considerable emphasis was placed on the establishment of close, supportive and friendly human relations (friendships, perhaps) among participants, within a relaxed and fun-oriented atmosphere. The vision of learning thus combines two of the elements discussed in Chapter 4, namely experiential learning and a deliberate attempt to create positive affective relations in the classroom.

The vision of the classroom found in the school and in students' attitudes combines two elements. One is that of the communicative classroom, which derives logically from the experiential view of learning. The other, which has already been alluded to, is the role of the classroom as a social and communicative reality in its own right. This is related to the idea of the classroom as socialisation. By its emphasis on fun learning and the establishment of friendly, socially satisfying relations among students and teachers, the school was fostering its own micro-society, which offered students a social outlet and chances of establishing a network of friendships and companionship. In terms of the distinction made in Section 5.5, this can be seen as a form of emergent socialisation: the school set up a framework and created possibilities for social interaction which were welcomed by the students, and which they sought to perpetuate. From the point of view of the teachers, with the apparent exception of Danny, this socialisation may be seen as imposed: it was the norm in the institution and they were expected to conform to it. The English classroom was thus a social reality in its own right where students came to learn English but also, and perhaps principally, to pursue personal interests within a pleasant and enjoyable social environment which could perfectly well be seen as an end in itself.

It was perhaps this aspect of the situation which some teachers had failed to realise and around which they had to negotiate their identities and classroom behaviours. In many educational settings, the goal (whether it is explicitly formulated or not) is to socialise students into a certain view of language learning and, very likely, a lot more than that. Within systems of this nature, the teacher is called upon to cooperate with this task of socialisation. In Duff and Uchida's study, the reverse is the case, with students (presumably supported by the institution) socialising teachers into a certain perspective on language learning and, more specifically, into the rules of a given micro-society: the language classroom itself.

## 8.3.5 Discussion

This study shows that the negotiation of classroom realities can operate in various ways depending on the role and relative influence of the participants involved. In particular, it shows how students can influence classroom dynamics, and that their role in the negotiation of teaching and learning procedures can be a powerful one. It also suggests that the ethos of a certain institution, what was referred to in Section 2.2 as an institutional rationality, can influence the negotiation of classroom realities between teachers and students. This may emerge with particular force in the present study because it is located in a private language school, i.e. a service provider which attracted students on the basis of a fairly well-defined ethos and approach to language teaching. In this way, the force of attraction of a school on students with similar underlying attitudes to language learning is likely to have given rise to a form of mutual reinforcement between the ethos of the school and the emergent culture of its (self-selected) students. The teachers who worked within this setting had to negotiate their classroom behaviours around these realities and, as we have seen, it was the teachers who had to give the most ground in the negotiative process.

Duff and Uchida's study shows how powerful a role students can play in negotiating teacher behaviours and classroom realities in the direction they wish.

- Have you encountered a situation in which you had to negotiate classroom realities according to an agenda developed largely by your students?
- Outline the nature of the negotiation and the aspects of teaching and learning around which it revolved.
- How did the negotiation unfold and what was its conclusion?

In more general terms, evaluate the way in which your approach to teaching has been modified or shaped by student reactions, whether over a longer period of time or within the framework of a given course.

## 8.4 A tale of two courses: Negotiating classroom realities among multiple participants

What takes place in the classroom is frequently influenced by actors who are physically far removed from the classroom itself. Teachers may thus find themselves having to reconcile different agendas and sets of priorities. One can come from the authorities that are responsible for the curriculum students have to follow and the objectives or examination against which their, and thus their teacher's, achievement is assessed. The other can arise from the perceptions, goals, and learning preferences of the students themselves, which may coincide more or less closely with the official agenda that they are required to follow. The teacher may therefore find it necessary to mediate between potentially differing conceptions of the nature and goals of language teaching as found in the programme, on the one hand, and the perceptions and goals of the students, on the other. The success of the course in question depends crucially on how well the teacher can mediate between the two, as effective learning is heavily dependent upon students being able to relate to course goals and methodology in a personally meaningful manner.

This section illustrates this type of situation by presenting a case study (Uvin, 1996) relating to the design and implementation of two versions of a workplace ESOL course for health-care workers of Chinese origin at a nursing home in Boston, USA. It shows how the author and course designer/teacher revised his first course to bring it closer to the needs of the students concerned while at the same time having to reconcile this change with the priorities and goals of a variety of other participants. The study shows that the negotiation of methodological procedures at classroom level frequently occurs within a context which is influenced by the perceptions and goals of participants who, although physically distant from the classroom as such, can exercise a very real influence on what is or can be done in the classroom.

### 8.4.1 The limits of a 'rational' approach

The official remit of the course, i.e. the way in which the course sponsors defined its objectives, was to improve the students' English skills within the context of their working lives as part of the broader goal of enhancing the effectiveness of service delivery in the institution concerned. The starting point of the course was an extensive needs analysis conducted by Uvin and which involved him devoting three weeks to examining the patient-care procedures used in the relevant institution. This included study of the technical aspects of health-care tasks, recording sample interactions, speaking to workers and residents, and a variety of other means of gathering information on the working conditions and procedures current in the institution in question. Specifically, Uvin set out to identify and understand the language requirements of the target health-care workers, and the tasks they had to perform. He then used this analysis to inform the setting of objectives and the preparation of teaching materials and activities (Uvin, 1996: 40–41).

What Uvin describes in terms of his initial approach represents a classic approach to ESP course design, and rests on a rationalistic view of language and of language learning. On one level, this approach yielded a number of positive results. For example, Uvin points to the objective relevance of course content, the clear direction it gave to classroom activities, and its usefulness in establishing objectives which gained the approval of funders, sponsors, and managers. In this way, the first course satisfied a number of objectively observable criteria as well as the demands for accountability of administrative and managerial participants. Uvin also, however, points to a number of shortcomings which emerged with the first course he developed. One was that it did not correspond to what the students themselves wanted. Another was that it addressed students' needs as operatives but not as the individuals they also were, both in their professional functions and as language learners. The course could thus be said to have fulfilled its goals in rational, objectively observable terms, as seen in the students' improved performance on external tests of their professional skills. The students still, however, found it difficult to relate to the course in a personally meaningful manner. Uvin suggests that this resulted from the initial definition of course goals failing to take account of important aspects of students' needs with respect to their use of the language and also in terms of their interaction with the learning process itself.

In what follows, I focus on the two sets of negotiative processes that Uvin initiated in the attempt to create a course which corresponded more fully to the students' needs. One of these was with the students themselves, while the other involved Uvin having to reconcile the priorities that emerged from his contact with the students with a framework of goals established by other agents, including managerial staff at the institution and funding bodies. This highlights the multi-faceted nature of negotiation in such situations. What takes place in the classroom between the teacher and students is one aspect of the process, but this is influenced, and often significantly so, by other parties and the parameters which they establish.

### 8.4.2 *An objective and the context of its realisation*

The problems which Uvin identified in the first version of his course related less to the objective relevance of the goals it pursued than to questions of student identity, and in this way to students' ability to relate meaningfully to course content and learning procedures. To begin with, the course addressed the work-related needs of the students, while the students themselves were looking for something more than this. Many students were recent arrivals in the USA and 'had language needs that went beyond the workplace' (1996: 43). These needs related to students' broader social and affective identity and included questions of culture shock and perceived social status. In other words, the first course adopted too narrow a definition of learners' needs.

Problems also arose with respect to the teaching–learning procedures set in place, which Uvin observed to be inappropriate in both cultural and personal terms. To begin with, he realised that the teaching–learning procedures originally chosen assumed educated learners, whereas some students had received little formal education and lacked basic learning strategies. Furthermore, these procedures differed in a number of respects from the preferred learning styles and strategies of Asian learners such as the students for whom the course was destined. In addition to this, strong teacher mediation of learning materials failed to provide students with the skills for coping autonomously in real-life situations. In other words, they failed to develop students' ability to transfer skills from in-class learning to their contact with the language outside of the classroom. Finally, Uvin found that the assessment procedures used were not always compatible with the needs and preferences of the students.

As a result of these mismatches, Uvin realised that the students were having difficulty in identifying both with the content of the course and with the teaching–learning procedures used, and that this was having negative effects on the quality of their learning. He also observes that the initial course structure was too inflexible and made it difficult to accommodate change. This meant that the course could not be made to respond to changes in students' learning needs over time. The solution which Uvin decided to adopt with respect to these problems was to involve the various participants (students, supervisors, residents, administrators, etc.) more directly in the process of course development. The move was thus from an objectively based and product-oriented approach to one that was participatory and process-oriented.

### 8.4.3 Negotiation I: Within the classroom

Uvin's second approach to the course involved the attempt to link course development more fully into students' identity both in their professional lives and within the learning process itself. He lists the following stages in the process.

1. Collaborate with learners to facilitate their participation as researchers in the investigation of their daily experiences.
2. Identify issues learners are facing.
3. Find out what needs to be done to resolve the issues we identified, and avoid them in the future.
4. Negotiate with learners as to which activities promote their learning in and outside the classroom, and fine-tune my teaching accordingly.
5. Involve learners in documenting their achievements and in evaluating the process.
6. Develop units or records of work (curriculum products) that account for the work done along the way.                    (1996: 45)

In order to achieve these goals, Uvin adopted a means of investigation designed to explore the students' subjective interaction both with their immediate working environment and their broader experience of life in the USA. This involved avenues of research such as keeping dialogue journals with students, taking part in meetings of supervisory and administrative staff, establishing classroom rituals like 'What happened today?' in order to allow students to discuss their personal experience of life in the institution, organising feedback sessions at the end of the class, listening actively to students both within the class and outside (e.g. on breaks), and organising visits to students' homes and to the communities in which students lived.

As a result of the insights he gathered in this manner, Uvin was able to gear the second course more closely around students' real needs and thereby make it better able to promote achievement of the goals set by the sponsoring bodies. At the same time he was able to respond more fully to the students' own perceptions of their needs in both content and process terms. Uvin points out that this collaborative approach 'enhanced [the students'] sense of ownership, motivation, and self-esteem' (1996: 52) and that it had positive effects on attendance (which had been somewhat erratic) and on the classroom atmosphere. All of this in turn had positive effects on students' performance both as language users and language learners. Uvin points out that this change required him to build up the necessary trust and mutual respect with students, and also that it called for more preparation and follow-up work. In essence, however, Uvin's comments indicate that the shift from an external, objectively based approach to needs analysis to one which was experientially oriented and which was open to input from students, produced significant gains in both the relevance of learning content and the effectiveness of learning activities.

This could be seen as the conclusion to the study. The course was revised in a certain direction, and the results were positive, which would point to the advantages of an approach to course development that is open to learner input and participation. This, however, would not give a complete picture of what Uvin had to do in order to achieve the positive results that he describes. In particular, it would give the impression that the within-class negotiation regarding learning content and methodology was all that was involved; however, this was not the case. In other words, it would leave out a major part of the negotiative process in which Uvin was involved.

### 8.4.4 Negotiation II: Beyond the classroom

It needs to be remembered that the course was of interest to participants other than Uvin and the students: there were other stakeholders, and their perceptions and goals also had to be taken into account. The students were following a course which was sponsored and paid for by their employers with the not unreasonable goal of helping them to become more effective health-care operatives and thus to contribute to the general quality of health-care in their institution. The negotiation of the course development and implementation procedures between Uvin and the students therefore had to take account of these objectively valid criteria, and also (which may not be quite the same thing) of how the relevant funding bodies and other interested parties interpreted these criteria. As Uvin himself points out, the course development process taught him that 'course design does not take place in a vacuum' (1996: 53–54).

A number of participants were present in a more or less immediate manner. One set of more readily visible participants were what Uvin describes as 'partners', namely residents, workers, supervisors, nurses, administrators, and managers in the nursing home. He points out that each of these groups of participants had different agendas, and that while these agendas sometimes overlapped, at other times they appeared to be in conflict with one another. Uvin's task therefore involved finding a balance between the agendas pursued by the various participants and reconciling their perspectives on the situation. In other words, there was a lot of negotiating to be done within the institution itself. He also points to the influence of factors such as staff changes, which meant that neither individual personalities nor levels of support for the project could be taken for granted. This meant that even within the institution itself, Uvin found himself negotiating on a moving stage with sometimes new actors playing new roles.

Uvin also had to take account of funding guidelines. In this respect, we are not talking about the role of identifiable individuals but rather of corporate groups (funding and sponsoring agencies) which had their own agendas and which operated according to their own perceptions and goal structures. Thus, even if they were relatively faceless, the influence exerted by these participants was nonetheless real for that. The impact of these groups in Uvin's study related to factors such as grant-application procedures (which influenced the manner in which course goals were formulated), and the need to have a quantifiable evaluation of outcomes not only with respect to learners' language abilities per se, but also in terms of their impact on the workplace in areas such as worker productivity, job performance and quality of work, worker attendance and safety. There were also requirements regarding the project management structure, including accountability towards the various parties involved. Uvin says that 'the impact of these guidelines on course design processes . . . and the development of materials was far-reaching' (1996: 56). Thus, while the bureaucrats responsible for developing the funding guidelines may have been physically distant from the situation itself, their influence on what could be done and how it had to be organised was very real.

Moving even further from the specifics of the target situation, Uvin also mentions the influence of the political, social, and economic climate. All the participants mentioned above were operating in a specific social and ideological context which gave rise to a number of more or less explicitly stated objectives and priorities.

> According to political and business leaders, workplace ESOL
> and literacy courses should support organizations (businesses,
> unions) at the local level, and the nation at the global level, in
> meeting the demands created by a more technically sophisti-
> cated manufacturing and service delivery process and restore or
> enhance their ability to compete. They should also help organi-
> zations cope with the implications of recent demographic
> changes, that is, assist them in upgrading the skills of minorities,
> immigrants, and refugees who are now making up the labor
> pool that organizations recruit from to fill entry-level positions.
>
> (1996: 57)

This perspective on the purpose of the course which Uvin was developing gave rise to a set of priorities which Uvin simply could not afford
to ignore, either in what he did or in how he presented this in official
documents. This social agenda thus exerted a powerful influence on
how Uvin had to define the goals of the course and on what he could or
could not do with his students. In other words, it set the global
parameters within which his more detailed level of negotiation with
students had to be conducted. In practice, it meant that Uvin had to
accommodate the demands for workplace relevance, improved service
delivery and efficiency, and objective accountability of learning outcomes (i.e., the 'official agenda' of non-classroom participants) with his
students' search for personal meaningfulness in the learning process
itself. His negotiative task therefore went beyond the classroom itself,
while at the same time it could never be divorced from the human
realities of classroom teaching and learning.

### 8.4.5 Analysis

This study shows a teacher and course designer, Uvin, succeed in
negotiating an approach to teaching and learning which was able to
satisfy the needs and demands of a variety of participants: the students
themselves, various institutional actors, and also the relatively distant
funding agencies. This task was a multifaceted one in which Uvin had to
take account of different perceptions of language, of the learning
process, and also of the nature and goals of the classroom.

The sponsors' vision of language was essentially functional: language
was a means for the students to perform their professional tasks as
health-care workers more effectively as part of a goal-oriented, service-
providing institution. This vision of language underpinned the first
course and Uvin was obliged to respect it in the second course as well.
The difference between the first and the second course was that the

latter incorporated a much richer vision of language, which allowed scope for the broader expressive agenda of the students as individuals and not simply as operatives in a mechanistic sense of the term. This made the language content of the second course more accessible to the students and thereby also (and not surprisingly) increased its effectiveness in functional terms. Uvin's efforts to open up the course content to students' personal concerns and to their own day-to-day experiences in the health-care institution was therefore anything but a distraction from the goals of the course as defined by the sponsors. The second course rested, in fact, on a richer view of language and, in particular, of functionality.

Uvin does not describe in detail the vision of learning which inspired the first course, other than to say that the approach was rather teacher-centred with respect to the mediation of materials, and allowed little scope for the development of student autonomy outside of the classroom. This makes it sound somewhat 'closed': the course had been developed in a rational manner on the basis of a needs analysis, but was insufficiently open to the learning needs of the students both within the framework of specific learning activities, and in terms of their everyday contacts with the language. The second version of the course, on the other hand, was experiential in a strong sense of the term, not only in terms of student participation on the micro-level of activity organisation, but also with respect to the students' role in the shaping of course content and objectives. This altered the status of the course from that of a 'simple' language course built around a pre-set syllabus to a process of reflection and learning which was shared between students and teacher, and which was open to the concerns and experiences of the students. As Uvin says: 'because [the students] had a say in what was learned, how and why, their learning went beyond the job-specific competencies' (1996: 52).

With respect to the vision of the classroom, it is necessary to distinguish between the role it had for the students, on the one hand, and the role it had for the sponsors, on the other. In other words, one needs to be aware of the tension between the pedagogical and the social roles the classroom had from the perspective of the various participants involved. In terms of the students, a change occurred between the first course, in which the classroom was intended to be a controlled learning environment, and the second, where it combined aspects of both the communicative classroom and the classroom as a school of autonomy. Students learned by active use of the language, not only within the framework of specific language practice activities, but also as part of their ongoing exploration of their experience of language use and the development of their own learning objectives. As a result of this approach to learning, students were able to develop reflective and self-directive skills both as language users and language learners.

From the point of view of the sponsoring agencies, the classroom, and the course as a whole, had a functional role. It was thus intended first of all as a controlled learning environment whose effectiveness had to be evaluated on the basis of clear, objectively verifiable criteria. It would also seem to have had a role in promoting a certain professional socialisation related to the official remit of the institution, which in turn reflected the prevailing political perspective on health-care and society at large. One of Uvin's most tricky tasks was thus to reconcile the vision of the classroom he found to be necessary for effective student learning with the vision of the classroom held by the funding bodies. To achieve this goal, he had to negotiate not only with the students and their concerns, but also with the numerous other participants involved and their concerns.

## 8.4.6 Discussion

This study could, and with good reason, be taken to show the advantages of adopting an explicitly negotiative approach to course development, i.e. one which opens up scope for the active inclusion of students' insights and concerns in the choice of learning activities and in programme development. The specific interest of the study in this chapter lies, however, in the way in which Uvin had to manage negotiative processes not just in the classroom itself, but also beyond it. Graves, in her commentary on Uvin's study, makes the following remarks in this respect:

> This situation underscores the fact that a needs assessment is not an objective, context-independent undertaking. It depends on how the analyzer defines (or is asked to define) *needs* [original emphasis]. In this case, needs were defined in terms of competencies, the language and behavior necessary to complete given tasks. A competency-based view of needs was the prevailing view in workplace course design at the time and partly an outgrowth of the necessity to document progress and outcomes for funders. This particular course was designed to correspond to a state examination for nursing home workers. Thus the students and their perceptions of their needs were only one part of the process of determining needs. (1996: 59)

Uvin's negotiation of course objectives at classroom level therefore had to take account of other relatively set conceptions of the nature of language and of learning.

This is a key factor in the study and it points to the often complex nature of decision-making in language teaching. Furthermore, as Graves (1996) rightly points out, Uvin was able to negotiate quite a lot, and he had fairly direct access to the participants whose conceptions of language teaching shaped the framework within which he had to work. Many teachers could not say the same thing, and they have to work within pre-set structures which they have little or no power to influence, and which are set up by distant participants to whom the individual teacher has little or no direct access. This means that the margin for manoeuvre of the average teacher may be slight. A set syllabus, prescribed coursebook, or the injunction to use a certain methodological approach in the classroom, can all become givens, non-negotiable elements around which the teacher has to work in the attempt to help students to find some form of personal meaningfulness in the learning process.

---

Uvin's study shows a teacher negotiating with two main sets of participants: the students who were physically present in the classroom, and various other participants who were more or less distant from the classroom in physical terms but who nevertheless exercised an influence on what was done in the classroom. With respect to one or more teaching situations with which you are familiar, identify the various sets of participants with which teachers have to negotiate classroom realities. Focus in particular on participants physically external to the classroom.

- In which ways do they influence classroom realities?
- To what extent can the classroom teacher influence the decisions made by these participants?

Uvin remarks that one of the things he learned from the course described was that 'course design does not take place in a vacuum' (1996: 53–54). What is your reaction to this comment?

---

## 8.5 Overview

The studies surveyed in this chapter show that language teaching is far from a neat, linear affair lived out in an ideal world of harmony and consensus. Language teaching and learning, and the classrooms in which they are lived out, are part of human life, and manifest the differences, disagreements and attempts of participants to reach a mutually acceptable modus vivendi which we find in most other aspects of human life. They also show (as if practising teachers would need to be reminded of this fact) that teachers cannot assume that they are able to call all the shots: other actors can exert a significant and sometimes decisive influence on what takes place in the classroom.

In Duff and Uchida's study, the teachers appear to have been negotiating around an agenda which was established primarily by the students and by the institution in which they were working, and which related to a variety of very detailed methodological choices and modes of interpersonal interaction in the classroom. Furthermore, the nature of the negotiation in which the teachers were involved was often indirect; for example, students turning up late for class as a means of indicating their dissatisfaction with the approach adopted by a given teacher. In Uvin's study we find a more active and explicitly negotiative figure who deliberately sought to mediate between the goals and expectations of a variety of participants. Uvin, however, was more than simply a class teacher. He was also a course designer who had an explicit mandate to design and implement a workable programme, and he had the status and practical possibility to influence what was done. Both studies, however, show that classroom realities are negotiated or constructed jointly by a variety of participants, teachers and students in the first instance, but also by other actors who may be physically distant from the classroom itself. In contexts where there is a broad consensus among participants as to the nature and goals of language learning, there may be little to negotiate. The greater the diversity which exists, however, the more there is that has to be negotiated, and diversity is the norm rather than the exception.

For this reason, language educators need to understand the various threads of diversity which meet in the classrooms in which they work and to be aware of the way in which the interaction of differing perceptions of the nature and goals of language teaching contribute to classroom dynamics. In addition to this, educational planners should be willing to acknowledge the very complex role of the classroom teacher as negotiator of classroom realities. The success of a language programme depends more than on any other factor on the meaningfulness which the programme assumes for the students physically present in the tens or hundreds of classrooms in which it is implemented. This, in turn, depends crucially on the sensitivity, adaptability, and the negotiative skills of classroom teachers. No coherent effort to understand language teaching as it is lived out in classrooms can ignore this aspect of classroom dynamics.

# 9 Living with complexity

A distinction was made in Chapter 1 between the technological and the ecological perspectives on language teaching. The former is positivistic in nature and posits a fairly linear relationship between methodological principle and pedagogical reality. The latter views situations holistically and evaluates methodological choices less in terms of theoretical principle than with respect to the way in which they interact with their context of use. This book is situated in the ecological perspective on language teaching and rests on the hypothesis that language teaching is a dynamic phenomenon which arises out of the interaction of classroom participants with one another, with methodology, and with the broader context in which they are working. The main source of the dynamic nature of teaching is that participants can and frequently do see the nature and goals of language teaching in differing terms. The meeting of these differing perspectives gives rise to a dynamic tension between students and teachers as they try to work out a shared understanding of language teaching and a sustainable modus vivendi in the classroom. This means that teachers have to do more than 'simply' impart knowledge or train skills: their task is more one of helping students to find a sense of personal meaningfulness in the learning process in a context which is often shaped by the perceptions, goals, and priorities of a variety of other participants. Language teaching is thus a strongly negotiative activity, and the dynamic process whereby teachers and students attempt to negotiate their classroom behaviours and identities is fundamental to classroom teaching and learning.

Language teaching is frequently discussed in terms of general principle, and methodology, i.e. considerations relating to the means by which the language is presented to students and learning activities are organised play a central role in the debate. Two points need to be made in this respect.

The first is that language teaching is always lived out 'locally'. General principle can, of course, provide insights and open up potentially productive lines of reflection. This having been said, effective teaching depends crucially on teachers' ability to understand and react to the particular group of students they have in front of them in a particular classroom (chalk-dust, broken chairs, and all). In other words, language teaching is a local activity. General principle can serve a role, but will not necessarily provide answers to the challenges posed by the specifics of a given group of students. These need to be sought for in the often untidy details of each teaching situation and in the dynamic interaction of students with the learning process.

The second point relates to the role of methodology, and it is clear that methodology plays an important role in classroom dynamics. It is the means by which the language is presented to students and learning activities are organised, and it influences many aspects of classroom interaction. Methodological choices therefore play a significant role in students' and teachers' negotiation of their classroom behaviours and identities. Methodology does not, however, operate in a linear manner, and it cannot be assumed that methodology as theoretical principle translates neatly into methodology as pedagogical reality. The latter arises out of the interaction of students and teachers with the method-ology in question, and this interaction is highly context specific. Exploring the meaning which methodological choices have for students and teachers is therefore crucial to understanding classroom teaching. Methodological choices thus interact dynamically with context.

In line with this perspective on language teaching, Chapters 3–5 surveyed a number of methodological perspectives on the nature of language, of learning, and of the classroom, and raised questions concerning the meaning which these perspectives can assume for students and teachers in the light of various aspects of context. The main point made in these chapters is that methodological choices need to be made not just on the basis of theoretical principle, but in terms of the meaning which these choices assume for the students and teachers present in a given setting. Chapters 6–8 focused on aspects of the dynamics of classroom teaching with reference to a number of case studies. Chapter 6 looked at the interaction between methodology and context, Chapter 7 argued for the active exploitation of students' culture of learning, and Chapter 8 focused on the negotiative nature of classroom teaching and learning. These chapters highlighted the complex nature of language teaching and the need to explore teaching situations in terms of the meaning which they have for participants in the full context of their lives within but also beyond the classroom. They also show that classroom realities emerge dynamically from students' and teachers' interaction with one another, with a variety of other participants, with methodology, and with various aspects of context. This chapter sums up the main implications which arise out of the perspective on language teaching developed in the previous chapters with the intention of providing teachers and other language educators with a few guidelines for exploring the dynamics of their own situations and in approaching decision-making in a locally meaningful and sustainable manner.

## 1 Acknowledge the complexity of language teaching in an open and constructive manner

Teaching is rarely a neat, tidy activity which fits conveniently into idealised curricular structures or elegant conceptions of best practice. Markee's (1997: 176) remark that innovation is 'an inherently messy, unpredictable business' applies equally to language teaching in general. Few practising language educators would seriously question that language teaching is a complex activity. All too frequently, however, this complexity is ignored or brushed under the carpet, and more often than not by participants who are not practising teachers and who have little or no experience of the realities of teaching as lived out in the classroom. The perceptions of these participants (planning authorities, aid agencies, institutional managers, client faculties, etc.) can, however, have a significant influence on the parameters within which teachers have to work, the goals they are required to achieve, or the methodology and materials with which they have to work.

It is, however, important for language educators – especially those who are responsible for programme development and teacher education – to insist on an open acknowledgement of the complexity of language teaching. This can involve arguing for appropriate teacher education and support in programme design, as well as the allocation of the necessary time for a detailed study of the target teaching context. It also calls for the willingness to look beyond the neat, elegant structures within which language teaching is often discussed and programme goals defined. Furthermore, it is important that teachers' professional education should provide them with the confidence to acknowledge and analyse the complexity of teaching without fearing that this will be interpreted as a sign of them having somehow or other failed to 'get things right'. This calls for openness within our profession and also for a strong advocacy of an acknowledgement of the real nature of teaching with non-teaching participants.

## 2 Acknowledge diversity in an inclusive and constructive manner

Language teaching can mean different things to the various actors who, in one way or another, exert an influence on what takes place in the language classroom and on the terms in which outcomes are evaluated. Teachers thus frequently have to work in a context which is influenced by the perceptions and goals of participants physically distant from the classroom itself. They are, however, most immediately confronted with diversity among their students, and effective teaching depends crucially on teachers' ability to help their students find a sense of personal meaningfulness in the teaching–learning process. This, in turn, depends on an inclusive and constructive acknowledgement of students' individuality, and thus of their diversity. It is for this reason that there is a growing realisation in our profession that no one method or approach is 'right' in absolute terms or even appropriate for all students in all contexts (Prabhu, 1990; Holliday, 1994; Kumaradivelu, 1994).

Diversity is a fundamental component of language teaching and a constructive accommodation of this diversity is an essential condition for effective teaching. Accommodating diversity, and especially the diversity which we encounter among our students, is not, however, always an easy affair. In certain circumstances, it can involve reconciling students' perceptions and goals with those which are imposed via the programme objectives or prescribed materials with which teachers have to work. It can also raise the more personal challenge to teachers of accommodating perspectives on language teaching and learning which differ from their own. A constructive and inclusive acknowledgement of human diversity is, however, essential to an effective and locally meaningful approach to teaching. Thus, despite the practical and attitudinal difficulties which can arise in the attempt to accommodate learner diversity, Murray (1992) is correct in suggesting that diversity should be viewed as a resource. Indeed, translating this insight into practice is probably one of the main challenges with which both our profession as a whole and each of us as teachers are confronted.

## 3 Work with situations locally, in terms of their own inner logic and dynamics

There is an understandable tendency in language teaching to look for general principles (which are often formulated in terms of methodology) and then to use these general principles as a basis for decision-making in specific contexts. As already pointed out, however, language teaching as lived out in the classroom is always a local phenomenon. General principle can, of course, provide insights and open up potentially productive lines of reflection, but the value of general principle needs to be evaluated critically in the light of each situation in its own terms. This implies that language teaching needs to be understood locally, in terms of the specifics of each situation, i.e. local details, untidiness, and all.

Adopting a locally based approach to pedagogical decision-making has at least two sets of implications. The first is a matter of attitude, and involves a positive valorisation of local realities combined with a critical evaluation of general principles in terms of their local meaning and appropriacy. The second is that it can call for consideration of a wide range of factors, some of which may not seem directly pedagogical in nature. Such factors can relate to general funding levels for language education, the status of the TL in the students' home community, the hierarchical structures present in the target institution, as well as a variety of social, economic or ideological factors and the way in which these impact on the attitudes and behaviours of students, teachers, or other participants (cf. Elson, 1996/97). It also, of course, calls for consideration of the traditions of teaching and learning current in the target context. A locally based approach to language teaching views situations holistically, so any factor which assumes importance in participants' minds or which can exert an influence on the practical realisation of teaching needs to be taken into consideration and accommodated in pedagogical planning.

## 4 Evaluate methodological choices in terms of their local meaning and interaction with context

One of the points which has been made frequently in previous chapters is that methodology interacts dynamically with students' and teachers' attitudes, beliefs and expectations, and with various other aspects of context. For this reason, methodology as theoretical principle does not necessarily correspond to methodology as pedagogical reality in the classroom. Methodological choices therefore need to be evaluated in the light of the meaning which they assume for students and for teachers and, in this way, in the light of the way in which they contribute to classroom dynamics. In other words, methodological choices need to be made not simply on the basis of theoretical principle, but also with respect to their interaction with context.

The factors which may need to be taken into consideration in this respect are varied. From the point of view of students, they can include the stage students are at in their learning career, their perceptions of the practical relevance to them of the TL, their sociocultural attitudes to the TL community, their culture of learning, their habitual modes of study in other subject areas, and the demands of a pragmatically relevant examination they have to take. With respect to teachers, potentially relevant contextual factors include their conditions of work and salaries, their role and responsibilities in their educational system, and the status of teaching in their community. Some of these factors may not seem to be directly pedagogical in nature. They do, however, contribute to forming the context within which teaching and learning are lived out, and can thus exert a significant influence on the meaning which methodological choices assume for students and for teachers.

## 5 Evaluate methodological choices from an ethnographic perspective

This point evidently has links with the last point in the sense that the ethnographic bases of methodological choices influence the meaning these choices have for participants. No methodological choice is un-marked. All rest on assumptions about the nature of language, of learning, and of the classroom; they therefore frequently have implica-tions of a broader sociocultural and ideological nature. For this reason, it is essential to evaluate the assumptions on which methodological choices rest, whether these assumptions are explicitly stated or, which is more often the case, remain implicit and unstated. This has two sets of implications.

The first is that an ethnographic analysis of the learning traditions of the target context should be an integral part of pedagogical planning. This strategy is of particular relevance to language educators from outside the context in which they are working. Making this analysis an integral part of pedagogical planning can contribute to an under-standing of local value systems and cultures of learning and, in this way, provide guidelines for the development of a locally meaningful ap-proach to learning. The second involves a critical and ethnographic analysis by language educators of their own culture of learning. Ethnography is not something which applies only to the traditions and culture of 'the other', and all language educators need to be able to analyse the bases of their assumptions and attitudes to language teaching. This advice is perhaps of particular relevance in the area of ELT, which frequently involves language educators from an Anglo-Saxon background working with students and teachers from different cultural backgrounds; this gives rise to the risk of culturally based misunderstandings. The main point here is that it can be very easy to misunderstand or to react judgementally to classroom behaviours that are different from those which we have been prepared to expect from our own educational socialisation. Harmonious classroom dynamics depend crucially on participants being able to reach a mutually mean-ingful understanding of the nature and goals of language teaching. This has little chance of arising if teachers and students are interacting at cross purposes, without being able to understand the different meanings which methodological choices have for one another.

## 6 Invest in teachers and in teacher education

It was suggested in Chapter 8 that teaching has a strongly negotiative element and that this arises out of different participants' attempts to work out a personally meaningful approach to language teaching and classroom interaction. Teaching therefore involves the attempt to help students find a sense of personal meaningfulness in the learning process, and the classroom teacher plays a crucial role in this task. Investing in teachers and in teacher education is thus one of the most important means of enhancing the quality of teaching in the classroom.

In part, this involves looking honestly at the practical conditions in which teachers work, including their salaries and the status of teachers in society. Inadequate training, low status, or poor salaries can seriously undermine teachers' ability to invest the time and energy which is required to help students find that essential sense of personal meaningfulness in the learning process. Chamnan and Cornish (1997), Cortazzi and Jin (1996), Johnston (1997), and Yeo (1997) all point to the effects of poor material conditions, low salaries, and low social status on teachers' attitudes and ability to invest time and effort in their pedagogical tasks, quite apart from their willingness to choose, or to remain in, the profession. And Hayes (1996: 182) pertinently points to the effects on teachers of a 'deskilling and devaluing of teachers' work [and] the assessment of individuals primarily in terms of their financial earning potential'. Considerations of this nature may seem to go beyond the normal domain of pedagogy, but their effect on classroom dynamics, and thus on the quality of classroom teaching, cannot be doubted.

It is also important to evaluate the coherence between what is asked of teachers in terms of programme goals and methodological development, on the one hand, and the setting-up of appropriate enabling conditions, on the other (cf. Basanta, 1996; Liu, 1998; Tudor, 1999a). In the dynamic, negotiative perspective on teaching which has been developed in this book, teacher skills are a crucial component of classroom dynamics, and teacher education and support are thus one of the most productive means of adding value to the educational process (Tudor, 1999b).

## 7 Be open and realistic about what one brings to the teaching process

This point relates to the individual teacher and his or her interaction with language teaching. In a technological view of language teaching, the role of the teacher is defined largely in terms of implementing the pedagogical plans of participants further up the educational hierarchy.

In an ecological perspective, the teacher is an active and involved participant in the creation of classroom realities. For this reason, what teachers bring to the teaching process – in terms of their own view of language teaching, their own value system and interpersonal preferences, and also their personal investment in their tasks – are all significant components of classroom dynamics. Allwright (1983: 196) suggests that the lesson is 'a socially constructed event', and the teacher plays a particular role in the process of co-authorship or negotiation of classroom realities.

It is therefore important for teachers to analyse their own culturally based conceptions of teaching and learning, as well as to look into their personal interaction with the teaching process: what teaching means to them and the way in which they define their goals (cf. Edge, 1996a, 1996b). In this way, they can come to understand the 'negotiating stance' from which they interact with their students, with other participants, and with the methodological perspectives found in curricula and in teaching materials. Consideration of factors of this nature needs to be part of teacher education and of teachers' ongoing interaction with their chosen profession (Sikes, 1985; Appel, 1995; Pennington, 1995, 1996; Sendan, 1999).

# References

Abraham, R. G. 1985. Field independence–dependence and the teaching of grammar. *TESOL Quarterly* 20: 689–702.

Adendorff, R. D. 1996. The functions of code switching among high school teachers and students in KwaZulu and implications for the teacher. In K. M. Bailey and D. Nunan: 388–406.

Allwright, D. 1983. Classroom-centred research on language teaching and learning: A brief historical review. *TESOL Quarterly* 17: 191–204.

Allwright, D. 1984. Why don't learners learn what teachers teach? The interaction hypothesis. In D. M. Singleton and D. G. Little: 3–18.

Almarza, G. G. 1996. Student foreign language teachers' knowledge growth. In D. Freeman and J. C. Richards: 50–78.

Anderson, J. 1993. Is a communicative approach practical for teaching English in China? Pros and cons. *SYSTEM* 21: 471–480.

Appel, J. 1989. Humanistic approaches in the secondary classroom: How far can we go? *ELT Journal* 43: 261–267.

Appel, J. 1995. *Diary of a Language Teacher*. Oxford: Heinemann.

Arnold, J. (Ed.) 1999. *Affect in Language Learning*. Cambridge: Cambridge University Press.

Arthur, W. B. 1989. The economy and complexity. In D. Stein: 713–740.

Arthur, W. B. 1990. Positive feedbacks in the economy. *Scientific American*. February, 80–85.

Atkinson, D. 1989. 'Humanistic' approaches in the adult classroom: An affective reaction. *ELT Journal* 43: 268–273.

Bailey, K. M., B. Berthold, B. Braunstein, N. J. Fleischman, M. P. Holbrook, J. Tuman, X. Waissbluth and L. J. Zambo 1996. The language learner's autobiography: Examining the 'apprenticeship of observation'. In D. Freeman and J. C. Richards 1996: 11–29.

Bailey, K. M. and D. Nunan (Eds) 1996. *Voices from the Language Classroom*. Cambridge: Cambridge University Press.

Ball, S. J. and I. F. Goodson. (Eds) 1985. *Teachers' Lives and Careers*. London: Falmer Press.

Barron, C. 1991. Material thoughts: ESP and culture. *English for Specific Purposes* 10: 173–187.

Basanta, C. P. 1996. Comment: In the name of the teacher. *ELT Journal* 50: 263–264.

## References

Benson, P. 1997. The philosophy and politics of learner autonomy. In P. Benson and P. Voller: 18–34.

Benson, P. and P. Voller (Eds) 1997. *Autonomy and Independence in Language Learning*. Harlow: Longman.

Block, D. 1996. A window on the classroom: Classroom events viewed from different angles. In K. M. Bailey and D. Nunan: 168–194.

Borg, S. 1999. Teacher's theories in grammar teaching. *ELT Journal* 53: 157–167.

Breen, M. P. 1984. Process syllabuses in the language classroom. In C. Brumfit 1984b: 47–60.

Breen, M. P. 1986. The social context for language learning. A neglected situation? *Studies in Second Language Acquisition* 7: 135–158.

Breen, M. P. 1987. Learner contributions to task design. In C. N. Candlin and D. F. Murphy: 23–46.

Breen, M. P. and A. Littlejohn (Eds) 2000. *Classroom Decision-Making*. Cambridge: Cambridge University Press.

Brindley, G. 1984. *Needs Analysis and Objective Setting in the Adult Migrant Education Program*. Sydney: New South Wales Adult Migrant Education Service.

Brindley, G. 1989. The role of needs analysis in adult ESL programme development. In R. K. Johnson 1989: 63–78.

Brookes, A. and P. Grundy (Eds) 1988. *Individualisation and Autonomy in Language Learning*. London: Modern English Publications.

Brumfit, C. 1982. Some humanistic doubts about humanistic language teaching. In *Humanistic Approaches: An Empirical View*. ELT Documents 113. London: British Council: 11–19.

Brumfit, C. 1984a. *Communicative Methodology in Language Teaching*. Cambridge: Cambridge University Press.

Brumfit, C. (Ed.) 1984b. *General English syllabus design*. ELT Documents 118. Oxford: Pergamon/British Council.

Brumfit, C. 1991. Problems in defining instructional methodologies. In K. De Bot, R. B. Ginsberg and C. Kramsch: 133–144.

Brumfit, C. and K. Johnson (Eds) 1979. *The Communicative Approach to Language Teaching*. Oxford: Oxford University Press.

Burkhalter, A. 1986. The expression of opinions: A preliminary needs analysis of discussion skills for academic purposes. M.A. qualifying paper, ESL Program: University of Minnesota.

Burnaby, B. and Y. Sun 1989. Chinese teachers' views of Western language teaching: Context informs paradigm. *TESOL Quarterly* 23: 219–238.

Burns, A. 1996. Starting all over again: from teaching adults to teaching beginners. In D. Freeman and J. C. Richards 1996: 154–177.

Campbell, C. 1996. Socializing with the teachers and prior language learning experience: A diary study. In K. M. Bailey and D. Nunan: 201–223.

Campbell, C. and H. Kryszewska 1992. *Learner-based Teaching*. Oxford: Oxford University Press.

Canagarajah, A. S. 1993. Critical ethnography of a Sri Lankan classroom: Ambiguities in student opposition to reproduction through ESOL. *TESOL Quarterly* 27: 601–626.

Canagarajah, A. S. 1999. *Resisting Linguistic Imperialism in English Teaching.* Oxford: Oxford University Press.

Candlin, C. N. 1987. Towards task-based language learning. In C. N. Candlin and D. F. Murphy: 5–22.

Candlin, C. N., C. J. Bruton, J. H. Leather and E. G. Woods. 1981. Designing modular materials for communicative language learning; An example: Doctor-patient communication skills. In L. Selinker, E. Tarone and V. Hanzeli: 105–133.

Candlin, C. N. and D. F. Murphy (Eds) 1987. *Language Learning Tasks.* Lancaster Practical Papers in Language Education 7. Hemel Hempstead: Prentice Hall International.

Carroll, J. B. 1966. The contributions of psychological theory and educational research to the teaching of foreign languages. In A. Valdman: 93–106.

Carter, R. A. 1992. Language in the National Curriculum. Presentation at Thames Valley University, Ealing, London.

Chamnan, P. and A. Cornish. 1997. Language and education in Cambodia. In B. Kenny and W. Savage: 33–43.

Chapelle, C. 1995. Field-dependence/field-independence in the second language classroom. In J. M. Reid 1995: 158–168.

Chapelle, C. and C. Roberts. 1986. Ambiguity tolerance and field independence as predictors of proficiency in English as a foreign language. *Language Learning* 36: 27–45.

Chick, J. K. 1996. Safe-talk: Collusion in apartheid education. In H. Coleman 1996b: 21–39.

Chomsky, N. 1957. *Syntactic Structures.* The Hague: Mouton.

Chomsky, N. 1959. Review of B. F. Skinner's *Verbal Behavior. Language* 35: 26–58.

Chomsky, N. 1965. *Aspects of the Theory of Syntax.* Cambridge, MA: MIT Press.

Clarke, N. 1989. Materials adaptation: Why leave it all to the teachers? *ELT Journal* 43: 133–141.

Clarke, D. F. 1991. The negotiated syllabus: What it is and how likely is it to work? *Applied Linguistics* 12: 13–28.

Coleman, H. 1989. *Approaches to the Management of Large Classes.* (Research Report 11) Leeds: Language Learning in Large Classes Research Project.

Coleman, H. 1996a. Shadow puppets and language lessons: Interpreting classroom behaviour in its cultural context. In H. Coleman 1996b: 64–85.

Coleman, H. (Ed.) 1996b. *Society and the Language Classroom.* Cambridge: Cambridge University Press.

Cortazzi, M. 1990. Cultural and educational expectations in the language classroom. In B. Harrison: 54–65.

Cortazzi, M. and L. Jin. 1996. Cultures of learning: language classrooms in China. In H. Coleman 1996b: 169–206.

Crookes, G. and S. M. Gass (Eds) 1993. *Tasks in a Pedagogical Context: Integrating Theory and Practice.* Clevedon, Avon: Multilingual Matters.

Cummings, M. C. 1996. Sardo revisited: Voice, faith, and multiple repeaters. In K. M. Bailey and D. Nunan: 224–235.

## References

Cunningsworth, A. 1995. *Choosing Your Coursebook*. Oxford: Heinemann.

Curran, C. 1972. *Counseling-Learning: A Whole-Person Model for Education*. New York: Grune and Stratton.

Curran, C. 1976. *Counseling-Learning in Second Languages*. Apple River, IL: Apple River Press.

De Bot, K., R. B. Ginsberg and C. Kramsch (Eds) 1991. *Foreign Language Research in Cross-cultural Perspective*. Amsterdam, PA: John Benjamin.

Deller, S. 1990. *Lessons from the Learner*. Harlow: Longman.

Dörnyei, Z. 1990. Conceptualising motivation in foreign language learning. *Language Learning* 40: 45–78.

Dörnyei, Z. 1994. Motivation and motivating in the foreign language classroom. *The Modern Language Journal* 78: 273–284.

Dörnyei, Z. 1998. Motivation in second and foreign language learning. *Language Teaching* 31: 117–135.

Doughty, C. and J. Williams (Eds) 1998. *Focus on Form in Classroom Language Acquisition*. Cambridge: Cambridge University Press.

Duff, P. A. 1996. Different languages, different practices: Socialisation of discourse competence in dual-language school classrooms in Hungary. In K. M. Bailey and D. Nunan: 407–434.

Duff, P. A. and Y. Uchida 1997. The negotiation of teachers' sociocultural identities and practices in postsecondary EFL classrooms. *TESOL Quarterly* 31: 451–486.

Easton, G. 1982. *Learning from Case Studies*. London: Prentice Hall International.

Edge, J. 1996a. Keeping the faith. *TESOL Matters* 6: 1, 23.

Edge, J. 1996b. Cross-cultural paradoxes in a profession of faith. *TESOL Quarterly* 30: 9–30.

Elliott, J. 1993a. Three perspectives on coherence and continuity in teacher education. In J. Elliott 1993b: 15–19.

Elliott, J. (Ed.) 1993b. *Reconstructing Teacher Education*. London: Falmer Press.

Ellis, G. 1996. How culturally appropriate is the communicative approach? *ELT Journal* 50: 213–218.

Ellis, G. and B. Sinclair 1989. *Learning to Learn English*. Cambridge: Cambridge University Press.

Elson, N. 1996/97. The making of educational change. *TESOL Matters* 6: 1, 4.

Erbaugh, M. S. 1990. Taking advantage of China's literary tradition in teaching Chinese students. *The Modern Language Journal* 74: 15–27.

Faerch, C. and G. Kasper (Eds) 1983. *Strategies in Interlanguage Communication*. Harlow: Longman.

Finocchiaro, M. and C. Brumfit 1983. *The Functional-Notional Approach*. Oxford: Oxford University Press.

Fortez, G. E. 1997. Language teaching in difficult circumstances. In B. Kenny and W. Savage: 15–32.

Freeman, D. 1996. Redefining the relationship between research and what teachers know. In K.M. Bailey and D. Nunan: 88–115.

218

Freeman, D. and J. C. Richards 1993. Conceptions of teaching and the education of second language teachers. *TESOL Quarterly* 27: 193–216.

Freeman, D. and J. C. Richards (Eds) 1996. *Teacher Learning in Language Teaching*. Cambridge: Cambridge University Press.

Freire, P. 1970. *Pedagogy of the Oppressed*. New York: Herder and Herder.

Giles, H., J. Coupland and N. Coupland (Eds) 1991. *Contexts of Accommodation*. Cambridge: Cambridge University Press.

Giles, H. and P. Smith 1979. Accommodation theory: Optimal levels of convergence. In H. Giles and R. St. Clair: 45–65.

Giles, H. and R. St. Clair (Eds) 1979. *Language and Social Action*. Oxford: Blackwell.

Gould, S. J. 1993. *Eight Little Piggies: Reflections in Natural History*. New York: W. W. Norton and Company.

Grady, K. 1997. Critically reading an ESL text. *TESOL Journal* 6: 7–10.

Graves, K. (Ed.) 1996. *Teachers as Course Developers*. Cambridge: Cambridge University Press.

Hall, D. R. 1997. Why projects fail. In B. Kenny and W. Savage: 258–267.

Halliday, M. A. K. 1973. *Explorations in the Functions of Language*. London: Edward Arnold.

Halliday, M. A. K. 1975. *Learning How to Mean: Explorations in the Development of Language*. London: Edward Arnold.

Harrison, B. (Ed.) 1990. Culture and the language classroom. *ELT Documents* 132. London: The British Council.

Hayes, D. 1996. Prioritizing 'voice' over 'vision': Reaffirming the centrality of the teacher in ESOL research. *SYSTEM* 24: 173–186.

Ho, J. and D. Crookall 1995. Breaking with Chinese cultural traditions: Learner autonomy in English language teaching. *SYSTEM* 23: 235–243.

Holliday, A. 1991. Dealing with tissue rejection in EFL projects: The role of an ethnographic needs analysis. Unpublished Ph.D. thesis, Lancaster University.

Holliday, A. 1994. *Appropriate Methodology and Social Context*. Cambridge: Cambridge University Press.

Holliday, A. 1996. Large- and small-class cultures in Egyptian university classrooms: A cultural justification for curriculum change. In Coleman 1996b: 86–104.

Holliday, A. and T. Cooke 1982. An ecological approach to ESP. In Waters 1982: 123–143.

Horwitz, E. and D. J. Young 1991. *Language Anxiety: From Theory and Research to Classroom Implications*. Englewood Cliffs, N.J.: Prentice Hall.

Howard, R. and G. Brown (Eds) 1997. *Teacher Education for ESP*. Clevedon: Multilingual Matters.

Howatt, A. P. R. 1984. *A History of English Language Teaching*. Oxford: Oxford University Press.

Hyland, K. 1993. Culture and learning: A study of the learning style preferences of Japanese students. *RELC Journal* 24: 69–91.

Hymes, D. 1972. On communicative competence. In J. B. Pride and J. Holmes: 269–293.

# References

Johnson, K. 1982. *Communicative Syllabus Design and Methodology*. Oxford: Pergamon.

Johnson, K. 1996. *Language Teaching and Skill Learning*. Oxford: Blackwell.

Johnson, K. and H. Johnson 1998. *Encyclopedic Dictionary of Applied Linguistics*. Oxford: Blackwell.

Johnson, K. E. 1992. Learning to teach: Instructional actions and decisions of preservice ESL teachers. *TESOL Quarterly* 26: 507–535.

Johnson, R. K. (Ed.) 1989. *The Second Language Curriculum*. Cambridge: Cambridge University Press.

Johnson, W. K. 1999. Observations of the anti-other: An avenue to self-censorship. *TESOL Matters* 9: 4.

Johnston, B. 1997. Do EFL teachers have careers? *TESOL Quarterly* 31: 681–712.

Kauffman, S. 1995. *At Home in the Universe*. Harmondsworth: Viking.

Kennedy, C. 1987. Innovating for a change: Teacher development and innovation. *ELT Journal* 41: 163–170.

Kennedy, C. and J. Kennedy 1996. Teacher attitudes and change implementation. *SYSTEM* 24: 351–360.

Kenny, B. and W. Savage (Eds) 1997. *Language and Development: Teachers in a Changing World*. Harlow: Longman.

Kershaw, G. 1997. Business visits in Papua New Guinea. In B. Kenny and W. Savage: 164–177.

Kinsella, K. 1996. Designing group work that supports and enhances diverse classroom working styles. *TESOL Journal* 6: 24–30.

Krashen, S. D. 1982. *Principles and Practice in Second Language Acquisition*. Oxford: Pergamon.

Krashen, S. D. 1985. *The Input Hypothesis: Issues and Implications*. Harlow: Longman.

Krashen, S. D. and T. Terrell 1983. *The Natural Approach*. Oxford: Pergamon.

Kubota. R. 1999. Japanese culture constructed by discourses: Implications for applied linguistics research and ELT. *TESOL Quarterly* 33: 9–35.

Kumaradivelu, B. 1994. The postmethod condition: (E)merging strategies for second/foreign language teaching. *TESOL Quarterly* 28: 27–48.

Lakoff, G. and M. Johnson 1980. *Metaphors We Live By*. Chicago/London: Chicago University Press.

Langfeldt, H-P. 1992. Teachers' perceptions of problem behaviour: A cross-cultural study between Germany and South Korea. *British Journal of Educational Psychology* 62: 217–224.

Larsen-Freeman, D. 1997. Chaos/Complexity science and second language acquisition. *Applied Linguistics* 18: 141–165.

Lewin, R. 1993. *Complexity*. London: J. M. Dent.

Lewis, M. 1993. *The Lexical Approach*. Hove: Language Teaching Publications.

Lincoln, Y. and E. Guba 1985. *Naturalistic Inquiry*. Newbury Park, CA.: Sage.

Littlewood, W. 1999. Defining and developing autonomy in East Asian contexts. *Applied Linguistics* 20: 71–94.

Liu, D. 1998. Ethnocentrism in TESOL: Teacher education and the neglected needs of international TESOL students. *ELT Journal* 52: 3–10.

LoCastro, V. 1996. English language education in Japan. In H. Coleman 1996b: 40–58.

Long, M. H. and G. Crookes 1992. Three approaches to task-based syllabus design. *TESOL Quarterly* 26: 27–56.

Long, M. H. and G. Crookes 1993. Units of analysis in syllabus design: The case for task. In G. Crookes and S. M. Gass (Eds): 9–54.

Mackay, R. and A. Mountford (Eds) 1978. *English for Specific Purposes.* Harlow: Longman.

Markee, N. 1997. *Managing Curricular Innovation.* Cambridge: Cambridge University Press.

McCargar, D. F. 1993. Teacher and student role expectations: Cross-cultural differences and implications. *The Modern Language Journal* 77: 192–207.

Melton, C. D. 1990. Bridging the cultural gap: A study of Chinese students' learning style preferences. *RELC Journal* 21: 29–54.

Mishan, F. 2000. Authenticity in language learning materials design. Unpublished doctoral thesis, Department of Languages and Cultural Studies, University of Limerick.

Moore, T. 1977. An experimental language handicap (personal account). *Bulletin of the British Psychological Society* 30: 107–110.

Moran, P. R. 1996. 'I'm not typical': Stories of becoming a Spanish teacher. In D. Freeman and J. C. Richards 1996: 125–153.

Moskovitz, G. 1978. *Caring and Sharing in the Foreign Language Classroom.* Rowley, MA: Newbury House.

Muchiri, M. 1996. The effect of institutional and national cultures on examinations: The university in Kenya. In H. Coleman 1996b: 122–140.

Mueller, T. H. 1971. The effectiveness of two learning models: the audiolingual habit theory and the cognitive code learning theory. In P. Pimsleur and T. Quinn: 113–122.

Munby, J. 1978. *Communicative Syllabus Design.* Cambridge: Cambridge University Press.

Murray, D. E. (Ed.) 1992. *Diversity as Resource.* Alexandria, VA: Teachers of English to Speakers of Other Languages, Inc.

Murray, D. E. 1996. The tapestry of diversity in our classrooms. In K. M. Bailey and D. Nunan: 434–448.

Norris, L. and S. Spencer 2000. Learners, practitioners, teachers: Diamond spotting and negotiating role boundaries. In M. P. Breen and A. Littlejohn: 195–203.

Norton, B. 1997. Language, identity and the ownership of English. *TESOL Quarterly* 31: 409–429.

Numrich, C. 1996. On becoming a language teacher: Insights from diary studies. *TESOL Quarterly* 30: 131–153.

Nunan, D. 1988. *The Learner-centred Curriculum.* Cambridge: Cambridge University Press.

Nunan, D. 1989. Toward a collaborative approach to curriculum development: A case study. *TESOL Quarterly* 23: 9–25.

Nunan, D. 1997. Designing and adapting materials to encourage learner autonomy. In P. Benson and P. Voller: 192–203.

# References

Nunan, D. and C. Lamb 1996. *The Self-directed Teacher*. Cambridge: Cambridge University Press.

O'Connor, O., A. Pilbeam and F. Scott-Barrett 1992. *Negotiating*. Harlow: Longman.

Okoye, I. 1994. Teaching technical communication in large classes. *English for Specific Purposes* 13: 223–237.

O'Neill, R., R. Kingbury, T. Yeadon and E. T. Cornelius 1978. *American Kernel Lessons: Intermediate*. New York: Longman.

Oxford, R. and M. Ehrman 1993. Second language research on individual differences. *Annual Review of Applied Linguistics* 13: 188–205.

Oxford, R., M. E. Hollaway and D. Horton-Murillo 1992. Language learning styles: Research and practical considerations for teaching in the multicultural tertiary ESL/EFL classroom. *SYSTEM* 20: 439–456.

Oxford, R. and J. Shearin 1994. Language learning motivation: Expanding the theoretical framework. *The Modern Language Journal* 78: 12–28.

Oxford, R., S. Tomlinson, A. Barcelos, C. Harrington, R. Z. Lavine, A. Saleh and A. Longhini 1998. Clashing metaphors about classroom teachers: Toward a systematic typology for the language teaching field. *SYSTEM* 26: 3–50.

Pennington, M. C. 1995. The teacher change cycle. *TESOL Quarterly* 29: 705–731.

Pennington, M. C. 1996. The 'cognitive-affective filter' in teacher development: Transmission-based and interpretation-based schemas for change. *SYSTEM* 24: 337–350.

Pennycook, A. 1997. Cultural alternatives and autonomy. In P. Benson and P. Voller: 35–53.

Pimsleur, P. and T. Quinn (Eds) 1971. *The Psychology of Second Language Learning*. Cambridge: Cambridge University Press.

Prabhu, N. S. 1984. Procedural syllabuses. In J. A. S. Read (Ed.): 272–280.

Prabhu, N. S. 1987. *Second Language Pedagogy*. Oxford: Oxford University Press.

Prabhu, N. S. 1990. There is no best method: Why? *TESOL Quarterly* 24: 161–176.

Prabhu, N. S. 1992. The dynamics of the language lesson. *TESOL Quarterly* 26: 225–241.

Pride, J. B. and J. Holmes (Eds) 1972. *Sociolinguistics*. Harmondsworth: Penguin.

Read, J. A. S. (Ed.) 1984. *Trends in Language Syllabus Design*. Singapore: SEAMEO-RELC.

Reid, J. M. 1987. The learning style preferences of ESL students. *TESOL Quarterly* 21: 87–110.

Reid, J. M. (Ed.) 1995. *Learning Styles in the ESL/EFL Classroom*. Boston, MA: Newbury House.

Richards, J. C. 1985. *The Context of Language Teaching*. Cambridge: Cambridge University Press.

Richards, J. C. 1992. The culture of the English language teacher: A Hong Kong example. *RELC Journal* 23: 81–102.

Richards, J. C. 1996. Teachers' maxims in language teaching. *TESOL Quarterly* 30: 281–296.

Richards, J. C. (Ed.) 1998. *Teaching in Action: Case Studies from Second Language Classrooms*. Alexandria, VA: TESOL Inc.

Richards, J. C. and T. S. Rodgers. 1986. *Approaches and Methods in Language Teaching*. Cambridge: Cambridge University Press.

Richards, J. C. and M. Sukwiwat. 1985. Cross-cultural aspects of conversational competence. In J. C. Richards 1985: 129–143.

Richterich, R. 1973. *Systems Development in Adult Language Learning*. Strasbourg: Council of Europe.

Riley, P. 1988. The ethnography of autonomy. In A. Brookes and P. Grundy: 12–34.

Robinson, P. 1991. *ESP Today: A Practitioner's Guide*. Hemel Hempstead: Prentice Hall.

Ruane, M. and D. P. Ò Baoill (Eds) 2000. *Integrating Theory and Practice in LSP and LAP*. Dublin: Applied Language Centre, University College Dublin and Irish Association of Applied Linguistics.

Rubin, J. 1987. Learner strategies: Theoretical assumptions, research history and typology. In A. Wenden and J. Rubin: 15–30.

Savignon, S. J. 1983. *Communicative Competence: Theory and Classroom Practice*. Reading, MA: Addison-Wesley.

Scovel, T. 1978. The effect of affect on foreign language learning: A review of the anxiety research. *Language Learning* 28: 129–142.

Selinker, L., E. Tarone and V. Hanzeli (Eds) 1981. *English for Academic and Technical Purposes*. Rowley, MA: Newbury House.

Sendan, F. 1999. Conceptual growth through reflection in EFL teachers. Paper presented at the conference IATEFL Teachers Develop Teachers Research 4: Reflective Learning, Katholieke Universiteit Leuven, 2–4 September 1999.

Shamim, F. 1996a. In or out of the action zone: Location as a feature of interaction in large ESL classes in Pakistan. In K. M. Bailey and D. Nunan: 123–144.

Shamim, F. 1996b. Learner resistance to innovation in classroom methodology. In Coleman 1996b: 105–121.

Sikes, P. 1985. The life cycle of the teacher. In S. J. Ball and I. F. Goodson (Eds): 27–60.

Simons, H. (Ed.) 1980. *Towards a Science of the Singular*. University of East Anglia: Centre for Applied Research in Education.

Sinclair, B. 1997. Learner autonomy: The cross-cultural question. *IATEFL Newsletter* 139: 12–13.

Singleton, D. M. and D. G. Little (Eds) 1984. *Language Learning in Formal and Informal Contexts*. Dublin: IRAAL.

Skehan, P. 1989. *Individual Differences in Second-language Learning*. London: Edward Arnold.

Skehan, P. 1991. Individual differences in second language learning. *Studies in Second Language Acquisition* 13: 275–298.

Slembrouck, S. 2000. Negotiation in tertiary education: Clashes with the dominant educational culture. In M. P. Breen and A. Littlejohn: 138–149.

# References

Stake, R. S. 1980. The case study method in social enquiry. In H. Simons: 62–75.

Stein, D. (Ed.) 1989. *Lectures in the Sciences of Complexity, SFI Studies in the Sciences of Complexity.* Addison-Wesley Longman.

Stevick, E. W. 1989. *Success with Foreign Languages.* Hemel Hempstead: Prentice Hall.

Stevick, E. W. 1990. *Humanism in Language Teaching.* Oxford: Oxford University Press.

Strevens, P. 1977. *New Orientations in the Teaching of English.* Oxford: Oxford University Press.

Sullivan, P. N. 1996. Sociocultural influences on classroom interactional styles. *TESOL Journal* 6: 32–34.

Susser, B. 1998. EFL's Othering of Japan: Orientalism in English language teaching. *JALT Journal* 20: 49–82.

Tremblay, P. F. and R. C. Gardner 1995. Expanding the motivation construct in language learning. *The Modern Language Journal* 79: 505–518.

Tudor, I. 1993. Teacher roles in the learner-centred classroom. *ELT Journal* 47: 22–31.

Tudor, I. 1996. *Learner-centredness as Language Education.* Cambridge: Cambridge University Press.

Tudor, I. 1997. Autonomy and the 'traditional' classroom. *IATEFL Newsletter* 139: 18–19.

Tudor, I. 1998. Rationality and rationalities in language teaching. *SYSTEM* 26: 319–334.

Tudor, I. 1999a. Assessing enabling conditions for reflective teaching and learning. Paper presented at the conference IATEFL Teachers Develop Teachers Research 4: Reflective Learning, Katholieke Universiteit Leuven, 2–4 September 1999.

Tudor, I. 1999b. Language teachers: Roles and requirements. Paper presented to the Quality Management in Higher Education Language Studies Working Group, Second Conference of the European Language Council, University of Jyväskylä, 1–3 July, 1999.

Tudor. I. 2000. Perception and authenticity in tertiary level ESP. In M. Ruane and D. P. Ò Baoill (Eds): 101–113.

Usuki, M. 1999. Promoting learner autonomy: A reconsideration of the stereotypical views about Japanese learners. *Independence* (Newsletter of the IATEFL Learner Independence SIG) Winter 1999: 7–10.

Uvin, J. 1996. Designing workplace ESOL courses for Chinese health-care workers at a Boston nursing home. In K. Graves (Ed.): 39–62.

Valdman, A. (Ed.) 1966. *Trends in Language Teaching.* New York: McGraw-Hill.

Van Lier, L. 1988. *The Classroom and the Language Learner.* London: Longman.

Van Lier, L. 1996. *Interaction in the Language Curriculum.* London: Longman.

Van Lier, L. 1997. Observation from an ecological perspective. *TESOL Quarterly* 31: 783–787.

Waldrop, M. M. 1992. *Complexity.* Harmondsworth: Viking.

Wallace, M. J. 1991. *Training Foreign Language Teachers*. Cambridge: Cambridge University Press.

Wallace, M. J. 1999. Using case studies in language teacher education. Paper presented at the conference IATEFL Teachers Develop Teachers Research 4: Reflective Learning, Katholieke Universiteit Leuven, 2–4 September 1999.

Waters, A. (Ed.) 1982. *Lancaster Practical Papers in English Language Education*, Vol. 5: *Issues in ESP*. Oxford: Pergamon Press.

Wenden, A. 1987. How to be a successful language learner: Insights and prescriptions from second language learners. In A. Wenden and J. Rubin: 103–117.

Wenden, A. and J. Rubin (Eds) 1987. *Learner Strategies in Language Learning*. Hemel Hempstead: Prentice Hall.

Widdowson, H. 1978. *Teaching Language as Communication*. Oxford: Oxford University Press.

Wilkins, D. 1976. *Notional Syllabuses: A Taxomomy and its Relevance to Foreign Language Curriculum Development*. Oxford: Oxford University Press.

Williams, M. 1988. Language taught for meetings and language used in meetings: is there anything in common? *Applied Linguistics* 9: 45–58.

Williams, M. and R. L. Burden 1997. *Psychology for Language Teachers*. Cambridge: Cambridge University Press.

Willing, K. 1988. *Learning Styles in Adult Migrant Education*. Adelaide: National Curriculum Resource Centre.

Willing, K. 1989. *Teaching How to Learn: Learning Strategies in ESL*. Sydney: National Centre for English Language Teaching and Research.

Woods, D. 1991. Teachers' interpretations of second language teaching curricula. *RELC Journal* 22: 1–18.

Woods, D. 1996. *Teacher Cognition in Language Teaching*. Cambridge: Cambridge University Press.

Yeo, S. 1997. The ESP coursebook: Effects on an in-service training programme in Slovakia. In R. Howard and G. Brown (Eds): 148–157.

Yin, R. K. 1994. *Case Study Research: Design and Methods*. Thousand Oaks, CA: Sage Publications.

Young, R. 1987. The cultural context of TESOL: a review of research into Chinese classrooms. *RELC Journal* 18: 15–30.

# Index

# Index

# Index

# Index

naturalistic learning 5, 78–79, 82, 85
naturalistic research 41–42
needs analysis 58–59, 112
  defining 'needs' 204
  immigrant learners of English 73–74
  objective *versus* experiential 197, 200
  practicalities of 59–60
negative stereotyping 170
negotiation
  ESOL in USA case study 184–85,
    196–97, 196–205
    analysis 202–4
    classroom, in and beyond 199–202
    objective and context 198–99
    'rational' approach 197–98
  language school in Japan case study
    185–96, 206
    analysis 193–95
    ethos of learning 185–86
    the negotiation 191–93
    participant conceptions of teaching
    and learning 187–91
  of messages 3, 82
  negotiative dynamics 182–85, 207
  teaching as 181–82
normality, assumption of 39–40, 46
Norris, L. 168
Norton, B. 72
notional/functional syllabuses 57
Numrich, C. 16
Nunan, D. 23, 24, 29, 40, 41, 106, 118,
  120, 125, 181, 182

O'Connor, O. 59
Okoye, I. 133
O'Neill, R. 147
opinion gap activities 80
otherness, exploring 70
Oxford, R. 12, 20

pedagogical choices
  acknowledgement of diversity in 3
  cultures of learning 159–60
  situation-external criteria questioned 2,
    4
  visions of language 75–76
  visions of learning 102–3
Pennington, M. C. 16, 214
Pennycook, A. 117, 118

personal meaningfulness
  activities 80, 84, 100, 115
  course content 197–99, 202–3
  learning 113–14, 174–75, 183
  methodological choice 103, 196
  quality of teachers 213
phonology 51, 53, 55
  in functional approach 59
political choices
  classroom realities 36–37
  course design 201–2
  varieties of TL 54
political correctness 188
'post-method' condition 23
Prabhu, N. S. 43, 45, 81, 210
predictability of language, and fluency
  93–95
private sector, institutional influences 38
problem solving 173
problematic situations, learning from 135
procedural syllabus 81
process syllabus 81, 84, 116
product-orientated learning 149, 150
'progressive' pedagogical undertaking 171
project organisation, by students 176
publishing houses, influence of 38, 154

rationalities 32–39
  diversity of participants 32–33, 43
  institutional and corporate 37–38, 195
  merging of different 40, 43
  methodological 34–35
  sociocultural 35–37, 38
  student 33–34
  teacher 38–39
  understanding classroom reality 47
reality, day-to-day of classroom
  accessibility 29
  researching nature of 41–42, 47
  'untidiness' 30, 46, 135
reflective teaching 5, 24
reform, effecting 44–45, 142–44, 167–70
refugees case study, humanistic approach
  66
Reid, J. M. 11, 20
relationships, humanistic approach 66, 97,
  99
research
  agenda, changing 39–42

Lightning Source UK Ltd.
Milton Keynes UK
UKOW01f0814310715

256124UK00001B/59/P